The
COMFORTS
of HOME

ALSO BY MERRITT IERLEY

Open House:
A Guided Tour of the American Home, 1637 to the Present

Traveling the National Road:
Across the Centuries on America's First Highway

With Charity for All:
Welfare and Society, Ancient Times to the Present

The Year That Tried Men's Souls:
A Journalistic Reconstruction of the World of 1776

A Place in History:
A Centennial Chronicle of North Arlington, New Jersey,
Birthplace of Steam Power in America

The
COMFORTS
of HOME

*The American
House and the
Evolution of
Modern Convenience*

MERRITT
IERLEY

CLARKSON POTTER/PUBLISHERS
NEW YORK

Research for this book was funded primarily by a grant from the Alfred P. Sloan Foundation. Additional funding was supplied by the Fairleigh S. Dickinson Jr. Foundation.

Published by Clarkson N. Potter, 201 East 50th Street, New York, New York 10022. Member of the Crown Publishing Group.

Random House, Inc. New York, Toronto, London, Sydney, Auckland
www.randomhouse.com

CLARKSON N. POTTER, POTTER and colophon are registered trademarks of Random House, Inc.

Printed in the United States of America

DESIGN BY RENATO STANISIC

Library of Congress Cataloging-in-Publication Data
Ierley, Merritt.
The comforts of home : the American house and the evolution of modern convenience / Merritt Ierley. — 1st ed.
    p.   cm.
Includes bibliographical references and index.
1. Dwellings—Environmental engineering—United States—History. I. Title.
TH6057.A6I37   1999
696'.0973—dc21   99-20434
                                                        CIP

ISBN 0-609-60299-3

10 9 8 7 6 5 4 3 2 1

First Edition

CONTENTS

FOREWORD

It seems safe to say that many of us would not find the homes of our grandparents and great-grandparents comfortable places to live. Perhaps heat came from a parlor stove. If Granny was lucky, a cake taken from the oven in the wood-fired kitchen range would be charred only on one side. She spent what little spare time she had reading while seated at the dining room table under the room's solitary gaslight, her book carefully positioned to avoid the dark shadows cast by the light fixture. And a call of nature meant a trip to a privy that stood at the back of the garden.

Were we to move further back in time, the living conditions would be even more inhospitable. The few comforts of home enjoyed by our ancestors would hardly have met our expectations of what makes life pleasant. It is the ease with which we obtain and how we use such amenities as heat, light, water, gas, and electricity that determine our well-being. In *The Comforts of Home*, Merritt Ierley makes it abundantly clear that "comfort" is a relative term.

Developments and improvements do not occur at a uniform rate; the change tends to come in fits and starts. Even incremental differences are significant, though, when tracing the history of the design and operation of the home. Obtaining water from a pump in the yard was an improvement over a well and bucket. But if the pump was located inside the house, coupled to a kitchen sink rather than a bucket in which to wash, this was an even greater improvement. Never mind that in either case waste was simply emptied into the yard. In hindsight these appear to be minor steps, but such advances and countless others made life easier.

In the past, even the most basic comforts often required hard work. For example, a warm home, with the peculiarly American tradition of central heating, required among other things laying in a supply of fuel, stoking a furnace at regular intervals, adjusting dampers, and finally removing the ash of spent fuel. No easy task, this — and creating cold was even more difficult. As the degree of effort needed to establish comfort gradually lessened, life moved toward a situation of positive ease. At the same time, the definition of "comfort" grew to include issues of efficiency, cleanliness, compactness, and safety.

Much of our comfort results from advances in science and technology. But in some instances the widespread acceptance of one development depended on the creation and evolution of other technologies. A flush toilet was of little use if there was a water supply, but no adequate sewerage system through which to remove the waste. Illumination provided by gaslights was a tremendous step forward over even the best oil lamps, but without an adequate system to deliver gas to the home, change was slow in coming. In many areas the danger posed by overturned and even explosive oil lamps was finally removed only with the installation of electricity.

Understandably, the conditions in which comfort was ultimately created appeared in individual homes at different times. Although cost has always been a consideration, there is also the component of daring. Approval of the new and unknown, bucking established ideas even if it was to make life easier has always been difficult. Not only were developments for indoor plumbing systems technically challenging, but beliefs associated with bodily functions, sources of disease, and health in general were strong forces working against their acceptance.

Sorting through a great amount of information, the author of *The Comforts of Home* has woven together an extremely thorough and delightfully readable story of the events, characters, and devices behind the comfortable home of the late twentieth century.

William E. Worthington, Jr.
Assistant Curator
History of Technology
National Museum of American History
Smithsonian Institution

INTRODUCTION

A very comfortable place, the modern American home. It meets virtually every creature need, for the most part with little creature effort. It is a remarkably efficient place for doing what it has to do — protect and sustain, feed and nourish; keep washed and refreshed, rested and relaxed; make warm in the cool season and cool in the warm.

As such, the home is the culmination of a process of improvement and refinement. There was once only what warmth could be gotten from the fireplace — a sentimental thing to sit in front of now, when central heat bears most of the burden, but a notoriously inefficient device when the fireplace was all one had for heat. Once only an open window provided relief on a hot day. And there was only "outdoor plumbing." The water needed for cooking, washing, and bathing was hauled in from a well, and an outhouse, or privy, was perhaps the greatest discomfort of home.

Comfort is real — it is felt, seen, sensed, appreciated, enjoyed. But it is also relative. Standards change. The devices and systems that make a home comfortable today were once beyond imagining. One made the most of what one had and, in the absence of a higher norm, supposed oneself comfortable. And indeed, in its own relative way, this was comfort.

It is something of an axiom that each innovation breaks down our connection with the past. Technology tends to cover its tracks. As a level of convenience is reached, the old ways are quickly forgotten. In the age of fully automatic appliances, a hand-wringer washing machine of the mid-twentieth century is as hard to find as a black-and-white television in the age of color. The coal-burning furnace, not so long ago the mainstay of home heating, is now virtually extinct. Rarely today are kerosene lamps used except for camping or as an occasional backup during a power failure. Yet all were once symbols of a "modern" age.

People today have an ever diminishing sense of what the old was even like, and almost no sense of how technology first came into use in the home. That is not to say there haven't been some thoroughly capable works written about household technology. But they have usually focused on one aspect—lighting, for example, or appliances or plumbing, and usually only on one period of history.

The purpose here is to make that leap backward and see how the whole of this comfortable house came about, seeking in particular the earliest manifestations of progress. That will be the focus here rather than a technical description of the house today, for a number of "how it works" books have been published. But the story of how household technology used to work and, more important, how it began, has inspired surprisingly little curiosity despite Americans' usual fascination with their nation's past.

To get started, let us take a quantitative look at comfort and convenience in the American home.

COMFORT IN NUMBERS

America is a land of 100 million homes—106 million to be more precise. And more to the point, it is statistically a land of 106 million *comfortable* homes.

To be sure, some are more comfortable than others, some much more; and a scattered few of them do not even have a kitchen sink. But on the whole, no society has ever dwelled in so much comfort and convenience.

Of those 106 million homes, 99 percent have heat and a kitchen sink, and 98 percent have a stove, a refrigerator, and at least one complete bathroom. Although climate in many areas hardly makes it a necessity of life, 74 percent have air conditioning in at least one room, and 47 percent have central air. Roughly seven out of ten homes have a washer and dryer. Some 88 percent of homes have water supplied by public utilities; almost all the rest also have running water, mostly from wells that use electrically driven pumps.

Electricity lets 59 percent of households cook, 38 percent heat water, and 28 per-

	1. New York 1856	2. Baltimore 1859	3. Middletown 1890	4. Major cities 1893	5. Homestead, Pa. 1910	6. Zanesville, Ohio 1925	7. 36 communities 1925	8. Middletown 1925	9. 63 cities 1934
Running Water	–	–	14%	–	52%	91%	95%	75%	91%
Electricity	–	–	–	–	–	–	74%	97%	99%
Indoor Toilet	9%	2%	2 doz. homes	29%	17%	–	–	–	81%
Tub/Shower	1%	7%	5%	–	–	61%	93%	–	–
Central Heat	–	–	–	–	–	42%	71%	–	–
Refrigerator	–	–	–	–	–	1%	2%	–	17%
Electric Range	–	–	–	–	–	–	3%	–	} 71%
Gas Range	–	–	–	–	–	90%	80%	–	
Electric Iron	–	–	–	–	–	59%	82%	–	–
Vacuum Cleaner	–	–	–	–	–	53%	60%	–	–
Washing Machine	–	–	–	–	–	28%	29%	–	–

1. and 2. New York and Baltimore. Water company records. Martin, *Standard of Living in 1860.*
3. Middletown is Muncie, Indiana. Lynd, *Middletown: A Study in Contemporary American Culture.*
4. New York, Philadelphia, Chicago, and Baltimore. *Seventh Special Report of the Commissioner of Labor,* Washington, 1894. Aggregate percentage of water closets in slum areas. Study showed that water closets were replacing privies in areas of concentrated population, but most, if not all, of these water closets were shared.
5. Homestead. Byington, *Homestead: The Households of a Mill Town.*
6. and 7. Eastman, *Zanesville and 36 Other American communities.*
8. Lynd, *Middletown.*
9. U.S. Department of Commerce, *Real Property Inventory,* 1934. The inventory encompassed sixty-four cities; the data here are from a report in *The New York Times,* August 26, 1934, on sixty-three of those cities.

cent keep warm. Gas does more of the home heating (50 percent) and more of the water heating (55 percent) but less of the cooking (40 percent).

Old and new energy sources are at the fringes. Coal, once the main fuel for home heating, is used in only about 2 percent of today's dwelling units while wood, the most common fuel before coal, remains enduringly useful, accounting for 11 percent of the

THE AMERICAN HOUSEHOLD AND THE
EVOLUTION OF TECHNOLOGY, 1940–1995

	1940	1960	1995
HEATING			
Central heating[1]	42%	66%	90%
Stoves, fireplaces, space heaters	47%	32%	9%
Dwelling units unheated	11%	2%	1%
COOKING[2]			
Gas stoves	49%	64%	40%
Electric stoves	5%	31%	59%
Stoves using coal, wood, and other fuels[3]	46%	5%	1%
PLUMBING			
At least one complete private bathroom	55%	83%	98%

1. Includes permanently installed, built-in electric units in floors, walls, and ceilings as well as furnaces heating a room immediately above or room(s) on one or both sides of room in which the furnace is located.
2. Assumes that statistically all housing units have cooking facilities.
3. There is no breakdown for coal in 1940, when it was still used significantly as a cooking fuel, or for 1960; for 1995 the figure is .006%.

fuel used. Solar energy, that promise of the future, remains just that, with slightly less use than coal.

From water supply to heat, from sink to oven, from tub to toilet, from air conditioning to washing machines, technology for the modern American home, matched by the availability of affordable fuel and power to run it all, makes for a very comfortable place in which to live.

It was, of course, not always so. In 1950, only 64 percent of American homes had full bathrooms. The postwar building boom would raise that total to 83 percent in just one decade. As of 1940 only slightly more than half of the households in America had a complete complement of tub and/or shower, toilet, and sink. Prior to 1940, only scattered data are available, but of course the percentages would be much smaller for those early years. Nevertheless, putting what we know in tabular form we find the American house steadily becoming a more convenient place in which to live.

FINDING THE RECOGNIZABLY MODERN

"Recognizably modern" will be a key term here. It is not within the scope of this book to pursue every development in household technology to its present state. Inevitably the primary focus will be on the nineteenth and early twentieth centuries, for that was the time of the greatest advances in comfort and convenience. In 1800, with very few exceptions, American homes were hardly technologically distinguishable from those of the colonial period. By 1900 it was not uncommon to find central heat, hot and cold running water, kitchen range, icebox, bathtub, water closet (toilet), electric lights, and electric fans—a house totally transformed from what it had been in 1800; a house, except for refinement of technology, recognizably modern even in the year 2000.

Since this book is about technology in the household, rather than technology generally, the emphasis will be different than in a general work. In looking at heating, for example, we will place considerably more emphasis on the development of hot-air heating rather than on steam or hot-water heat, simply because evolution has produced a clear preponderance in that direction. Nearly two-thirds of today's homes are heated with warm air. (The earlier term was "hot air"; the meaning is the same.)

We will also emphasize the middle-class house, but we must refer frequently to the homes of the wealthy, for that is where new forms of technology usually first appear.

Particular importance will be attached to essential systems—heating, plumbing, water supply, lighting, the bathroom—as opposed to appliances, for this core technology has had the greatest impact on the modern house. Large appliances, like washing machines, will be discussed; small appliances, like hair dryers, will not, except in passing. Nor will telephones and personal computers be covered, since their use transcends household convenience.

We will examine the history and transformation of household technology in three phases. In Part 1 we will begin with the opening of the nineteenth century and the growing awareness in America of the "genteel modern house" (quoting a real estate ad in the *Times* of London in 1790) that was evolving in England—a house notable for its implications of what technology might one day do for convenience in the household. We will look in, so to speak, as Benjamin Latrobe, America's first professional architect and himself an English immigrant, in 1805 advises client William Waln of Philadelphia on what a house nowadays should be like. To make it modern, he explains, you must make the house express "the very comprehensive word 'comfort.'" But what exactly does "comfort" mean in 1805? How many people are comfortable? What about the vast majority who aren't (at least by Latrobe's new standard)? What are their houses like at the dawn of this new age? And how did these various degrees of comfort reach the level of development that justifies calling this the beginning of the modern era of comfort and convenience?

Part 2 will focus on 1860, by which time the "modern house" seemed to have surpassed even something from the Arabian Nights, as quoted in *Eighty Years' Progress*, a survey of "modern times" published in 1869:

> *With the improved style of houses there is a constant ambition to occupy a "modern house," or one with the "modern improvements," which may be enumerated as, warming apparatus, whether by hot-air, water, steam, or gas; the water-pipes in all the rooms, connecting with the cooking-range for facility of heating; water-closets and bath-rooms connected with street sewers to carry off the waste water; bells, speaking-tubes, telegraphs [sic], ventilation, burning-gas, dumb-waiters to communicate with different floors, and all the luxury of arrangement and embellishment which makes a modern private dwelling so far in advance even of the fairy palaces of the Arabian Nights' Entertainments.*

For most Americans, however, such a home was still a fantasy.

Part 2 opens with another architect, one who is building his own house. James Gallier Jr. was fully aware of what made a house modern, and he made his home just that. In a brief tour, we will take a closer look at household technology a half a century after Latrobe. The year 1860 itself is significant. There had been considerable development of technology — "giant strides . . . the miracles of antiquity are between each thumb and finger now," as it seemed to Samuel Goodrich in 1856. But the new was, for the most part, available only to the wealthy, Gallier being no exception. The development of mass production spurred by the Civil War would change that; indeed, in the 1860s alone, the number of industrial firms in America increased by 80 percent, the largest one-decade increase in American history. This new era of mass production would raise the standard of living until middle-class homes throughout the country eventually replicated the Gallier house.

By the 1920s, which saw a building boom in the wake of the First World War, it seemed that "comfort had been brought up to perfection," or so said *House & Garden* magazine in January 1926. And indeed, most of what makes today's houses modern and comfortable was now in place, plugged in, turned on, and working. The modern house as it existed early in the twentieth century, along with further improvements still to come, takes us through Part 3.

PART 1

THE COMING
of MODERN : 1805

All we require is the greatest possible compactness, & convenience for the family,
expressed in the very comprehensive word "comfort."
—BENJAMIN LATROBE, 1805

In a genteel way, befitting a genteel age, architect Benjamin Henry Latrobe had some advice for a client that in later times might have been put more bluntly as "Get with it. The times are changing. Build a *modern* house. And above all, make it comfortable and convenient."

The client was William Waln, and we will see to what extent he took Latrobe's advice. Technologically, most houses at the time were little altered from the postmedieval house that came to America with its earliest settlers. By 1805 architectural styles had changed and the average house looked different than it had in the seventeenth century, but it still worked much the same way. In terms of comfort and convenience the average house of 1805 was not much more advanced than that of the 1600s. People still hauled water inside from a well; what they used for cleaning and kitchen chores they then dumped outside. Cooking was done at the fireplace. Personal washing was performed in the bedroom, using a pitcher of water and a basin. For the occasional bath—and usually it was very occasional—they might set up a small portable tub in the kitchen, where they could heat water in the fireplace. Heat was supplied by the inefficient fireplace or, occasionally, by a stove. And there was that epitome of inconvenience, the outdoor privy.

With the nineteenth century came the dawn of a new era. It had begun in Europe—England, in particular—late in the eighteenth century, and through the perceptiveness of architects like Latrobe and clients like Waln, this century of technological revolution began to transform the house in America. The average home that was essentially postmedieval in 1805 would, by the beginning of the twentieth century, be recognizably modern, from kitchen to bathroom, from central heating to electric lights.

What made a house modern in 1805? An occasional kitchen might have water pumped in from a well or, in a very few cities, from a public water supply. A boiler on the hearth might provide hot running water. Perhaps the homeowner would have the latest technology—a Rumford roaster, a water closet, or a bathtub. Lighting might include the recently invented Argand lamp, six to eight times brighter than candles. For heat, there might be a stove instead of, or in addition to, a fireplace.

PREVIOUS PAGE: *In the early 1800s Peale's Museum in Philadelphia, the world's first popular museum of natural science and art, was a showplace for all that was new. Beyond signifying a new appreciation of science, the museum made science relevant in 1815 by using that newest of technologies, gaslight, to illuminate its displays. It was here that thousands of Americans first glimpsed what would one day light the household. The painting is* The Artist in His Museum *(1822) by Charles Willson Peale—Peale the unique artist who created a unique museum.* (**Courtesy of the Pennsylvania Academy of the Fine Arts, Philadelphia. Gift of Mrs. Sarah Harrison [the Joseph Harrison Jr. Collection]**)

Actual examples of these new conveniences were still scattered, owing in part to a lack of awareness; only a cognizant few Americans knew, and understood, what was coming into use in Europe. There was also the matter of affordability. The most advanced kitchen appliances, a "Rumford Kitchen" and a stove, cost $268.11 when the Christopher Gore home was being built in 1806–1807 in Waltham, Massachusetts. An entire year's wages for a laborer at roughly this same time averaged $264. Water closets, bathtubs, heating stoves, indoor water supply, Argand lamps, and other manifestations of a revolution in comfort were simply beyond the means of all but the very well to do in 1805. Within a century,

Philadelphia in the early 1800s. The scene here is Third Street seen from Spruce. (**Engraving by William Birch. Library of Congress**)

these and other more sophisticated devices would be common. Getting to that point took first steps. Beginning with the house that Benjamin Latrobe built for William Waln, and another nearby designed for John Markoe, let us explore the evolution of comfort and convenience that eventually produced the comfortable American home.

PHILADELPHIA: 1805

It was the Athens of America. Notwithstanding its having stepped down as both national and state capital within one year (the state government departing for Lancaster in 1799 and the federal for the new city of Washington in 1800), and the consequent economic upheaval, Philadelphia in 1805 was still the commercial, scientific, cultural, social, artistic, and intellectual capital of the nation. And the technological capital too.

The city's commercial prosperity was signified by its docks. More than thirty ships a week, about a third of them foreign, arrived in port, while a like number departed with goods and agricultural products bound for foreign lands and other American ports. For a population of some 90,000, the largest in the country, there were the blessings that went with commercial success. Walking from the docks toward the center of town one would find not the muddy morasses that passed for streets in some cities but many broad lanes uniformly paved with clean, round stones taken from the bed of the Delaware River near Trenton Falls. Along the principal streets were Lombardy poplars planted in the 1780s, which had now risen to the fullness of their benevolence. "They serve," said a contemporary observer, "not only greatly to ornament the city, but to promote public health by the circulation of air they produce, and the shade they afford during summer." At night this same walk—elsewhere so often taken in shadow—was here protected all night long by streetlamps, some 1,100 in all, each one an oil lamp enclosed in a glass mantle atop a post along the footpath. Those by the markets were lighted every evening at dusk and allowed to burn until daylight; others were lighted only on nights when there was not enough moonlight to suffice. Moonlit and moonless nights combined, this took some 14,000 gallons of lamp oil a year.

The high quality of life in Philadelphia was evident in the presence of three libraries and two museums. Peale's Museum now occupied the upper floors and tower of the recently vacated State House, later known as Independence Hall. The inspiration and labor of love of Charles Willson Peale, one of the country's great painters, the museum was unlike anything else in America, or anything else in the world, for that matter. It was the world's first popular museum of natural science and art. Here, mostly in glass cages, some with habitat backdrops meticulously painted by Peale himself, were stuffed mammals, birds, fish, and insects representing hundreds of species, from the grizzly bear and alligator to the whooping crane and flamingo. There were also some four thousand framed insects, many so tiny that they were exhibited in microscopic wheels. At the other extreme was the museum's premier attraction: the skeleton of a mastodon dug up by Peale in 1801 in Ulster County, New York.

In a few years this museum also would give thousands of visitors their first glimpse of gaslight—appropriately so, since it was Philadelphia that had brought gaslight to America in 1796. The scene for that introduction was an amphitheater maintained by Ambrose and Company, manufacturers of fireworks, for pyrotechnic displays. In August 1796 Ambrose staged "a grand fire-work by means of light composed of inflammable air" issuing from jets in pipes bent to simulate shapes of emblems and houses. The "inflammable air" would later be used as illuminating gas.

This was a modern city in other ways as well. There were two hospitals, including Pennsylvania Hospital, the country's first general hospital and still its largest. There was a health officer to enforce health regulations and nine companies of firefighters. With its bustling port, it is not surprising that Philadelphia merchants had a wide variety of goods for sale, about as fine a selection as could be found anywhere in the land.

Perhaps the city's greatest convenience for residents—at least for the most affluent—was its public water supply, which went into operation in 1801 and by 1805 was connected to some 685 homes. Philadelphia's water system was technologically significant as the first major use of steam power (for the pumps) in America; it was also chiefly the work of the architect and engineer Benjamin Latrobe. All in all, this Philadelphia of 1805 was a modern city by any measure—a good place to look for the modern house of its day.

ARCHITECT OF CHANGE

If Philadelphia is a good place to look for the beginnings of a new era of comfort and convenience, Benjamin Henry Latrobe is uniquely appropriate to introduce that era. Born in England of a mother from Bethlehem, Pennsylvania, and an English father of French Huguenot descent, Benjamin Henry Latrobe spent his early professional years in England and then transplanted himself in 1796 to the New World. He settled in easily and forthwith made a reputation as an architect and engineer. As an architect, he gave America its first Gothic Revival structure (Sedgley, a residence in Philadelphia, 1799) and its first Greek Revival building (the Bank of Pennsylvania, also in Philadelphia, 1798 to 1800), thereby spanning the aesthetic extremes of early-nineteenth-century architecture in two fell swoops. He went on to take charge of construction of the U.S. Capitol, 1808 to 1817, and to contribute to the completion of the White House. He also designed such distinguished houses of worship as the Basilica of the Assumption of the Blessed Virgin Mary in Baltimore and Saint John's Episcopal Church in Washington. In an age

Benjamin Henry Latrobe. (Plate 131, Glenn Brown, *History of the United States Capitol*)

when the purview of an engineer chiefly encompassed roads and bridges and canals, Latrobe helped to expand the profession to embrace mechanics, particularly the use of steam power. Significantly, it was Latrobe, beginning in 1799, who designed and engineered the Philadelphia waterworks. In coming years he also took a role in the development of canals, and he collaborated with Robert Fulton in the development of steamboats.

Six feet two, he had a military bearing, and yet a personal charm that commanded friendship—with Thomas Jefferson, among others. But whereas Jefferson was the consummate amateur architect, as were most architects, consummate or otherwise, in the early nineteenth century, it was Latrobe, with his advanced training in England, who raised architecture to a profession in America and who is generally recognized as America's first professional architect. Add to this the fact that during his training in England, and in the course of travel and study in France, Latrobe had accumulated a working knowledge of what was au courant in the home and we have an excellent observer of household technology at the beginning of a century during which our fundamental expectations of comfort and convenience were to be revolutionized.

BROADENING CONCEPTS

Comfort was a broadening concept in 1805. Of course it is always a relative matter. The vast number of householders in 1805 who cooked at an open hearth, had fireplaces for heat, stored food in a cold cellar, used candles for light, washed in basins, and trekked to outhouses enjoyed what passed for comfort at the time. But a fortunate few, having been exposed to new ideas, had more sophisticated ideas about fashion, taste, and comfort.

Latrobe himself wrote in his journal, after first visiting Philadelphia in 1798: "As far as I did observe, I could see no difference between Philadelphian and English manners. The same style of living, the same opinions as to fashions, tastes, comforts, and accomplishments. Nor can it be well otherwise. The perpetual influx of Englishmen, the constant intercourse of merchants — here the leaders of manners and fashions — with England, must produce this effect."

An advertisement for the "genteel modern house," Times, London, July 22, 1790: one of a growing number of English dwellings that served as models for the modern house in America.

Home buyers want up-to-date houses, and in England at the beginning of the nineteenth century real estate advertisements made a point of mentioning the newest features. An advertisement in the *Times* of London in 1790 described the "genteel modern house" as one that included a "water closet and cistern, supplied from the main." Other ads of the 1790s and early 1800s extolled the virtues of "airy bed-chambers," "convenient kitchen," "kitchen with pump and sink," "breakfast par-

The Waln House: Watercolor by Richard H. Kern, 1847. (Courtesy of the Library Company of Philadelphia)

lour," "laundry," "pantry," "numerous closets," "powdering room," and "water closets on each floor."

Among those who might appreciate these finer things of life, given a little knowing encouragement, was a wealthy China-trade merchant named William Waln for whom the busy docks of Philadelphia had been a source of prosperity.* In 1805 he was engaged to Mary Wilcocks, who happened to have been Mary Elizabeth Latrobe's closest friend since childhood. (Mary Elizabeth was Latrobe's second wife; his first wife, Lydia, died in England in 1793.) Waln had property at Chestnut and Seventh Streets and wanted a house for himself and his bride-to-be. Would Latrobe take on the project? He would not merely take it on, the architect replied; since the future Mrs. William Waln was "a Lady, more loved and esteemed by Mrs. Latrobe than any of her friends," this "has given me a motive for the exertion of my best talents & industry." This inspiration prompted Latrobe to write to Waln on March 26, 1805, his dictum about the word "comfort." On another occasion Latrobe wrote that the Waln house was "such a house as I should build for myself."

Such comments raise great expectations for us. But as we assess the comforts that Latrobe planned, we must keep in mind the house as it existed generally in 1805. The Georgian style that dominated the eighteenth century had produced great architectural refinement over the postmedieval house of the 1600s, but few increases in con-

21

THE
COMING OF
MODERN:
1805

---

*The Walns were among the founding families of Philadelphia. Part of William Waln's fortune accrued from shipping opium from Turkey to China. Waln and other Philadelphia merchants with established trade routes to China were selling as much as $100,000 worth in 1805.

venience and comfort other than those that derived, for example, from windows placed so as to produce cross ventilation.

It is against this that we must see the Waln house, for what Latrobe thought should and should not be included. Also, we don't know exactly what the house was like in its final form since it has long since been demolished. Only its exterior appearance is preserved in an 1847 watercolor. We rely on Latrobe's own words—chiefly his letter of March 26, 1805—for the architect's vision of the ideal house for a favored client or for himself.

COMFORT IN DESIGN

Convenience to Latrobe, as to other architects of the nineteenth century, resulted not only from technology but also from design—from freer use of space—and that is most evident here. Spaciousness—at least in the sense of airiness if not necessarily greatness of area—takes on desirability in its own right, not merely as a by-product of Georgian symmetry. Providing larger and more numerous windows with thinner muntins was a common way of attaining airiness. Convenience also meant ease of movement from one space to another, and this was achieved through thoughtful placement of doors and stairways.

We should not expect to find that any great effort was made to provide convenience in the kitchen, since it was understood that the Walns would have domestic help. Even so, Latrobe declared that "The kitchen is spacious, well lighted. . . . From the kitchen a door leads to the Back stairs, which communicate immediately with the Dining room, and the Lady's apartment above stairs. At the foot of these stairs is a small room, which can be well adapted to the purpose of a bath."

Still another aspect of convenience is to be found in new room uses, often reflecting a greater informality. Hence we find "a [small] parlor [that] will probably be the common family breakfasting room." The idea of an informal eating area separate from the dining room, if there was one, or from the kitchen was new in England and still innovative in America.

COMFORT IN TECHNOLOGY

More overtly technological was Latrobe's insistence on a "Water closet, which the command of Water afforded in Philadelphia by the Waterworks will render perfectly inoffensive if carefully put up." The water closet was one of the new conveniences that Latrobe brought with him from England and France, where it had been in use, albeit to a limited degree. Philadelphia, with its ample water supply from Latrobe's water-works, was especially appropriate for its use in America; but there were water closets elsewhere at this time making use of cisterns that were either roof-fed or filled by pumps using well water.

Three years later and three blocks away, at Chestnut and Tenth Streets, Latrobe undertook another commission that would reflect new notions of convenience. This house was built for John Markoe, also connected to the Latrobes through marriage. Designed in 1808, the house was completed in 1811.

Here there was virtually a modern bathroom, albeit not in one room. On the second floor (or chamber story), adjacent to a dressing room serving the master bedroom, were separate enclosures containing a bathtub with stove-heated cistern for hot water and a separate water closet, also with its own cistern. Water, as in the Waln house, was readily

RIGHT: *Latrobe's drawing of the Markoe House, dated December 23, 1809. Second floor. Note the bathtub and water closet adjacent to the dressing room serving the principal bedroom.* (Courtesy of the Library Company of Philadelphia)

BELOW: *The Markoe House: An undated drawing showing the original appearance of the house.* (Free Library of Philadelphia)

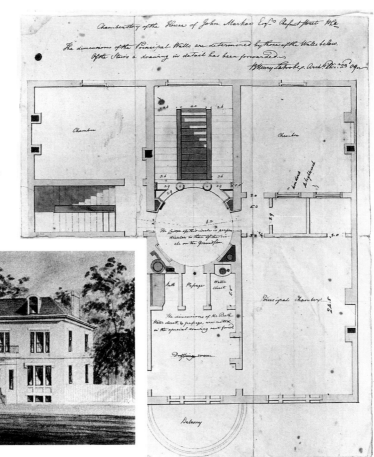

available. Other features included folding doors between the drawing room and the parlor and a plentitude of closets, another convenience feature that was relatively recent.

These were the comforts and conveniences that made a house modern in the eyes of America's first professional architect. Let us compare them with those London real estate ads touting "airy bed-chambers," "convenient kitchen," "kitchen with pump and sink," "breakfast parlour," "laundry," "pantry," "numerous closets," "powdering room," and "water closets on each floor." These are features we have seen incorporated into the plans for Waln and Markoe houses. (A powdering room was chiefly a place for powdering wigs, but it sometimes had a water closet, suggesting a possible origin of the modern term.) The Waln and Markoe houses did not require kitchens with pumps because of the Philadelphia waterworks, and yet there is no mention of a kitchen sink in either Philadelphia home.

The kitchen sink was among the slower-to-appear aspects of household technology in America. Latrobe might nonetheless have provided a built-in hot water supply for the kitchen, without a sink. The George Read II House in New Castle, Delaware (1804), which had no access to a public water supply, did have a pump room adjacent to the kitchen that drew water from an outside well into a 30-gallon boiler in back of the kitchen hearth, thus making hot water continually available in the kitchen at the turn of a stopcock, albeit apparently without any sink to go with it. Buckets were the traditional means of storing and using water in a kitchen, as were pitchers and basins elsewhere in the house. Why did Latrobe not provide the Walns with built-in hot water, or if he did, why did he not mention it in any of his letters or specifications? Surely he was aware of the Read house; Latrobe lived for a time in New Castle. Why no hot water? We do not know.

Meanwhile it is through a contemporary of Latrobe's, then in England, that we are afforded another look at the quintessence of modern at the turn of the nineteenth century.

A House Elysian

I have been inhabiting Elysium the last eight days . . . a life sweeter than you can possibly imagine.
—Marc-Auguste Pictet, 1801

"Elysium" was the home of Benjamin Thompson, Count Rumford, who makes an interesting comparison with Latrobe in that Rumford was born in America and emigrated to England; and in that his expertise was in kitchen, lighting, and heating technology, precisely those areas in which Latrobe showed little interest. His house was at

45 Brompton Row, just outside London, and Professor Marc-Auguste Pictet, a Swiss scholar visiting there, left a description dated August 15, 1801:

> *I have been inhabiting Elysium. . . . The agreeable and the useful have been combined in this abode with much ingenuity and success.*
>
> *You divine at once that everything that concerns the use of fuel, whether for the kitchen or for warmth, has been carried to the highest degree of economy and perfection. . . . Panels of wainscoting at the right and the left of the fireplace are hung on sunken hinges, and you raise one or the other of these, in the style of a table, when you wish to write or read near the fire. The same arrangement is adapted to the piers which separate the windows, and you can at your will produce either a table or a simple panel, when you allow it to fall back again. . . .*
>
> *The bedchambers are disguised in the same way, that is to say, the bed is concealed under the form of an elegant sofa. . . . Under the sofa are two large and deep drawers which contain the bedding, coverlet, and night-gear, and which are hidden by a fringed valence. In a few minutes the sofa is converted at night into an excellent bed, and in the morning the bed becomes for the day an ornamental piece of furniture. . . .*
>
> *The windows have a double glazing, and the exterior makes a three-sided projection, in which are placed vases of flowers and odorous shrubs, which you may have at your pleasure within or outside the apartment, according as you open or close the inner sash. . . .*
>
> *The house is equipped with the most perfect simplicity and the most complete order, and a person could not conceive a more pleasant life, nor one more comfortable than that which is led here.*

All these, along with specially designed appliances for cooking and assorted other devices, made this a truly remarkable house, way beyond the ordinary house of its day.

But no wonder. Count Rumford, physicist extraordinaire and by a curious twist of fate the Bavarian ambassador to England (hence living in London in 1801), was a giant among household innovators. And yet his name is today hardly a household word. He might have been honored with a statue as one of a singularly great generation of American heroes. But though he was born in 1753, and a contemporary of American heroes like James Madison and Alexander Hamilton, whose intellect he matched, his inclinations pointed

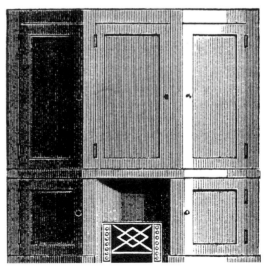

ABOVE LEFT: *Count Rumford, as Bavarian ambassador to England, 1798.* (George E. Ellis, Memoir of Sir Benjamin Thompson, Count Rumford)

ABOVE RIGHT: *The ultramodern kitchen, 1801: Count Rumford's own house in London. This, according to Rumford, was "a concealed kitchen . . . on entering it, nobody would suspect [it] to be a kitchen." An open fireplace is surrounded by a paneled wall that conceals a roaster on the upper right and a "family boiler" on the left. The panels were lined with sheet iron and were installed two to three inches distant from the built-in stoves so that cooking might "be carried on with perfect safety with the door shut." Most visitors were undoubtedly impressed, but scientist and editor Thomas Thomson, after visiting Rumford's home in 1802 recalled that he "was very much surprised to observe that not one of the utensils had ever been put to use . . . his notions of cooking were theoretical rather than practical." In the case of Rumford's own kitchen, that may have been so; but the usefulness of Rumford's kitchen technology—roasters, ranges, steam kitchens, coffeepots, and so on—may be judged by its immediate popularity in both Europe and America.* (Rumford, Complete Works, vol. 3)

him away from rebellion and toward reconciliation with the mother country. A Loyalist, he fled the colonies in 1776 and took up residence first in England and then in Bavaria. It was a choice for which he was never forgiven in his homeland, and he remains little remembered in America. One must go to Munich to find a statue of him.

In Munich Rumford made his reputation as a provider of modern conveniences, both as head of the Bavarian war department, with chief responsibility for the living conditions of soldiers, and as head of Munich's House of Industry, which saw to the poor, whose plight seems genuinely to have evoked Rumford's sympathy. What he accomplished helped both the troubled masses of the poorhouse and a government that was sensitive to their misfortune as long as the cost of sensitivity was not too high. On one occasion Rumford wrote that "Nothing surely is so disgraceful to society and individuals as unmeaning wastefulness," and as if balancing these two spheres of inter-est he set out to reduce costs while improving conditions. He built, at the workhouse, a kitchen that included two rows of four boilers each, set in brickwork. They were heated by one fireplace, using flues and dampers to distribute the heat. The result, he calculated, was a considerable saving in fuel and also a more efficient way to feed a thousand or so people a day.

ANOTHER WORD FOR COMFORT

From almost every incident that now comes before the public, we date the origin of some important addition to our language. We therefore frequently meet with advertisements, &c. wherein we are told, that persons may have their kitchen fireplaces and culinary utensils Rumfordized.
— EUROPEAN MAGAZINE, JANUARY 1809

From the success of Rumford's workhouse kitchen and a similar installation at the military academy, recognition flowed, resulting in commissions by wealthy individuals throughout Western Europe for Rumford kitchens of smaller size but equal efficiency. In England he designed for Sir John Sinclair, a founder of the Board of Agriculture, a model kitchen that went on public display at the board's headquarters. In 1798 he devised, for a tradesman named Summers, an ingenious roaster that Summers constructed for customers to see. In less than three years Summers had built and installed at least 260 of these devices, which became known as Rumford roasters. The roaster came into use in America after publication in Boston in 1804 of "On the Construction of Kitchen Fire-Places" (volume 3 of Rumford's *Essays*). However, the device was so sophisticated for its time and such a bold departure from traditional methods of cooking that few people, even among the wealthy, chose to own one. Even those who did install a roaster routinely kept an open hearth as well, both for heating and for traditional cooking.

But Rumford's influence could be felt beyond the kitchen—literally felt. His reputation was largely made on his improvement of the fireplace as a source of heat. The late-eighteenth-century fireplace was still the inefficient boxy structure it had been in the postmedieval house. Most of its warmth went straight up the chimney, but a solution to that problem was elusive. Stoves sent more heat out into the room, but at the expense of losing "Sight of the Fire, which is in itself a pleasant Thing," as Benjamin Franklin pointed out in behalf of his own Pennsylvania fireplace, better known as the Franklin stove. Fireplaces were also expensive. Having one built as part of the house was more economical, but could it be redesigned to send more heat into the room and to use less fuel?

The Count showed that it could, and the Rumford fireplace began to gain popularity in the early 1800s. Rumford simply reduced the overall size of the fireplace, in particular the depth of the inner hearth. He then angled the sides to make the opening in front three times the size of the back, and he considerably reduced the size of the throat. The result was a noticeable increase in the amount of heat that radiated into the room.

This solution satisfied Rumford himself, who admitted to being "still child enough to be pleased with the brilliant appearance of burning fuel." Yet he was also "sanguine enough to expect" the time when an open fire would cease to be the chief means of heating. He helped to fulfill his own prophecy by experimenting with central heating. For the theater of the Royal Institution in London he designed a steam heating system in 1802. He explained that "The theater is warmed in cold weather by steam, which, coming in covered and concealed tubes from the lower part of the house circulates in a large semicircular copper tube 8 inches in diameter and about 60 feet long which is concealed under the rising seats of the pit." Although the system was eventually dismantled, it had apparently worked reasonably well. But both steam and hot water as commonplace methods of heating were still some years off.

As for lighting, Rumford had the advantage of building upon a major recent development—the Argand lamp, patented in England in 1784, which was many times brighter than a candle. Never satisfied with what existed, Rumford produced a new lamp using the same basic principles but changing the wick. He was also among the first to recognize the impact of glare on illumination—to see that it was not only the intensity of the light source but the significance of light versus shadow that influenced the quality of illumination. The result was a lamp with a translucent shade made of silk—this at a time when the uncovered flame of a candle or oil lamp was virtually universal. Translucence, Rumford said, might also be extended to windows by using ground glass instead of clear window glass. He proposed just that in the course of presenting a paper to the Institute of France in 1807. The institute's auditorium faced a small court that was surrounded by high buildings. In cloudy weather or late in the day there was a troubling deficiency of light. If ground glass was used in the windows, suggested Rumford, "the amount of light in the hall would be much increased, and the light will be more equable, softer, and more agreeable." His audience laughed, but in time, Rumford would be proven right, and his understanding of the dynamics of illumination would be fundamental to modern lighting.

Meanwhile, one of Rumford's contemporaries, though his sense of the comfortable and convenient was not his chief legacy, deserves more than a mere mention in the company of these innovators: Thomas Jefferson.

CONTRIVANCE AND CONVENIENCE

[Jefferson's] local and domestic arrangements were full of contrivances, or conveniences *as he called them, peculiarly his own and never met with in other houses . . . and even in the President's House [the White House] were introduced some of these favorite contrivances, some of them really useful and convenient.*
—MARGARET BAYARD SMITH, 1809

In his own house, Monticello, and to a lesser extent in the White House during his time there, Jefferson took delight in incorporating conveniences both of his own design and of European model. During his tenure in France from 1784 to 1789, Jefferson encountered much that was new, for Paris in the late eighteenth century was also experiencing a thrust toward modern notions of convenience, and Jefferson spread the word. For example, he wrote from Paris in 1784 to his friend, Charles Thomson, secretary of the Continental Congress, that "There has been a lamp called the cylinder lamp lately invented here. It gives a light equal, as is thought, to that of six or eight candles."*

Jefferson was among the earliest advocates of the water closet. When he moved into the White House in 1801, there was only a privy out back. He requested installation of a water closet, something he perhaps used for the first time in Paris.

As minister to France, Jefferson lived in a recently completed town house owned by the Comte de Langeac. The financially troubled Langeac could not afford to use the spacious mansion himself and was undoubtedly happy to have so respectable a tenant as the U.S. minister.

Thomas Jefferson. **(Library of Congress)**

The Hôtel de Langeac had many of those spatial amenities we have seen in England and in American homes based on English models. On entering the house, one passed through a reception hall into a circular room with a skylight. Adjoining this was an oval drawing room that overlooked the Champs-Élysées. Also on the main floor

---

*The Argand lamp. In the same letter, Jefferson told of another modern convenience: "I should have sent you a specimen of the phosphoric matches but that I am told Mr. Rittenhouse has had some of them. They are a beautiful discovery and very useful. . . . The convenience of lighting a candle without getting out of bed, of sealing letters without calling a servant, of kindling a fire without flint, steel, punk, &c., are of value."

were the principal dining room, a smaller and presumably less formal dining room, and a bath room, for bathing only. The kitchen was in the basement, reached by a back staircase. On the second floor were three spacious bedchambers, each with its own dressing room, two with walk-in closets. There was also a *lieu à l'anglais*—a water closet. (The English called their privies jakes, colloquial for *jacques*, and the French returned the favor with their "English places.") No details are known about this particular water closet, but one illustrated in A. J. Roubo's *L'art du menuisier* (page 68) would appear to fit well into the room layout. The town house itself was demolished in 1842, but the floor plans are preserved in the Bibliothèque Nationale.

Although a water closet was finally installed at the White House in 1804, Jefferson never got beyond sketching a plan for one at Monticello. A drawing, probably done sometime before 1808, shows a scheme for piping in water to serve both a greenhouse and water closet, but nothing came of the plan. The most likely reason is that water supply was always a problem at Monticello, a mountaintop dwelling. As part of the enlargement of Monticello begun in 1796 and completed in 1809, Jefferson did include three indoor privies using a sophisticated venting system that included a 160-foot basement-level air tunnel and shafts venting through a chimney flue. These indoor facilities are distinguished from their outdoor counterparts by the convenience of their location and by the fact that waste could not be allowed to accumulate, as in a privy pit. Waste had to be removed regularly, but exactly how this was done is not known; certainly it fell to one or more of Monticello's many servants. In a sense these were fancy chamber pot rooms. Unlike a water closet, there was no flushing action of water.

The architecture of the Hôtel de Langeac also inspired features of Jefferson's 1796 enlargement of Monticello. The Paris residence had two small private staircases in addition to the formal staircase, and Jefferson found these so convenient that he included similar stairways at Monticello. He also added a smaller, less formal dining area—the tea room—just off the main dining room. Langeac's skylight also was an inspiration. The alcove beds that are such a familiar part of Monticello were also based on French models, and on his return from Paris Jefferson brought with him two Argand lamps for Monticello.

But Jefferson needed only so much inspiration. He could devise quite well for himself. Margaret Bayard Smith, a socialite and the wife of a publisher, recalled a visit to the White House:

There was in his dining room an invention for introducing and removing the dinner with the opening and shutting of doors. A set of circular shelves were so contrived in the wall, that on touching a spring they turned into the room loaded with the dishes placed on them by the servants without the wall, and by the same process the removed dishes were conveyed out of the room.

At Monticello, there were other things that would strike a contemporary observer and historian alike as ingenious. Examples include the clock with cannonball weights to show the day of week as well as time of day, the turntable closet at the foot of Jefferson's alcove bed, the writing table with revolving top in his bedroom suite, and the high-backed chair facing it.

Still another convenience that Jefferson contemplated but never tried to implement was central heat. An undated drawing (page 52) shows a central furnace with ducts to convey hot air to various rooms above. It has all the essential elements of a modern hot-air heating system except a mechanical blower. But Jefferson appears never to have gone beyond contemplating this. In both the original section of Monticello, begun in 1768, and the enlargement of the late 1790s, he relied on fireplaces and stoves, preferring the latter. One stove built to his specifications and installed in 1812, apparently in the tea room, proved quite satisfactory. "I have set it up," Jefferson wrote, "and find it to answer perfectly. The room is very small where it is placed, and it is fully warmed up by it in a few minutes."

At the other thermal extreme was Monticello's capacious and efficient icehouse, a stone-lined cistern 20 feet deep (16 feet below ground and 4 above) and 8 feet in diameter. Its wooden lid was covered with a layer of earth for additional insulation. Completed in 1802, the icehouse was first filled the following winter, using ice from the Rivanna River. According to Jefferson's records, sixty-two wagonloads of ice were needed to fill it. The ice rested on a lattice of boards covered with straw. As the ice was dumped in, it would have been customary to place straw around the perimeter; Jefferson substituted wood shavings because carpentry work at Monticello was producing piles of them and he was glad to find a use. The top was also covered with a layer of shavings. When it was time to obtain ice, a workman would enter through a door at the top of the cistern and use an ax to chop away what was needed. During the average season, ice could be expected to last until the fall. At first melted ice water was removed with buckets; by 1807 Jefferson had a pump in place for the purpose.

GETTING THERE

This was just the beginning of a remarkable century, within the span of which the house was transformed from essentially postmedieval to basically modern. Before 1800 the average home contained almost nothing that could be called technology, but by the early 1900s, the house had most of what makes it modern, from kitchen to bathroom, from central heat to electric light. As important as these new conveniences was the evolution of power, fuel, and water supply that made the new technologies work.

Power, Fuel, and Water Supply

Moving toward the Future

The windmill was brought down to Boston, because, where it stood near Newtown, it would not grind but with a westerly wind.
— Governor John Winthrop, Massachusetts Bay, August 14, 1632

Always a still month, August — the stillest of the year. In the Massachusetts Bay area, however, Governor Winthrop had a right to expect a little more of a stir. Boston is breezier than most of the country, and parts of coastal Massachusetts register some of the highest average rates of wind power in the United States. Even so, the first site for the mill at what is now Watertown left something to be desired; hence it was hauled to Copps Hill in Boston. Four years later another mill was erected in Boston, and subsequently others appeared on various hills in town. Indeed, during the colonial period — beginning with the earliest one known, which was erected at the Flowerdew Hundred Plantation near Jamestown, Virginia, in 1621 — many windmills were in use in the colonies.

Windmills had been relatively common in England, so it is no surprise that the settlers in Winthrop's colony, finding they had landed in a breezy place, constructed windmills to perform the chore for which they were so well suited: grinding grain. Its gristmill function was primary, but wind-driven machinery also appears to have worked for fulling mills.

In the colonial period, and indeed well into the nineteenth century, windmills were modeled on what the colonists had known in Europe, and they changed very little during the early years. The colonial windmill was a productive source of power, but it was also labor-intensive. Someone had to watch over it almost continually. It was also expensive to build. Smaller, more efficient windmills that adjusted themselves to the wind automatically would change all that, as we will see, and make wind a widely used source of energy for the individual household, especially in the Midwest, in the later nineteenth and early twentieth centuries.

Animal power, chiefly horse and mule, was another option, but less for the individual homeowner than for the farmer. Geographer and traveler John Melish, visiting the Harmony Society settlement in Pennsylvania in 1809 observed "a dog turning a wheel [presumably a treadmill] for blowing the bellows" at a blacksmith's forge.

And of course there was that perennial source of power closest at hand, so to speak—the human arm. Humans hauled water from a spring, pumped water from a well, hauled water into the house, washed things with water, got the fire going, put things on the fire, took things off the fire, and so on. Before the introduction of steam and electricity, it was the human arm that most often made things work.

Wind and water, horse and human. For the individual household, it was still only the human who was significant.

THE COMING OF STEAM POWER

Steam power was first used in America in 1755 to operate a drainage pump in the principal shaft of the Schuyler family copper mine in Bergen County, New Jersey, then the largest copper mine in North America. The engine was a Newcomen atmospheric engine built in England by Joseph Hornblower, a colleague of Thomas Newcomen, and was typical of the engines in use at the time. It was atmospheric in that power did not come directly from steam pressure, as in later engines, but through the use of steam to create a vacuum and let atmospheric pressure do the work. The engine's single cylinder was allowed to fill with steam from a boiler below. Through a valve on the cylinder,

PREVIOUS PAGE: *The Old Windmill, Nantucket, Massachusetts, 1746.* (Historic American Buildings Survey)

a jet of cold water was then injected, causing the steam to condense. This created a vacuum, which resulted in atmospheric pressure forcing downward the piston in the cylinder, and this in turn operated the pump. Primitive though it was, it is estimated this system could pump at a rate of 180,000 gallons a day. Wood was used for fuel.

John Schuyler placed the order for the engine through his London agent in 1749, and by 1755 the engine was ready. Sometime around the middle of March—the exact date is no longer on record—the engine was fired up, representing the first use of a modern form of power in the New World.

Except for Philadelphia's water supply, or a rare instance like a steam jack for turning meat over a hearth, patented in 1792 by John Bailey, these early uses of steam had no direct bearing on the household. They are significant, though, in that they represent the coming of new technology that will have considerable impact later in the nineteenth century.

ELECTRICITY: BARELY A HINT

What in modern times is central to nearly all of household technology was still an abstract idea at the end of the eighteenth century. Neither Benjamin Franklin, despite his famous kite experiment in 1752, nor the other learned scientists of the time had any idea how drastically electricity would transform their way of life. Franklin gave merely a hint of the impact of electricity on household life when he suggested in 1749 that "a turkey be killed for our dinner by the *electrical shock*, and roasted by the *electrical jack* [a rotating spit, in the nature of a modern rotisserie], before a fire kindled by the *electrified bottle* [a Leyden jar]." But the use of electricity for cooking, even in primitive form, was more than a century away. And little, if any, thought appears to have been given to the possibility of electricity being useful in day-to-day life around the house.

FUEL: STILL MOSTLY WOOD

In the absence of power-driven appliances, those staples of modern life, fuel for domestic purposes was for heating and lighting; and, except for the very occasional use of coal, fuel meant wood. The earliest colonists left behind a Europe threatened with the increasing depletion of its forests. In England, for example, the dwindling supply of wood was obvious by the sixteenth century. The Europeans must have been awed by the prospect of a vast continent with seemingly infinite reserves. Wood became the standard fuel for cooking and heating, and continued as such well into the nineteenth century.

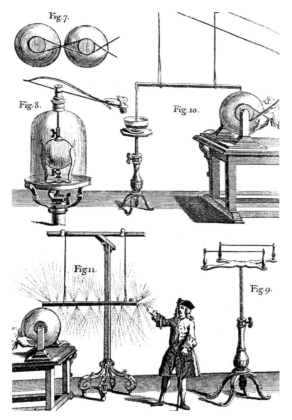

Experimentation with electricity in the eighteenth century— barely a hint of what was to come. (**Universal Magazine**, London, November 1747, Library of Congress)

Coal was in use by the mid-eighteenth century, but only to a very limited degree. Most of what was used was imported from Great Britain, and in 1769 this totaled 8,558 tons. Some coal also was produced in the colonies. In 1765 alone, 712 tons of coal mined in America were sent from James River ports in Virginia to ports in Massachusetts, Rhode Island, New Jersey, and Pennsylvania. The two totals combined give a rough idea of the amount of coal burned annually in the colonies. Use of coal was probably most common near ports of entry, and particularly in major cities. Of the 8,558 tons imported in 1769, roughly 79 percent (6,757 tons) went to the ports of Boston, New York, Philadelphia, and Charleston, and was probably used in or around those cities. There is no way of knowing how much was used domestically and how much commercially. Certainly some homes used coal for fireplace heating. As one example, the house that Thomas Heyward Jr. built in Charleston, South Carolina, in 1772 had only coal grates in the fireplaces. The price of coal was such that only the wealthy could afford it, however. For those who could, it was worth the expense; it produced greater heat than wood and required less tending.

VERY USEFUL WORKS

In the . . . house [a mill using a water wheel] they were now arranging water-works, which were to drive the water up the steep hill, and then through pipes distribute it to every house. . . . This will be a very useful work . . . for hitherto it has kept a man busy from morning till night to carry the water up the hill to the houses.

—THE REVEREND ISRAEL ACRELIUS OF SWEDEN, VISITING
BETHLEHEM, PENNSYLVANIA, JUNE 18, 1754

Water supply as technology in America may be said to have started in Bethlehem in 1754. Here was the first organized effort using pump, pipes, and a reservoir — the essentials of modern water supply. There had been a primitive attempt as early as 1652 in Boston, when the Water Works Company constructed a series of wooden pipes to carry water by gravity flow from a spring to a central reservoir. Since the reservoir was only twelve feet square, the system was obviously of limited use. There was no use of pumps.

Bethlehem's water system was more ambitious, using a pump to tap the Monocacy Creek, a tributary of the Lehigh River. The system was built by Hans Cristopher Christiansen, a Danish millwright, along the lines of similar waterworks in Europe. Bethlehem's system used water power — an overshot waterwheel in the millhouse — to operate a pump that forced water up a steep hill to a water tower at the grade level of the town itself. The pipe through which the water was pumped was made of hollowed-out hemlock trunks. After a trial run the system went into regular operation on June 27, 1754. There may have been connections to a few nearby houses using wooden pipe, but most residents probably carried water from the tower in buckets.

The majority of people in the colonial period got their water from wells, springs, and streams. Sites for houses in a town, indeed the locations of towns and villages themselves, were often chosen because of their proximity to water. And, in rural areas for the duration of the colonial period, wells and streams were sufficient. In towns and cities there were public pumps in addition to wells. Swedish scientist Peter Kalm, after visiting Philadelphia in 1748, wrote that there was a well in every house along with several in the streets, although that is clearly an overstatement.

Only in the latter part of the eighteenth century, however, did public water supply systems really begin to develop. And it was no coincidence that a number of cities all became concerned with water supply at the same time, nor that Philadelphia was preeminent among them. Its experience, as related by John Watson, was typical: "There was little or no desire expressed by the citizens of Philadelphia, for any other than their *good* pump-water, till after the yellow fever of 1793. Then, when the mind was alive to every suggested danger of ill health, the idea of pump-water being no longer good found its increasing supporters."

Yellow fever had been known since early colonial times but outbreaks were sporadic. Epidemics could be severe, however, as in Philadelphia and Charleston in 1699 and New York in 1702. At the very end of the eighteenth century, there came outbreaks in one city after another; and now the search for a cause was accelerated. In Philadelphia there had been epidemics before, especially of smallpox, but nothing resembling the terror unleashed by yellow fever in 1793. There was panic as crowds fled the city. Some infected victims were left to die along the roadside; people in out-lying districts were too afraid to offer help. In 1794 yellow fever struck Baltimore and New Haven and, a year later, devastated New York City. Over the next several years smaller towns like Portsmouth, Newburyport, and Providence fell victim. New London, then a town of 2,800, was stunned in 1798 as one in every eight of its residents was stricken and one in every twenty-eight died between mid-August and mid-October. Clearly this was a crisis. Was yellow fever spread by the water? With its transmittal by mosquito only established in 1900, it could not be discounted.

Many, and perhaps most, people were certain that yellow fever was contagious. As Philadelphia publisher Mathew Carey observed, "Acquaintances and friends avoided each other in the streets, and only signified their regard by a cold nod. The old custom of shaking hands fell into such general disuse that many shrunk back with affright at even the offer of a hand." Those who held to the contagion theory argued that the threat came from outside the country, and they pressed for the use of quarantines as the primary defense. Baltimore responded to the crisis in 1794 by appointing a committee on health that imposed quarantine regulations the follow-ing year.

Others disagreed. The pumps in Philadelphia were many (along the footpaths at intervals of 60 to 70 feet on nearly every street) and the water was clear. "But," observed Benjamin Latrobe, in a letter on April 29, 1798, "this very circumstance, the inexhaustible supply of clear water to be found in every possible spot of ground, and which must have appeared the most tempting inducement to its projector, Penn, to found here a city, is the great cause, in my opinion, of the contagion which appears now to be an annual disease of Philadelphia, the yellow fever."

Elsewhere there was also suspicion about water as the cause of the spread of yellow fever. Even before Latrobe gave his opinion, Boston recognized an increase of pollution in wells and thus accepted the need for a new source of water. The Massachusetts General Court chartered the Boston Aqueduct Corporation in February 1795 to supply the city with water from outlying Jamaica Pond in Roxbury. By 1798 the center of Boston was being served either by wood pipe in the house or by retail for a penny a pail.

In 1796 Salem, Massachusetts, built a gravity-flow system to supply water from nearby Spring Pond. Customers could have water piped into their homes to a tap in the cellar, kitchen, or scullery. In New Hampshire the Portsmouth Aqueduct was incorporated in 1797 and, by 1800, was serving most of downtown Portsmouth, with a total of 214 customers, including both houses and stores. Water was conveyed through wooden pipe from a spring about three miles distant. That water-supply system was substantially the work of Benjamin Gilman, an Exeter, New Hampshire, silversmith and maker of precision tools, who had earlier been involved in constructing the aqueducts in Boston and Salem as well as Exeter and New London, Connecticut. The Portsmouth system had perhaps a unique feature. According to historian Charles W. Brewster, "Within a few feet of the wharf [terminus of the system] was a carved statue of a man, with extended arm, and from his forefinger a stream of water was continually issuing. This was a fanciful vent of the Portsmouth Aqueduct."

A water-supply system using an aqueduct was developed by the Shaker community at Hancock, Massachusetts, shortly after its founding in 1790. The system supplied water for operating workshop equipment as well as for drinking and household needs. An anonymous visitor described the system in 1818:

> *A small stream of water comes down the mountains north of the town, near the source of which a dam is erected . . . the stream is conducted by an aqueduct under ground to the middle of the village, where it is made to pass through a hollowed tree for the purpose of turning a large overshot wheel that serves to work their machinery. From this wheel the water is conveyed underground to the washing rooms, and also for watering the horses, stables, works, etc. . . . . It also supplies the mill that saws firewood, pounds their wood that is split for basket making, and is afterwards conveyed to the different fields to water the cattle, & etc. Thus is everything under their control so directed that nothing is wasted.*

The first use of steam power in the Western Hemisphere, as we have seen, was for draining the principal mine shaft at the Schuyler copper mine in New Jersey in 1755. Pumping water was the first essential use of steam power in Europe as well, although not only to keep mine shafts working. By the 1720s there were steam engines in use for water supply at Passy, France, tapping the river Seine for the city of Paris, and at Toledo, Spain.

New York City in 1774 commissioned Christopher Colles, an engineer and cartographer, to construct a system of waterworks using steam power. The project was

The steam-powered Philadelphia waterworks, Centre Square pumping station, 1801. Water was conveyed to customers from here by way of wooden pipes. (**Free Library of Philadelphia**)

interrupted by the Revolutionary War and never completed. It was therefore Philadelphia that first used steam for water supply in America — in the waterworks that Latrobe designed and constructed. The project was begun in 1799, and not without controversy. Was steam power safe? It was one thing to use it in a distant mine shaft, but in the middle of a city? A letter to the *Philadelphia Gazette*, July 31, 1800, raised the specter of "general calamity to our city, to wit: a reliance upon steam engines in the proper supply of water. They are machines of all machinery the least to be relied on, subject to casualties and accidents of every kind."

Still, within a year Latrobe had presented to the Philadelphia Common Council, and the council had accepted, a bold plan for circumventing the need for wells, which drew upon, said Latrobe, "the stratum in which the water runs, and which the action of the pump draws to itself from all parts round it . . . the filth . . . of the neighborhood." Instead Latrobe would draw water from the clean-flowing Schuylkill River. His plan called for two steam engines — one at the riverbank, the other in Centre Square, site of the present City Hall. Working in series, these engines, capable of pumping more than 700,000 gallons every twenty-four hours, conveyed water from the river through brick tunnel, 6 feet in diameter and 1,408 yards long, to the engine house at Centre Square, where the second engine raised it to a 16,000-gallon tank, from which the water flowed by gravity. Water was delivered to customers by wooden pipe, the standard of the day.

The process of making pipe was described by James Mease in 1811: "The pipes are bored by placing the log in two cast iron rings and centered by regulating screws. As the log turns the augers enter at each end and meet in the middle, a pipe of fifteen feet long can be bored and the joints made for the connecting cylinders in fifteen minutes. The connecting cylinders are of cast iron widening at both ends that as the log is driven up the joints become tight." Pipe for the distribution system mostly had bores of 3 or 4½ inches — quite small by modern standards.

This system, which went into service on January 21, 1801, was easily the largest application of steam power yet attempted in America. Yet all this infrastructure existed at the outset for the convenience of only sixty-three houses, four businesses, and a sugar refinery — little more than a quarter the number of customers that the Portsmouth Aqueduct was serving at the time. That changed quickly. Five years after it opened, the Philadelphia waterworks had nearly 850 customers and, by 1811, more than 2,000. As it acquired business, however, it also acquired problems. The engines were subject to frequent breakdowns and costly repairs; and the system as originally planned quickly became insufficient for the needs of a growing city. By 1822 an entirely new water system was in operation with a reservoir on Fairmount Hill.

The Philadelphia water-supply system, whatever its failings, pointed the new century in the direction of technologically managed mass water supply that would be indispensable to the vast population growth ahead.

HEATING

OVERCOMING "INCONVENIENCIES"

Staying warm has priority over keeping cool. For the most part, we can cope with hot weather without technological assistance. If a handheld fan doesn't help, there is the shade of a tree or even the cool of a stream; or, within the bounds of modesty or necessity, we can divest ourselves of enough clothing to enable us to cope with sweltering heat and let the body's natural defense mechanism of perspiration do the rest. We may not be as comfortable as we might like, but we will survive.

To keep warm, however, the body often needs help. Even in a moderate climate we need at least some warm clothing, produced through some form of technology, however simple. In colder climates in dead of winter we absolutely require a source of heat, produced by technology of a more complex form, to keep us from freezing to death or succumbing to pneumonia.

Heat was the first adaptation in our basic shelter to raise our home above the primitive level. Even the crude shelter of prehistoric man managed to accommodate fire for heating and cooking. In the evolution of the American house, we find evidence of technology in heating prior to any other application of ingenuity. (Because it was much more difficult to achieve, cooling technology came much later.) The heating stove, for example, represents a higher level of comfort and convenience than the open fireplace, and a correspondingly higher level of technological advancement. Although hardly common, stoves were in use when water supply still consisted of hauling water into the house in buckets, when refrigeration consisted at best of a cellar, when bathing meant using a simple basin in one's bedroom, when the privy and the chamber pot were all that existed of the bathroom, and when cooling and ventilating were only as sophisticated as opening a window. Although most people had to be content with the open hearth for heating and cooking, a few enjoyed the greater comfort and fuel efficiency of a small heating stove. Dr. John Clarke of Boston had three of them by the early 1660s, as evidenced by his will, executed in 1661, which stipulated that they were to go to his wife. Samuel Sewall, also of Boston, had one stove. In his diary on January 16, 1702, he wrote that there was "Comfortable moderat wether: and with a good fire in the Stove warm'd the room."

The use of stoves during the colonial period was generally more common among German settlers. The oldest existing heating stove in America that is still in its original site and original condition is believed to be at Schifferstadt, Frederick, Maryland, the home built by Elias Brunner, of Schifferstadt, Germany, in 1756. The Germans are known to have had heating stoves by the mid-fifteenth century.

One of the earliest known references was recorded by the French chronicler Gilles le Bouvier (1386–1457?): "For the cold that grips Germany in winter they have stoves that heat in such a manner that they are warm in their rooms . . . and it takes not much wood to heat them."

During the colonial period, most of the nineteenth century, and even into the twentieth, the fireplace was the primary source of heat. At the beginning of European settlement the fireplace was still essentially medieval, still a cavernous structure, virtually a small room, large enough to walk into, which was in fact required to tend to the bake oven in the back wall. There might even be space for a chair within and to one side of the fire, and this was the one place in the house that was actually all-over warm in the frigid deep winter. By the eighteenth century the dimensions of the fireplace had been gradually reduced, somewhat improving efficiency, and the bake oven had been relocated to the front and to one side of the hearth.

The open fireplace of today is a quaint and nostalgic addition to a home that has a central heating system on which to rely for actually keeping warm. In such a setting

OPPOSITE PAGE: *A perspective view of Gauger's fireplace.* (Nicolas Gauger, *La mécanique du feu*, Paris, 1713)

it is hard to imagine what it was like to have to rely on the fireplace alone. Because much of its heat went straight up into the sky above, the traditional fireplace was singularly inefficient as a source of heat. This shortcoming was keenly felt when there was still not much one could do about it. In his 1744 tract publicizing what eventually became known as the Franklin stove, Benjamin Franklin carefully cataloged all the disadvantages of the fireplace:

> *Their Inconveniencies are, that they almost always smoke if the Door be not left open; that they require a large Funnel, and a large Funnel carries off a great Quantity of Air, which occasions what is called a strong Draft to the Chimney; without which strong Draft the Smoke would come out of some Part or other of so large an Opening, so that the Door can seldom be shut; and the cold Air nips the Backs and Heels of those that sit before the Fire, that they have no Comfort, 'till either Screens or Settles are provided (at a considerable Expence) to keep it off, which both cumber the Room and darken the Fireside. A moderate Quantity of Wood on the Fire in so large a Hearth, seems but little; and, in so strong and cold a Draught, warms but little; so that People are continually laying on more. In short, 'tis next to impossible to warm a Room with such a Fire-place: And I suppose our Ancestors never thought of warming Rooms to sit in; all they purpos'd was to have a Place to make a Fire in, by which they might warm themselves when acold.*

Many people regarded stoves with suspicion, however. They were considered unwholesome compared with the open fireplace, and they were thought to have an unpleasant smell. Furthermore, it was feared that a stove would actually make the room too warm, thus causing people to catch cold on going outside.

A COPERNICAN THEORY OF THE HEARTH

Coinciding with the European settlement of America was the glorious revolution of science that was the age of Galileo and Newton. And while exploring the eternal mysteries of the heavens hardly ameliorated the chill in one's parlor, the emphasis on mathematics inherent in astronomy contributed to a renewed interest in mathematics and science generally, and eventually there was impact on the household. The diagram on page 45 is almost a Copernican theory of the hearth, redefining relationships in the fireplace, as Copernicus did for the heavens and earth.

The common way of building fireplaces with the jambs parallel, and the breast inclined, is not proper for reflecting heat into a room.

—NICOLAS GAUGER, LA MÉCANIQUE DU FEU, 1713

Gauger likewise shakes up old beliefs. Of Nicolas Gauger we know little except that he was born in France about 1680, had a natural curiosity about science, experimented with the physics of light, and wrote a tract on thermometers and barometers before turning to the science of heating. He died, probably in Paris, in 1730.

Gauger's experimentation started with the shape of the fireplace itself. What had been an open bonfire, confined only by andirons, in the middle of the medieval great hall eventually moved to one side of the hall, where it was partly enclosed by a boxlike structure made up of perpendicular surfaces. This became smaller, but it was still the fireplace in Gauger's time, as it would be for years to come. If we examine this fireplace, said Gauger, we can prove that most of the heat is reflected back into the hearth and then up the chimney. Gauger argued that since angle of incidence equals angle of reflection, most rays of heat warm only the inside of the fireplace itself while only a few are reflected outward into the room. In any case, quoting the original translation, those that remain in the room "have lost most of their strength before they can get thither." But if we build the fireplace in the shape of a parabola instead of a simple rectangle, we can redirect many of those straying rays of warmth in our direction. In time, the focusing quality of the parabola found application in reflecting telescopes, radar antennas, searchlights, and automobile headlights. And indeed, the configuration of

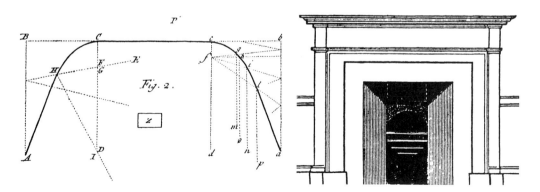

ABOVE: *Plate from* La mécanique du feu, *explaining the significance of the parabolic shape of Gauger's fireplace relative to traditional box-shaped fireplace.*

RIGHT: *Sharply slanted sides and an opening taller than it was wide were distinguishing characteristics of the fireplace designed by Count Rumford at the beginning of the nineteenth century. Here was an essential principle of Gauger's fireplace made both practical and popular.* (**Rumford, Complete Works**)

the fireplace did change more or less along these lines, except that Gauger's solution of using sheet metal to create the effect of a parabola never caught on, and the practicalities of laying brick or stone simply didn't lend themselves to parabolic shapes. But bricks or stones can be set at simple angles. It was Count Rumford nearly a century after Gauger who popularized this seemingly simple yet effective way of increasing warming efficiency.

The Z Factor

If we look closely at Gauger's parabolic fireplace of 1714 (see diagram on page 45), we will notice the small square labeled Z toward the front and center. Here is an even clearer manifestation of the impact of science on the development of heating.

The Z factor is air, as presented through a vent. As we have seen, stoves had been in use for some time, but they were closed, self-contained units. As they heated the air in the room they also dried it out, leading to laments about unwholesomeness and odor. Here now we have outside air being drawn into the heating process: a trapdoor connected to outside air by means of a hollow passage. As Gauger explains: "When this trapdoor (Z) is lifted up a little way, the air from without will go through a vent hole . . . rush in violently and not only light the fire but cause it to flame even though the wood should be green, and also forcibly drive the flame and rays of heat so as to make them beat back into the room after one or two reflections, when the fire is lighted."

Overstated, but to the point. The introduction of outside air, while increasing combustion, serves the greater purpose of enhancing the distribution of heat as well as the quality of the air. The means of this is the plate of iron (or brass or copper) that forms the back wall of Gauger's fireplace. This allows for "a void space about four inches deep [behind the heat], divided by several partitions, which form several cavities, cells or square tubes, the first communicating with the second, the second with the third, and so on; making all together as it were a sort of recurved canal . . . so that the air can go in at the lower end and go out at the upper end of it."

Gauger explains it this way: "The cold air, which will come at the lower entrance, will begin to grow warm in the first cavity; then as it comes through the second, its heat will increase, still it will grow hotter in passing through the third, &c., so that it will come out [into the room] very warm, through the upper hole. As long as there is any fire in the room, there will by this means be a constant circulation of the air through those warmed hollows, because the air in them being rarefied, will be succeeded by the more dense, and therefore stronger air which comes in at the bottom . . . which it may do, until it has acquired what degree of warmth you please. . . ."

Here we have convection. Gauger describes a system that promises to spread that heat throughout the room by creating currents of warmth. In theory at least, one does not have to sit immediately in front of the Gauger fireplace, warming only one's front. This device is meant to heat an entire room, not merely the space in front of the fire. Here is a significant beginning of modern heating.

GAUGER "NEW-INVENTED"

Gauger did not claim to have invented the vent hole. "The invention is not new," he acknowledged, "for I myself used it five and twenty years ago, having seen the use of it in other places." Indeed a century earlier, in 1624, Louis Savot developed a fireplace in which air was drawn through passages under the hearth and, once warmed, allowed

to exit through a grille in the mantel. This was a innovative idea in 1624, but when Gauger found use for it "in other places" in the 1690s or so, it was still of limited application.

Gauger is barely remembered; but one who attempted to translate his ideas of heating into daily life was Benjamin Franklin. Franklin clearly knew the English translation of Gauger's *La mécanique du feu*, first published in Paris in 1713. Gauger's work inspired the Franklin stove, which was first offered for sale in the *Pennsylvania Gazette* on December 3, 1741: "To be sold at the Post-Office Philadelphia, The New Invented Iron Fire-Places; Where any Person may see some of them that are now in Use, and have the Nature and Advantages of them explain'd."

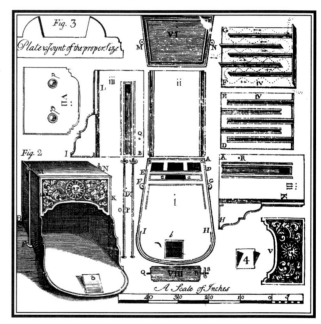

Benjamin Franklin's Pennsylvania fireplace, as first illustrated in 1744 in An Account of the New-Invented Pennsylvanian Fire-Places. *The various parts, once assembled, form the finished structure at lower left. The trapdoor in front, analogous to Gauger's Z vent, was designed, said Franklin, so that "Air rushes in from the Hollow under the Bottom Plate, and blows the Fire." At the upper right are the components of the air box.* (Courtesy of the Library Company of Philadelphia)

In fact the Franklin stove was neither a fireplace nor a stove in the traditional sense, but its nature and advantages followed closely in the lineage of Gauger and represented a promise of comfort over the usual means of heating the home in 1741. Franklin himself enumerates these usual means in his 1744 tract, *An Account of the New-Invented Pennsylvanian Fire-Places:*

1. *The large* open fireplace *"used in the Days of our Fathers," a carryover of the medieval hearth*
2. *The* "newer-fashioned *Fire-places, with low Breasts, and narrow Hearths" (a trend toward compactness of the fireplace for greater efficiency)*
3. Fireplaces as "described by Mons. Gauger . . . *for warming the Air as it comes into the Room"*
4. Holland stoves
5. German stoves
6. "Iron pots, *with open Charcoal Fires, plac'd in the middle of a Room"*

The most significant of these in retrospect was Gauger's, but it was probably unknown in America other than to technophiles like Franklin. The large open fireplace was the most commonplace and the most inefficient. As Franklin explained: "[It] has generally the Conveniency of two warm Seats, one in each corner [but] 'tis next to impossible to warm a Room with such a Fire-place." The "newer-fashioned" fireplaces were showing the way to the future by concentrating the heat source, though still only in a token way. While the eighteenth-century fireplace was smaller than the cavernous seventeenth-century fireplace, it was still large by comparison with what would evolve in the nineteenth century, and it shared with its predecessor a propensity for letting most of the heat fly "directly up the Chimney. . . . Five sixths at least of the Heat (and consequently of the Fewel) is wasted, and contributes nothing to the warming of the room."

The Holland stove was essentially what we think of today as a heating stove: a fully closed iron box with a door and a flue connected to the chimney. It was more fuel-efficient than the open fireplace and relatively successful at warming a room. But, lamented Franklin, "There is no Sight of the Fire, which is in itself a pleasant Thing. One cannot conveniently make any other Use of the Fire but that of warming the Room. When the Room is warm, People not seeing the Fire are apt to forget supplying it with Fuel 'til 'tis almost out, then, growing cold, a great deal of Wood is put in, which soon makes it too hot."

The German stove, known as a five-plate, consisted of "Five Iron Plates scru'd together . . . like a Box, one Side wanting." Such a stove might be installed so that the missing side abutted a chimney, or a stone or brick wall of the room, on the other side of which was a door through which the fire was tended. The Holland and German stoves offered more comfort than the fireplace. But, again, there was no sight of the fire, nor could it be used for cooking or other tasks. At least as important was the question of air quality in the room. The German stove didn't draw air into the room, as did a fireplace; hence there was no exchange of air and one was obliged, said Franklin, "to breathe the same unchang'd Air continually."

Charcoal fires in pots were used chiefly in the shops of craftsmen, and such restricted use was fortunate, for the "sulphurous Fumes from the Coals [might sometimes] produce fatal Consequences."

That leaves us with one man:

> Sieur Gauger [whose] Invention was very ingenious, and had many Conveniencies: The Room was warm'd in all Parts, by the Air flowing into it through the heated Cavities: Cold Air was prevented rushing thro' the Crevices, the Funnel [of the chimney] being sufficiently supply'd by those Cavities: Much less Fuel would serve, &c. But the first Expense, which was very great; the Intricacy of the Design, and the Difficulty of the Execution, especially in old Chimneys, discouraged the Propagation of the Invention; so that there are (I suppose) very few such Chimneys now in Use.

Taking the best of Gauger, but making such modification as might reduce the cost and make construction and installation somewhat simpler, Franklin developed what was first called the Pennsylvania fireplace but which has come to be known as the Franklin stove. In its original form, it was an open cast-iron stove that could be inserted into an existing fireplace or made part of a new one. It had the virtue of a sight of the fire, the absence of which Franklin lamented as a shortcoming of Dutch and German stoves. But its chief virtue was that whereas a traditional fireplace or cast-iron stove transmitted heat by direct radiation and conduction, the Pennsylvania fireplace also heated by convection — by creating currents of air that circulated about, now plausibly heating the whole room. This, of course, derived from Gauger. His fireplace, it may be recalled, had "square tubes, the first communicating with the second . . . and so on, making all together as it were a sort of recurved canal." This is what Franklin called the air box. Both Gauger's square tubes and Franklin's air box can be seen clearly in the accompanying illustration.

Franklin's stove was relatively simple, yet more efficient than either the fireplace or the traditional stove. The air box, which made this invention significant in the evolution of heating, eventually disappeared, and what came to be known as the Franklin stove often was just an ordinary open stove, albeit one that was inserted into a fireplace rather than made to be freestanding. But as we shall see, that air box that disappeared seems to have inspired a significant step in the evolution of domestic hot-air central heat.

FROM STOVE TO FURNACE

Although the concept dates back to the hypocaust system in the homes of the wealthy during the Roman Empire, it was only late in the eighteenth century that significant attempts were made to provide central heat in modern times. One early example was the hot-water heating system designed for the Bank of England in 1792.

Early in the nineteenth century, domestic central heating began to come into use in America, and here the air box shows its significance. An important pioneer in central heating was Daniel Pettibone, of Roxbury, Massachusetts, an inventor whose list of credits ranges from a machine for mixing biscuit dough (1797) to a machine for casting half a ton of musket balls a day (1806).

Of these and other products of an inventive mind, he apparently wrote nothing other than patent applications and the like. The two published tracts for which he is known—and that are virtually all we know of him—are both on

A *diagram of the Pennsylvania fireplace. The dark vertical section is the air box (sometimes known as the fire box). Smoke from the fire travels up and over this to reach the flue at right. Fresh air meanwhile enters from below and circulates through the caliducts (the square sections) of the air box. When it is warm it issues out through the uppermost duct. Many later so-called Franklin stoves lacked an air box and functioned only as fireplace inserts. The true Franklin stove, or Pennsylvania fireplace, made use of the circulation of air through the air box to create convection.* (Robert Meikleham, **On the history and art of warming and ventilating rooms and buildings,** vol. 2 [London: 1845])

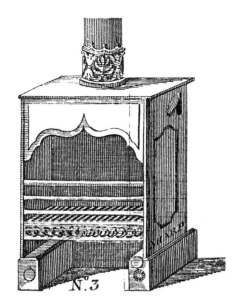

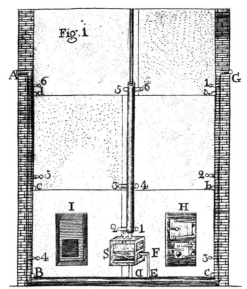

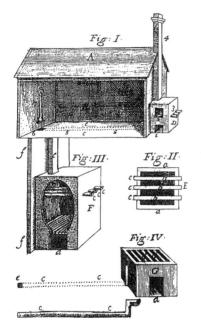

ABOVE LEFT: *The modern home in America at the beginning of the nineteenth century reflected English precedent, but the influence was not entirely one way. There was also very limited exportation of technology in the form of the "American stove," based on Franklin's Pennsylvania fireplace. This stove was offered for sale by James Sharp in London in the 1780s. It was intended both as a fireplace insert and as a freestanding stove; in either case, connection to a fresh air supply was required.* (James Sharp, **An Account of the Principles and Effects of the Pensilvanian Stove-Grates** [London: 1790])

ABOVE RIGHT: *This conception of central heat for a residence was devised by Oliver Evans in 1795. Evans made use of a double flue: The inner flue, or smoke pipe, allowed the smoke to exit from the stove (the boxlike shape at bottom center). The flue, or air pipe, enveloping the inner flue allowed heated air to rise and enter the rooms through valves on every floor, which could be opened and closed as needed. The stove itself could also be used to "bake bread, meat, &c." The major distinction between this and later types of central heating was that the latter used ducts connected directly with the various rooms rather than a central air pipe. Yet Evans's concept anticipated later systems in the configuration of the stove (H), which, with its separate doors for feeding the fire and removing ashes, is essentially what the hot-air furnace would look like well into the twentieth century.* (Oliver Evans, **Young Mill-wright and Miller's Guide** [Philadelphia: 1795])

BOTTOM: *An early conception of hot-air heat. This illustration is John Evelyn's 1691 device for heating a greenhouse with a simple stove or furnace. The illustration seems to indicate that the furnace is underneath the greenhouse, but this is a quirk of the illustrator's technique. The area below was simply a convenient place for an enlargement (Fig. III). The furnace is actually on the same level as the structure and is shown there as 3. Warm air was to be conveyed through its end wall into the greenhouse by air pipes (shown as D at far right and as C in the enlarged view). There was also an "air ground pipe" (5) under the floor. Barely visible on the lefthand wall is a "Thermometer hanging over the Nose of the Ground-pipe, by which to govern the heat"—obviously a primitive thermostat. Fig. II is the "Furnace air pipes," and Fig. IV is the "Ash hearth." A very sophisticated concept for its time.* (John Evelyn, **Kalendarium Hortense** [London, 1691])

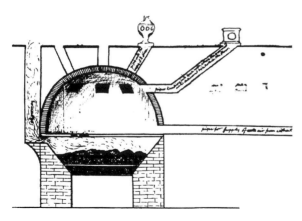

Another concept, presumably from the early 1800s, is this undated drawing by Thomas Jefferson. Here now is a central hot-air system as it existed throughout the nineteenth century and into the twentieth. Ducts from the furnace convey hot air to the rooms above. The horizontal duct at right is for the supply of fresh air; the vertical shaft at left is the flue. Although all the essentials were there in concept, Jefferson appears to have made no attempt to install central heat at Monticello during the enlargement and renovation of the house between 1796 and 1809. He relied instead on fireplaces and stoves. (**Library of Congress**)

heating, suggesting that Pettibone himself regarded this as his major accomplishment. *Description of the Improvements of the Rarifying Air-Stove* was published in 1810, and *Pettibone's Economy of Fuel* in 1812, both in Philadelphia. (Rarefied air is simply air that is less dense by virtue of being heated and which therefore rises.)

In the two tracts we find, not surprisingly, that Pettibone is a disciple of both Gauger and Franklin. Indeed, the 1812 tract begins forthrightly: "The principle upon which [my] stoves act, is described by the Sieur Gauger, in his Book, entitled *"Mechanique du Feu,"* published in 1709 [sic]; the first patterns in cast iron upon this principle were the invention of the celebrated and ingenious Dr. Benjamin Franklin." With such auspicious parentage one expects much; in fact what came about was the first clearly documented use of central heating in America. Pettibone himself had Franklin stoves in several rooms of his home and was highly pleased. In *Economy of Fuel* he wrote, "My dining-room, in particular, which has a large old-fashioned chimney, was formerly so cold as to be disused by my predecessors in cold weather; for the largest fires that could be made did not warm it; but since the same room has had an American [Franklin] stove, which is near twenty years, it has been as comfortable with respect to warmth as any room can be made."

Here it should be noted that Pettibone's dining room was not kept at a steady 68 to 70 degrees or anything remotely close to the modern standard of comfort. One early observer was highly impressed with a Franklin stove because it kept the room in the 50-degree range, a clear improvement over the usual fireplace-heated room, and this was probably true of Pettibone's dining room.

Before he wrote his paean to the Franklin stove, however, Pettibone began experimenting with central heat. Why, if he found a stove so comfortable? Perhaps he recalled reading in Gauger: "Not only the air of the room, in which the fire is, may be warmed by such a circulation; but if you bring in air from another room (in which there is no fire) . . . after a few circulations, it will be sufficiently warmed. . . . This way of warming a room, gives heat to all the people in it, though at a distance from the fire."

There is no reason to believe Gauger was expressing other than theory in this instance. Pettibone, however, lived at a time when technological theory was being turned into reality. It was coming to be realized that central heat, by employing one fire to serve a number of rooms, is more economical in its use of fuel. To which may be added economy of effort: it is easier to tend one fire serving four rooms than four separate fires in four separate rooms. And finally came that consummate realization for an inventor: a good invention is good business.

HOSPITAL-TESTED

Probably the first of Pettibone's heating systems in actual use was installed in February 1810 at Pennsylvania Hospital in Philadelphia. It was apparently based on an 1808 patent of his and was simply a trial run in which a central furnace was used to heat only

Pennsylvania Hospital, Philadelphia, 1800. (Engraving by William Birch. Library of Congress)

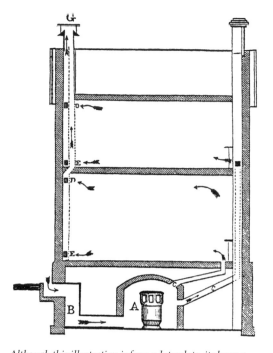

*Although this illustration is from a later date, it shows a typical hot-air heating system dating to the time of Daniel Pettibone. It consisted of a large stove (A) within a brick enclosure, or air chamber, from which heat rose through ducts to the rooms above. Outside air was admitted through B. This installation also shows a ventilating system for release of stale air through G. (**A. J. Downing, The Architecture of Country Houses**, 1850)*

six rooms of the hospital. On April 30, 1810, Josiah Hewes, president of the hospital's board of managers, reported that the managers "are so far convinced of the advantages to be derived from it, that they have purchased of him [Pettibone] the liberty to use the invention which he claims, throughout the hospital." The distinguished physician Benjamin Rush, a signer of the Declaration of Independence, also gave a personal endorsement: "I have examined the construction and principle of Mr. Pettibone's method of warming rooms, and am satisfied that it is calculated to produce its intended effect, with less expense of fuel, than an open fire, and with none of the inconveniences to some people of a close stove."

While there was experimentation at this time also with both steam and hot-water heating, early central heating systems in America were very similar to Pettibone's prototype. But a typical early system needs to be distinguished from modern hot-air heating; there was not only a considerable difference in effectiveness but in appearance as well. And here is where the air box comes in. Let us first have Pettibone describe it:

> *[My] improvements consist in using any stove . . . or other apparatus for heating air . . . set in bricks, similar to a still, or retort; receiving into it, at, or near the bottom, the external air into the [brick] cistern, or reservoir [surrounding the stove] . . . the heat then may be conveyed, in tin pipes, to any rooms or apartments which are to be warmed. . . . All these pipes, or tubes, must have stop-cocks, so as to regulate the passage of the heat at pleasure. (Description . . . of the Rarifying Air-Stove [Philadelphia, 1810])*

This was essentially the hot-air furnace as it existed for most of the nineteenth century. Pettibone described a brick chamber (later known as an air chamber) surrounding a large stove. Cold air entered the chamber at the bottom, was heated by the stove, and then, once rarefied, rose through tin pipes to the rooms of the house above. It worked basically the same as a later hot-air furnace except that the air was heated not in the furnace itself but in the chamber.

This was a remarkably simple arrangement, from a later point of view. Its innovativeness, however, owes substantially to its heritage. Here was the Pennsylvania fireplace taken to a new level of development. In effect Franklin's air box now became the stove itself. Air came in at the bottom (analogous to the hollow of Franklin's fireplace), rose over and around the stove (analogous to the air box), and then, once heated, found its way through the tin pipes to the rooms above.

Central hot-air heat was in use in homes by 1820. One of the earliest hot-air systems documented for residential use was installed by Reuben Haines III, the sixth-generation owner of Wyck in Philadelphia, built around 1710. In November 1820, Haines recorded in his diary that he had hired a mason to construct a "furnace in front cellar for Schuylkill coal." Here we also have evidence of the word "furnace" beginning to supplant "stove" for what was essentially the same apparatus. Basically this was the configuration of a typical hot-air heating system through the later nineteenth century.

Haines continued also to use fireplaces with coal grates even in the rooms served by his primitive central heating system. Even in midcentury, when central hot air was becoming more common and more efficient, it was still not unusual to have fireplaces in addition to the furnace, at least in rooms in the north side of the house. The fireplace not only supplied supplemental heat but also helped draw heat into the room from the central system.

LIGHTING

A LIGHT, LATELY INVENTED

I f the late eighteenth century was a time for discovering convenience generally, lighting was no exception. Early experimentation with gaslight was one element of this, and even before gas there was the development of the Argand lamp, which would have greater impact over the short term. The creation of Aimé Argand, a Swiss scientist who developed it in France and patented it in England in 1784, the lamp's essential element was its hollow cylindrical wick. This allowed a better flow of air through the burner and thus better combustion and more light than existing lamps. The burner consisted of two concentric metal tubes. Argand rolled a flat wick into a cylinder and inserted this through the concentric tubes, creating the effect of a hollow cylindrical wick. The oil supply was usually stored in a separate reservoir. An important feature of the Argand lamp was its chimney, which increased the draft, thereby also increasing combustion. The chimney rested on a perforated flange below the burner.

The Argand lamp would be refined in the early nineteenth century, but even in its original form it was a marvelous achievement. Gaslighting would be even more amazing, but it was still largely experimental.

Meanwhile, as this new century opened, the standard for most Americans remained as it had been throughout the colonial period: the light from the fireplace, candles, and lamps that burned various fuels. By about 1810 even candles were being transformed by technology. The modern candle is nearly smokeless and dripless. The earlier candles had to be snuffed frequently and the charred end of the wick trimmed to keep it from falling into the molten wax, thus lessening the light. By about 1810 braided wicks soaked in boric acid were coming into use. These tended to burn away more completely, improving the light and reducing the amount of snuffing needed. But common homemade candles of the old sort probably still had to suffice for most people.

The main source of light in the home throughout the colonial period and well into the nineteenth century remained the candle. The scene here is the Silas Deane House (1766) in Wethersfield, Connecticut. (Photograph by the author)

OPPOSITE PAGE: *A silver-plated Argand lamp used by George Washington in the 1790s.* (Smithsonian Institution)

Most lamps of the eighteenth century were quite primitive. The Betty lamp, as it was often called, burned fish oil or animal fat. Lamps were generally just shallow dishes that held a wick and offered only a feeble flame. Candles were no brighter but a little safer. If a lamp was overturned its fuel would spill whereas a candle might simply go out. Lamp fuel and candles were expensive to buy, and making candles was a time-consuming chore. Hence they were used discriminately — hardly ever during the day and with moderation even at night. Except when the wealthy showed off their illuminative power at parties, there must have been very little light, night after night — a sight that is difficult to imagine in modern times.

An Argand lamp in the age of electricity is quaint; in the age of candles and fish oil lamps, it must have been a very welcome addition to the household.

INFLAMMABLE AIR

One night in 1806 a wood-and-brick house at the corner of Pelham and Thames Streets in Newport, Rhode Island, may have appeared to be on fire. An eerie glow may have been visible within, a glow too pervasive to be candlelight, and visible not just in one window but in much of the house.

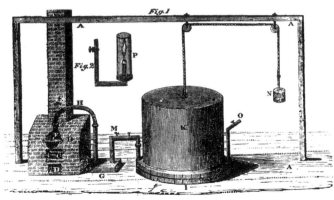

ABOVE: *A contemporary illustration shows what David Melville's gas-generation apparatus probably looked like.* (Thomas Cooper, *Some Information Concerning Gas Lights* [Philadelphia: 1816] Smithsonian Institution.)

LEFT: *David Melville in his later years.* (Smithsonian Institution)

This was the dwelling of David Melville (1773–1856), by vocation a pewterer and hardware merchant. By avocation Melville was an inventor who lately was known to be experimenting with something he called inflammable air. Was this as ominous as it looked?

In fact, he had things well under control. His inflammable air was what we might called illuminating gas, and Melville was previewing one of the nineteenth century's most significant achievements.

This combustible substance he liked to experiment with was hardly new. It could be found in nature—in the latter seventeenth century in Lancashire, England, for example, in the form of gas bubbling out through a small spring. The Reverend John Clayton was intrigued. He tried holding a candle near it and observed with wonderment that "the Spirit which issued out caught fire . . . and continued burning with Violence as it issued out in a stream, which I blew out, and lighted again." Clayton delighted in capturing the vapor in a bladder, which he then pricked with a pin and lit for the entertainment of friends. David Melville, however, had a more serious reason for experimenting with gas: he wanted to create light.

Gas had already been used to provide light—by William Murdock, who lit his home in Cornwall, England, with coal gas in 1792. Now Melville was demonstrating the same use in America. Indeed, Melville provided gaslight not only for some of the rooms in his house but also for a lantern on the street out in front. This, it should be noted, was before the first use of gaslight on the streets of London (1807). Melville was aware of Murdock's experiments and related work going on in England; and, based on what he had read, he devised his own apparatus for the manufacture of illuminating gas. It consisted of a small furnace in which coal was heated. As the coal burned it produced "hydrogenous gas, or inflammable air" (coal gas), which was passed by way of a pipe through a bath of lime water to remove impurities. The gas was then piped into a "gasometer," or storage tank, where it was kept for use. Essentially this was how gas would be produced for home use throughout the gaslight era, although it would be produced from various substances besides coal.

Melville's home was the first in America to be lit by gas, but he was not the first to make use of illuminating gas. That distinction goes to a Philadelphia fireworks manufacturer, Ambrose and Company, which gave a demonstration of gaslight in 1796. It was announced in an advertisement in the Philadelphia *General Advertiser* on July 29, 1796.

By Authority

MESSRS. AMBROSE, & CO. have the honor to inform the PUBLIC in general, and their friends in particular, that they will exhibit, on MONDAY the FIRST DAY of AUGUST, if the weather permits

A Grand Fire-Work,

In a stile altogether new, and never before executed in AMERICA, by the assistance of light composed of INFLAMMABLE AIR: This new invention has been received with the greatest applause in all the cities of EUROPE. During the evening, SIXTEEN SUPER PIECES will be exhibited, which by the great variety of changes, the mechanism of the pieces, and the variety of the colours of the fire, will give entire satisfaction . . .

To COMMENCE PRECISELY at HALF AFTER SEVEN O'CLOCK in the evening—the doors open at SIX.

The site was an amphitheater, apparently maintained by Ambrose for pyrotechnic displays. The "Grand Fire-Work" exhibition was preceded by a demonstration of sky rockets. Tickets ranged from a quarter to a half-dollar. The gaslight displays used tubing bent into various shapes, including an Italian country home and Masonic figures and emblems. The gas, which almost certainly was coal gas, issued from orifices in the tubes.

This was not a demonstration of gaslight so much as it was a demonstration, undoubtedly dramatic for its day, of the technology that made gaslight possible.

More nearly approaching gas illumination was a demonstration in 1802 in Baltimore by Benjamin Henfrey. An Englishman, Henfrey had come to America in the late eighteenth century and in 1797 had attempted to form a coal mining company. He is known to have experimented with coal gas, and, in March 1802, he demonstrated what he called a thermolamp. As related in Baltimore's *Federal Gazette* on March 11, 1802, Henfrey used a small cylinder suspended in a fire to heat about two pounds of coal, which produced a "gas vapor" that passed through a tin conductor into an adjoining room and into a lamp constructed of four tubes, where "it took fire and burned with a beautiful and brilliant light." In a second demonstration, Henfrey used his apparatus to produce light in a hanging fixture. Henfrey's displays produced no financial backing, however. There was a proposal in 1802 to install gaslight on streets in the neighborhood of Centre Square in Philadelphia under Henfrey's supervision, but nothing is known to have come of that plan. Still, Henfrey's work resulted in the granting of a U.S. patent on April 16, 1802, for a "cheap mode of obtaining light from fuel."

Melville received patents for gaslighting in 1810 and 1813 and, having focused more attention on this new technology, is better known than Henfrey. And he continued experimenting. In February 1813 Melville announced his plans for public demonstrations in an advertisement in the *Newport Mercury*. The occasion, he said, would "gratify public curiosity" and also allow him "to be to some degree remunerated for the very great expense" of his experimentation. The price of admission was twenty-five cents. In his ad he assured the public of the efficacy of gaslight ("in no way offensive, and very agreeable to the eye," "infinitely less trouble" than lamps) and of its safety ("free from the inconvenience and danger resulting from the sparks, and frequent snuffing of lamps and candles [thus reducing] the hazard of fire").

The demonstrations brought people by the thousands. Orders came in from cotton factories in Providence, Rhode Island, and Watertown, Massachusetts. But the cost of installation and operation turned out to be prohibitive. Potential customers expressed interest and then politely demurred when apprised of the cost. Melville kept his own apparatus in operation until 1817 for the occasional gratification of strangers, but otherwise turned to promoting the use of gas for lighthouses. The federal government awarded him a contract for a lighthouse near Newport, but then reneged under pressure from whale oil interests. Melville went back to his pewter trade and hardware business. It was not until 1853 that Newport streets were lighted by gas, by which time hardly anyone remembered what a luminary Melville had been.

Certainly the most widely seen display of gaslight in its early days—and the first in a large public building—was presented in that place of wonders, Peale's Museum. The museum had relied on Argand lamps, which at first seemed sensational enough. But since the museum prided itself on being in the forefront of science, it was only logical that its wonders of science be observed in the most modern lighting. Rubens Peale, the son of Charles Willson Peale, was now responsible for the museum. He began installing gaslighting at the old State House early in 1815. By late April, complete with gasworks, tubes, tubs, and 500 feet of soldered tin pipe, the system was ready for an awed public. The Long Room, nest eternal for a thousand stuffed birds, from pheasants to flamingos, must have been particularly dazzling with its five great ceiling fixtures glistening with cut glass.

The public was thoroughly impressed. Within weeks, so many paying customers came to observe the new wonder that the cost of materials and installation was virtually covered. By 1816, Rubens's brother Rembrandt Peale had gaslight in a separate, smaller Peale's Museum that had opened two years earlier in Baltimore. This was followed on February 5, 1817, by the chartering of the Gas Light Company of Baltimore, with Rembrandt Peale among the incorporators.

Gaslight had less success in Philadelphia, however. Under pressure from city officials, who feared fire or explosion, Rubens reluctantly dismantled the Philadelphia museum's gaslighting in 1820. Just as its first appearance surely whetted public interest, so did removal of gaslight under a hue of hazard undoubtedly dampen its acceptance. But as we shall see, this was only a temporary setback.

BATHING

THE EVOLVING BATHROOM

One of the most significant advances in the evolution of the house is the bathroom. In 1805 the bathroom in its modern sense simply did not exist—that is, there was no single room that contained a water closet, bathtub, and sink. The functions of ablution and elimination, separate and unconnected from time immemorial, remained so in America.

But change was in the making. Benjamin Latrobe's John Markoe House in Philadelphia had a bathtub and a water closet on the second floor, in separate cubicles but in close proximity. In England by this time an early version of the bathroom had evolved—at Donington Park in Leicestershire, in the home of the Earl of Moira, for example. Built between 1790 and 1800, the house included a "powdering room" with both a bathtub and a water closet. Powdering still pertained to wigs, though the term came to be used for a small bathroom in the twentieth century. The significance, however, is in the room itself. Here is a very early instance of ablution and elimination being combined in one room, as is now so taken for granted.

Traditionally elimination was for outdoors. One used a privy or, for reasons of convenience, a chamber pot that had to be taken outdoors and emptied. Elimination was, in every sense, removed from the house.

Washing oneself or taking a bath had nothing to do with elimination. It could be done outside, but it was clearly convenient to do it primarily indoors. One used a wash-basin, usually in one's bedroom, for personal washing and, if one was so inclined and had the means, a tub for more complete bathing in whatever room or space might suffice. The kitchen was probably the most common place since the hearth provided a place to heat the water. When a Boston merchant named Nathaniel Waterman in 1846 advertised for sale "every thing appertaining to the kitchen" he routinely included bathtubs. But, as was probably quite common, one might just forgo getting wet all over. Elizabeth Drinker of Philadelphia recounted in her diary how the family had purchased a shower bath and that she had tried it out. With some wonderment she recorded in July 1799 that "I bore it better than I expected, not having been wett all over att once, for twenty-eight years past."

The disinclination to bathe, of course, is attributable to more than just the absence of the technology of convenience. There was still an innate reluctance, indeed almost a dread, going back to the Middle Ages in Europe, when bathing was thought to be deleterious to the health. Yet by the mid-eighteenth century attitudes had begun to change, as exemplified by evangelist John Wesley's reminder that "cleanliness is next to godliness."

Elizabeth Drinker's shower bath was almost certainly meant to be used outdoors and consisted of a framework with a container of water above. Elizabeth offered no detailed description except to say that she "pulls at a cord and the water falls upon her through a cullender." The custom with the Drinkers was to let the water stand in the container "some hours" so that it was reasonably warm when the cord was pulled (no one used these outdoor devices in the winter). Elizabeth also explained that a woman using it wore a thin gown and "an Oyl cloath cap." In this way, except for her hair, her whole body could get wet at one time. By 1803 the Drinkers also had a "bathing Tub . . . made of wood, lined with tin and painted—with Castors under ye bottom and a brass lock to let out the water." The castors made the tub easy to move around.

OPPOSITE PAGE: *Slipper bath (no date, early nineteenth/possibly late eighteenth century). Formed from sheet metal in the shape of a slipper or boot, it enabled the bather to have no more than head and shoulders exposed, thus preserving modesty as well as the warmth of the bath. Based on the* sabotière *popular with French aristocracy in the eighteenth century, it is said to have been introduced to America by Benjamin Franklin. It was filled through the funnel at the top and emptied through a stopcock at the bottom front.* (**Photograph by the author, Museum Village, Monroe, New York**)

Tubs were normally used indoors, and an affluent family might even have a separate bathing room. In 1806, Gore Place in Waltham, Massachusetts, had a copper-lined tub set in a wooden enclosure. The tub at the Markoe House used water from its own heated cistern. The George Read II house in New Castle, Delaware, modern enough when completed in 1804, included a 7½-foot-long bathtub among a number of improvements in 1811. The tub was on the second floor, convenient to Read's bedroom, and had hot running water piped up from the kitchen. This was luxury perhaps unparalleled for 1811, but the technology went just so far. There was no pipe to empty the tub. When Read finished his bath, his servants had to empty the tub with pails, just as more modest tubs were emptied and filled. Read also had a shower, probably similar to Elizabeth Drinker's, but Read's was an accessory to the bathtub. While his bathing room was primitive by our standards, it offered a rare preview of what would someday be regarded as comfort and convenience in every home.

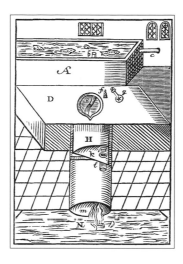

THE WATER CLOSET

FROM CHUTES TO DITCHES

The essential components of a water closet were in place in ancient times. The remains of houses dating from 2800 to 2500 B.C. in the city of Mohenjo Daro in the Indus Valley of Pakistan contain what seem to be brick water closets built into the outer walls. They appear to have emptied into either a street drain or a cesspit.

Elsewhere among early civilizations up through Roman times, from Egypt to Crete, water closets existed, some for sitting on and some for squatting over; anything from a wooden plank to elaborately carved marble might serve as a seat. Some of these primitive devices were flushed by water through a chute, others by jugs or dippers, draining through stone channels or vertical chutes into brick sewers, and still others into cesspits or the nearest street. Rome at its grandest had public baths supplied with water from its famous aqueducts. These communal facilities made use of water closets that could serve ten to twenty at a time, men and women separately. Waste from these facilities fell into a drain below and was washed by aqueduct water into a sewer. The homes of very wealthy Romans contained private facilities; less affluent residents used chamber pots in their apartments or trekked to these public *latrinae.*

Water closets effectively disappeared during the Middle Ages, which instead showed a clear proclivity to "cast and put into Ditches, Rivers and other Waters, and also within many other Places, within, about and nigh unto divers Cities, Boroughs and Townes of the Realm . . . annoyances, issues, dung, intrails or other ordure . . . that the air there is greatly corrupt and infect, and many Maladies and other intolerable Diseases do daily happen"—to quote from a proclamation of England's Richard II in 1388. The consequences of inadequate sanitation, if not fully understood, were at least recognized. Little else can be said about convenience in the Middle Ages except for those fortresses of civilization, the castles and monasteries. The recourse there was sometimes an indoor privy commonly known as a garderobe that was built into a thick outer wall or an extension beyond the main wall. Waste matter fell into a cesspool or a stream channeled to run underneath, or possibly into the castle moat (in which case the accumulation of filth presumably enhanced the moat's deterrent effect).

This was also the age of throwing the contents of one's chamber pot out the window, provided, in theory, one took the precaution of first shouting a warning. In France that warning was "gardez à l'eau," which became Anglicized to "gardyloo," from which came the British term *loo*, meaning a water closet.

THE METAMORPHOSIS OF THE JOHN

Of the prototypical water closets of ancient times, we have scant archaeological evidence—various grooved slabs and stone seats with holes having only one possible use—but nothing to show exactly what the device was like or how it worked. To a godson of Elizabeth I we owe proof on paper of something on the order of the water closet being revived in more modern times; and thus with him we can credibly begin the exploration of the water closet's evolution, chiefly in England.

In *Metamorphosis of Ajax*, published in London in 1596, Sir John Harington described a device to replace the outdoor privy, the chamber pot, and its more elegant counterpart, the close stool of the wealthy—usually a chair with a covering of cloth or cabinetwork around the bottom to conceal the pot. Resorting to euphemism, as has been its continuing legacy, Harington called his device an ajax, a play on "jakes," which is what the English called the privy. "Jakes" was itself a play on "jacques," used in scorn of the French and obviously a predecessor of the modern term "john."

Harington's device may not have been entirely new (he alludes to having seen something of the sort in Italy), but it is at least a prototypical water closet of which there

PREVIOUS PAGE: *Sir John Harington's water closet as illustrated in his* Metamorphosis of Ajax *(1596), the first documented attempt at a water closet reflecting modern principles.*

is a record preserved in detail. And while primitive, it has all the essentials of the water closet to come. Its essential feature, in Harington's own words, was "a vessel of brick, stone or lead of an oval form [corresponding to the later toilet bowl], as broad at the bottom as at the top [placed] very close [under] your seat, like the pot of a close-stool." Water was supplied from a cistern, admitted into the vessel by a small cock. The device was flushed using "a stem of iron as big as a curtain rod with a strong screw at the top of it." When the screw valve was turned, water flowed through the "stoole pot" and down a sluice into the equivalent of a privy vault. That was to be emptied "noone and night." There were such niceties as a lockable "scallop shell" to cover the screw valve when the privy was not in use so that "children and busy folk disorder it not." The cistern, according to Harington, could be filled by using "force . . . [you] force it [water] from the lowest part of your house to the highest." This apparently meant the use of a force pump, and is believed to be the earliest such reference on record in England.

How well did Harington's water closet work? Prior to the publication of *Ajax*, Harington said he had one built for his residence at Kelston, near Bath. Late in 1592, after becoming high sheriff of the county of Somerset, he was visited by his godmother, the queen, who is said to have seen the unusual device and, finding it quite to her liking, requested that one be built for Richmond Palace, where there was no scarcity of offensive odors to tweak her displeasure. There would certainly have been a lingering reek from close stools used behind wicker screens about the palace, the considerable number of which reflected the size of Elizabeth's retinue. There was also, as physician Andrew Boorde remarked in his *Brevyary of Health* in 1547, much "pissing in chimneys." The burning of incense and perfume helped only so much. Harington's assurance was therefore alluring: "If water be plenty, the oftener it [the water closet] is used and opened, the sweeter; but if it be scant, once a day is enough, for a need, though twenty persons should use it. . . . And this being well done, and orderly kept, your worst [water] privy may be as sweet as your best chamber."

Elizabeth thus seems to have had one built in Richmond Palace, and it apparently worked, at least more or less, for the queen is supposed to have had a copy of Harington's book hung on the privy wall. She never had another one constructed at any of her various residences, however, so perhaps it was not as sweet as advertised. Indeed, so far as is known, Harington never built another one anywhere.

Yet sometime in the next century water closets, quite possibly based on Harington's design, did come into limited use in England. There was one at the estate of Sir James Carew in Bedington, Surrey, by 1673, and we may reasonably suppose it was not

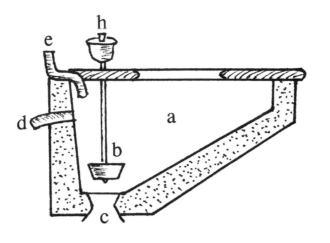

TOP: *Osterly House near London, c. 1730. The simplest type of mechanical water closet. It consisted of a marble trough* (A) *filled to the level of the overflow pipe* (D) *with water from the supply pipe* (E). *When the handle* (H) *was pulled up, a plunger* (B) *was raised, releasing contents into a lead waste pipe* (C). **(Redrawn from Glenn Brown, Water-Closets, 1884)**

BOTTOM: Cabinet d'aisance, *Paris, c. 1770, a French water closet of the same period as Whitehall's and a design essentially the same as that used at Osterly House nearly half a century earlier. It was made of marble or some other suitable stone hollowed out in the shape of a basin. Water was admitted by the cock at the right, and the closet was emptied by the plunger device. The overflow is at left. Cabinetry—including the seat and a type of cover—is shown.* **(A. J. Roubo, L'art du menuisier, vol. 2 [1770], [Paris: 1769–1775], plate 69. New York State Library, Albany, New York)**

unique, though other examples must have been rare. We have a brief description of Carew's privy from the antiquarian John Aubrey, who, under royal patent, toured Surrey in 1673 for the purpose of writing a history of it. His copious notes remained unpublished until after his death in 1697, finally appearing as a three-volume work published in 1718 and 1719. Of his visit to the James Carew estate in 1673, Aubrey writes, "Here I saw a pretty Machine to cleanse an House of Office [privy], viz. by a small Stream, no bigger than one's Finger, which run into an Engine, made like a Bit of a Fire-Shovel, which hung upon its Center of Gravity; so that when it was full, a considerable Quantity of Water fell down with some Force, and washed away the Filth."

That description leaves no doubt that it was a water closet of some sort. Was it inspired by Harington's *Ajax,* copies of which obviously existed here and there? Or was it derived from some relic of the Roman world—some vestige of a water-flushed latrine—as indeed Harington's may well have been, since he talked of seeing something like it in Italy? The use of such facilities elsewhere in the Mediterranean basin was given some notice just a few years prior to Aubrey's tour by another accomplished writer and traveler of his day, John Ogilby. His book, *Africa* (1670), included this observation of the city of Fez: "Round about the Mosques are a hundred and fifty Common-

Houses of Easement, built Four-square, and divided into Single-Stool-Rooms, each furnished with a Cock and a Marble Cistern, which scowreth and keeps all neat and clean, as if these places were intended for some sweeter Employment." In fact, the "pretty Machines" of both Carew and Harington, by whatever line of descent, almost certainly owed much to Roman and even earlier prototypes. Yet they also begin a new line, for it is from these and whatever few like them existed that the modern water closet eventually evolved in England and America.

It was likely a device similar to Carew's — or perhaps exactly the same — that Celia Feinnes saw on one of her peripatetic outings through the length and breadth of England. She wrote (c. 1703) of a visit to Windsor Castle and of observing in Prince George's dressing room "a closet that leads to a little place with a seate of easement of marble with sluces of water to wash all down." Perhaps this was the simple type that was in use by 1730 at Osterly House near London. It consisted of a marble trough with a plunger mechanism. Water was admitted by turning a cock; the trough was emptied by pulling up a handle, thus raising a plunger device sealing a hole in the bottom of the trough. Two of these were still in existence at Osterly House in the late nineteenth century. During a lecture for England's National Health Society in 1881, plumbing authority S. Stevens Hellyer reported that when he was there "a year or two ago, I found two such water closets. A niche in a fair-sized room was formed to receive the marble closet pan, and a door, shutting up close to the seat, hid the whole arrangement from sight. A lead soil-pipe was connected with the outlet plug-waste of the pan, and continued from it to the drain, which was brought into the house to receive it. The soil-pipes had no ventilation."

This device, quite archaic by 1881, was probably *the* water closet of the eighteenth century. Accounts of the death of George II on October 25, 1760, provide evidence that there was one, almost certainly of the same kind, at Kensington Palace. He had retired to a water closet just before he collapsed and fell, striking his head and dying before court physicians could reach him. Similar water closets were appearing in France and likely elsewhere in Europe. One that is virtually identical to that at Osterly House is illustrated in volume 2 of A. J. Roubo's cabinetmaker's manual, *L'art du menuisier*, published in Paris in 1770 (construction of such devices was considered more a matter of cabinetry than of plumbing by virtue of their being built into often elegant settings). Presumably this was the water closet as Jefferson knew it during his years in Paris.

A device of this same design was the first known water closet in America and probably the only one of its kind for a number of years. This closet was included in the plans

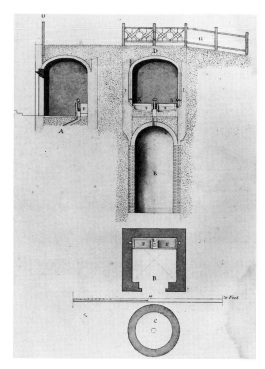

Whitehall, Annapolis, Maryland, c. 1765: the earliest documented water closet in America and perhaps the only one of its kind until the late 1790s. The rendering is by the architect Joseph Horatio Anderson. The water closet itself is similar to that at Osterly House, but here the entire facility is pictured in detail. A is a transverse section; B, the floor plan; C, a section of what corresponds to a privy vault or cesspool; and the structure from D to E, a side view of the entire installation. The device itself (F) was a double trough of marble, over each half of which would have been a seat of some sort. Water from a cistern was conveyed to the troughs by pipes (I) through cocks (K) on both sides of the water closet as shown in the side view. Between the troughs was a plunger device, or "plugg hole" (L in the floor plan), which, when raised, released the contents of the trough into the vault below. There was seemingly no way to empty the vault; its height, nearly twelve feet, was apparently thought sufficient not to prompt concern. Owing to the site on which Whitehall was built, this wing of the house was partly below grade; hence the garden fence (G) above and the indication of stairs (H) at left. The rendering itself is one of the most significant documents relating to the evolution of household technology in America. (Courtesy of the Winterthur Library, Joseph Downs Collection of Manuscripts and Printed Ephemera, No. 205)

for Whitehall, the home built around 1765 by colonial Governor Horatio Sharpe at Annapolis, Maryland, and there is no reason to believe it was not actually installed. A detailed account of how it worked is included with the architect's drawing, though nothing of the water closet remains. It was located in a small enclosure at the end of an arcade connecting it with the house. Nothing is left of that part of the house. The water closet arcade and a matching extension on the other side of the house were torn down in the 1790s to provide building material with which to enlarge the main section. During mid-twentieth-century restoration work at the house, however, owner Charles Scarlett Jr. uncovered wall tiles and a two-inch-thick slab of marble floor tile inconsistent with any part of the house except the water closet. The finding of these, along with the detailed drawing and specifications of the original architect, Joseph Horatio Anderson, led to the conclusion that there was indeed a water closet at Whitehall, and it was probably the first one in America.

A New Generation

This device's successor in the evolutionary process represented something of a technological jump. It was a sophisticated mechanism, by comparison, first seen in 1775 with the earliest English patent for a water closet. The patent holder, surprisingly, was a watchmaker, Alexander Cumming, who described it as "a water closet upon a new construction."

How is it we have a watchmaker to thank for this invention? For one thing, there was as yet no such specialty as plumbing. There was no existing discipline from which would naturally spring forth new ideas in that field. A watchmaker was no more and no less an authority on water closets than, say, a cabinetmaker, which in fact would be the occupation of the man responsible for the next major advance in water closets. Cumming (1733–1814), while specializing in watchmaking, had a broad knowledge of mechanics generally. A native of Scotland, he moved to London about 1765 and was called upon several times to give mechanical exhibitions for King George III, who for many years rewarded him with a pension of 200 pounds annually. He was a member of the Philosophical Society of Edinburgh and of the Royal Society.

Cumming's advance was a more complex valve (as opposed to a plunger) action to empty the bowl. The valve was a horizontal slide that projected and retracted within an outlet pipe. An S-trap, or siphon trap — or stink trap, as Cumming called it — supplied an ingenious way of keeping sewer gas from backing up through the water closet and into the house and has been an essential part of plumbing ever since. Yet Cumming's valve suffered from a serious defect. By its nature, a sliding mechanism, and especially one with the weight of the bowl — or basin, as it was called — resting on it, was prone to sticking. Any degree of corrosion made it difficult if not impossible to move; there was likewise the effect of freezing in cold weather.

A variation of Cumming's closet was shortly being produced by William Allen in his shop at 129 New Bond Street, London, and was advertised in the *London Evening Post* on February 4, 1776, as a "Patent Water Closet, of an entirely new construction . . ." requiring not "a tenth of the water of those of common construction" while being "perfectly sweet and easier managed." In Allen's employ at the time was a cabinetmaker named Joseph Bramma, originally from a village in Yorkshire but for the past few years taking advantage of the considerably greater demand for skilled craftsmen in London. Among his tasks for Allen was the fitting up of some of these new closets. He looked closely at Allen's product and at the Cumming closet on which it was undoubtedly based and, using his innate inventiveness, set about giving practicality and dependability to what was still little more than a novelty for the very wealthy. By late the next year he had completed a new design, much of which he worked out in his head while convalescing in bed after a bad fall at work, and on January 27, 1778, he received a patent of his own. The patent also represented the first use of a changed spelling of his

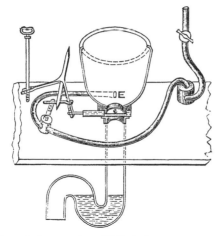

Cumming's water closet, 1775, the first to receive a patent in England. The handle-operated valve mechanism was relatively complex compared with a simple plunger, but the whole was still primitive by modern standards. The marble trough had now become a lead bowl, emptied through a slider valve actuated by the valve mechanism. Cumming's closet was notable as the first use of a siphon trap or S-trap (stink trap, Cumming called it). (Glenn Brown, Water-Closets, 1884).

name: he was now Joseph Bramah (1748–1814).

Whether the new spelling, signifying a broader pronunciation (probably BRAH-mah), also signified his sense of rising in the world, or whether it was coincidental, rise he did. He went on to receive a number of patents, and while the total is not remarkable, all were ideas ahead of their time. Most significant was his invention of the hydraulic press, patented in 1795, which had far-reaching importance in industry. Virtually as significant was the Bramah lock, a great improvement over anything that had existed and regarded as the best lock in the world for many years to come. Bramah offered a reward of 200 pounds to the first person who could pick it, and the reward went unclaimed until long after Bramah's death, when an American named Hobbs managed the feat at the Great Exhibition of 1851. Bramah also held patents on fountain pens, carriage brakes, fire engines, and printing machines.

Bramah considerably improved the water closet by getting rid of the sliding valve and substituting a hinged valve operated by a crank, a much more dependable mechanism. His other improvements included a flap over the inlet to spread water around the bowl as it was flushed (the forerunner of the modern flushing rim that encircles the bowl) and a second valve located in the overhead cistern, actuated by the same mechanism that emptied the bowl, to refill the bowl after flushing. The overall operation may be seen in the illustration on page 86.

The Bramah water closet was arguably the standard by which others were judged for years to come. Bramah is estimated to have produced some six thousand water closets by 1797. As J. Bramah & Sons, his firm continued producing water closets well into the nineteenth century.

In and Around the Kitchen

Science Made Savory

Little had changed in the kitchen since the early seventeenth century. Its focal point in 1805 remained the fireplace, which supplied heat as well as a means of cooking. Once nearly the size of a small room, sometimes even with a bench to one side within the opening, it was at least now more compact and a little more efficient. A significant improvement in the kitchen was moving the bake oven from the back wall of the walk-in fireplace to the front at the side of the opening—no small help considering the difficulty of using the oven. It was a ritual all its own. A separate fire had to be built inside the oven, and that fire had to burn until the bricks were red-hot. Then the fire and ashes had to be removed using a long, flat-bladed shovel and the bottom brushed clean, perhaps with a broom of hemlock twigs. Food to be baked, from bread to beans, from pudding to cake, went in and out according to baking time and the heat required. The oven was self-regulating in that it was continually cooling down. Foods that needed the most heat went in first, and so on. Only an experienced cook with good judgment could produce crisp bread and perfect pudding.

Vast and significant changes were on the horizon, however. Clearly the most important figure in this change — the one who, more than any other, brought the kitchen out of the Middle Ages — was Count Rumford.

Although he is regarded as primarily a scientific and technical genius, the essence of Rumford is that he had the instincts of an epicure as well as an engineer. It is not by happenstance that his technical writings are seasoned with such phrases as "rich and savory," "juicy and delicate," "wholesome," "well tasted," "nutritious." Perhaps nowhere in his writings is this any clearer than in his explanation of why he designed a new kind of coffeepot, a virtual prototype of the modern drip coffeemaker: "Nobody, I fancy, can be fonder of coffee than I am. I have regularly taken it twice a day for many years; and I certainly take care to have the very best that can be procured, and no expense is spared in making it good" (*Of the Excellent Qualities of Coffee*, London, 1812).

Indeed, what is particularly notable about Rumford is that the whole thrust of his work was so doubly directed. It was not enough that food could be prepared with more efficient use of time and fuel; it should also be savory.

Parenthetically it may be noted that Rumford was perhaps the first real kitchen planner, a calling that would come into its own only in the twentieth century. At the beginning of the nineteenth, he proposed determining the design of the kitchen by using chalk to draw on the floor what one wanted to have where. Or even better: cut thick pasteboard into pieces representing boilers, saucepans, roaster oven, and so on and see how it all looks before you actually build the kitchen — an innovative way of doing things.

But it is those boilers, saucepans, and roaster ovens that are the real Rumford. Food in his day, said Rumford, was most commonly prepared by boiling in an open vessel. This he condemned not just because it was inefficient but also because "This unscientific and slovenly manner of cooking [means] the food is rendered less savoury, and very probably less nourishing and less wholesome."

Concentrating the Heat

Rumford concentrated the heat on what was being heated, the corollary of which (in cooking, as opposed to heating) is that many small fires are more efficient than one

PREVIOUS PAGE: *A common method of making coffee in the early 1800s was to put ground coffee in a pot of water, boil it, remove it from the heat, wait for the grounds to settle, then pour off the brewed coffee. Count Rumford invented a better way: the drip coffeemaker, shown here as illustrated in his treatise* Of the Excellent Qualities of Coffee. (**Rumford, Complete Works, vol. 4**)

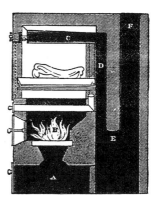

large one, primarily that notoriously inefficient fireplace. Rumford therefore designed four types of cooking apparatus, not all of which would necessarily be included in every kitchen:

- *the roaster — or Rumford roaster, or Rumford oven, as it is commonly called today, the best known of Rumford's many devices*
- *the enclosed fireplace — the progenitor of the stewing range, used in many houses of the early nineteenth century and a forerunner of the modern kitchen stove*
- *the register stove — an obvious forerunner of the modern range*
- *the family boiler — an improvement on the steam kitchen*

The most sophisticated of these devices — and it was virtually gourmet cooking for its day — was the roaster. It consisted of a hollow cylinder of sheet metal, usually roughly 18 inches in diameter and 24 inches long, set into a brickwork enclosure connected to a flue. Above the cylinder was a steam tube, regulated by a damper; the tube controlled moisture by the degree to which steam in the oven was allowed to escape from the cylinder (the oven proper). Below were two blowpipes regulated by in-and-out stoppers; these controlled the degree of browning. The heat of the oven was adjusted by a register in the ashpit door of the firebox below the oven. Smoke

Rumford's "enclosed fire-place" consisted of a series of separate fireboxes, each with its own opening, or boiler, into which was placed a pot or kettle. Each could be adjusted by its own damper. An adaptation of this was the stewing range found in some American homes of the early 1800s. This drawing from Rumford's On the Construction of Kitchen Fire-places and Kitchen Utensils *illustrates both.* (**Rumford, Complete Works, vol. 3**)

from the fire passed over and around the cylinder, resulting in even heating. When browning of meat was desired, the stoppers in the blowpipes were partly drawn out or removed and the steam tube was opened, conducting out moist air and allowing for deep browning of the meat. If very moist rather than very brown meat was desired, the settings were reversed.

The roaster was first described in Rumford's *On the Construction of Kitchen Fire-places and Kitchen Utensils* (London: 1799–1800). It came into use in America largely after the work was reprinted in Boston in 1804 (although copies of the London edition undoubtedly were available in America before that time). Both editions, as well as a number of subsequent ones, contained drawings and a detailed description of the roaster; and since Rumford selflessly sought no patents on any of his devices, anyone who wished to build one was free to do so. And many did. Homewood, the residence of Charles Carroll Jr. in Baltimore, is believed to have had a Rumford-inspired kitchen when it was completed in 1803 but evidence of it is lost. In 1804 the Gardner-Pingree House in Salem, Massachusetts, had a roaster. Some older residents of Salem recalled that Rumford, still known only as Benjamin Thompson, arrived in town at age thirteen to serve his apprenticeship under Salem merchant John Appleton. Records of construction at Gore Place, Governor Christopher Gore's home, in Waltham, Massachusetts, document the installation of a Rumford kitchen in 1806. That same year, merchants in Portsmouth, New Hampshire, were advertising the availability of Rumford kitchens "as cheap as they can be purchased in Boston." In January 1808, Portsmouth tradesman John Badger sold a complete "Rumford works," including a roaster, to merchant James Rundlet for his new home. The roaster, apparently built from the description and diagrams in Rumford's published work, adheres closely to the prototype. It is still in place in its original location adjacent to the hearth. There has long been conjecture that not all Rumford roasters were used regularly — that the complexity of operation left many a housewife or servant scratching her head and going back to the open hearth. That the Rundlets' roaster was used is evident in that it had to be repaired and reset in its enclosure in 1834 and repaired once again in 1858.

The Rundlet kitchen also has a "Rumford range" along a wall adjacent to the fireplace. It is a brickwork enclosure with three boilers, each with its own firebox accessible through a cast-iron door. Into each boiler could be set a covered pot or kettle. The heat for each boiler could be individually regulated by a damper on its firebox. Over the range Rundlet built a masonry hood that was intended to draw smoke and steam from the range and funnel it into the chimney — an obvious forerunner of the modern range-top hood.

The Rundlet range is an example of how the second of these Rumford devices, the enclosed fireplace, came into use in America. This fireplace was originally designed for institutional use — notably Rumford's modernization of the kitchens of the House of Correction in Munich and the Hospital of La Pietà at Verona, Italy. Cooking, whether in a public institution or a peasant's cottage, was usually the same in kind if not in scale — done at the open fireplace. And in either case, the failing was the same: "The loss of heat and waste of fuel in these kitchens," said Rumford, "is altogether incredible." Furthermore, there were "noxious exhalations," especially when charcoal was used as

Rumford used this illustration in the first publication of his On the Construction of Kitchen Fire-places *to show the "enclosed fire-place." This was the kitchen of Baron von Lerchenfeld, Munich, which Rumford designed in the 1790s. Each of the openings atop the brick enclosure is a boiler into which is placed a pot or kettle. Under each is a separate firebox, adjustable by its own damper. Flues from the separate fireboxes converge at the chimney in back.* (**Rumford,** Complete Works, **vol. 3**)

fuel, and a certain tendency "to cook the cook more than the food."

What more logical, therefore, than to enclose the fireplace? Instead of one large, vertical opening, have a number of small ones — say, four or five on top of each half of a semi-circular structure half-surrounding the cook. Each of these openings would have its own firebox underneath so the heat of each could be individually controlled.

Into each would be set a covered pot or kettle. Not all of these would necessarily be used at any one time. For a given meal, perhaps three or four would suffice. The other fireboxes would not be lit. In this way, only as much heat would be generated as would actually be used, and all of it would be concentrated exactly where it would be doing the most good. The smoke from each firebox would travel through conduits in the brickwork (generating some additional heat for each cavity it passed) and be released up a common chimney at the back.

On a large scale, the enclosed fireplace was the centerpiece of the kitchens Rumford created for the House of Correction and the Hospital of La Pietà; on a smaller scale, it might be anyone's "modern" kitchen. And indeed, Rumford, as his renown grew, created scaled-down versions of his kitchen for the homes of European nobles. In his *On the Construction of Kitchen Fire-places* he used as an illustration a kitchen he designed for Baron von Lerchenfeld in Munich.

On a smaller scale still, the enclosed fireplace became the Rumford range, or stewing range, in the Rundlet kitchen and a number of other American homes of the early nineteenth century; and with the course of evolution, the kitchen range, gas or electric, of the twentieth century.

Another progenitor of the modern range — and in fact resembling it much more than does the enclosed fireplace — is Rumford's register stove, also first described in *On the Construction of Kitchen Fire-places*. Here we have a rectangular brick structure with a cast-iron plate on top. In the top are two registers, which look at first like the burners of a modern range. Indeed this device, right down to its general dimensions,

Perhaps the first cooking stove that could be conveniently regulated was Rumford's register stove, which was in use at least by 1797 in his own home in Munich. The stove used circular registers set into an iron plate to regulate how much flame from the stove protruded through to a stewpan placed immediately above the register. The register was adjusted by the handle shown. (**Rumford, Complete Works, vol. 3**)

*The methodical Rumford: "These will be thought trifling matters," wrote Rumford, "but it must not be forgotten that convenience and the economy of time are often the result of attention to the arrangement of things apparently of little importance." To ensure the tight fit of a saucepan in its circular opening in his enclosed fireplace, Rumford insisted that the handle be attached on the inside. (**Rumford, Complete Works, vol. 3**)*

prefigures today's range more than does anything else of its time. The example described in *Construction* is 4 feet 6 inches long and 2 feet deep. It differs markedly from the modern article only in height—2 feet 6 inches.

Here is how it worked. Using the firebox door, which looked like a modern oven door, the user built a fire within, regulating it by a register on the ashpit door. Copper stewpans could then be suspended over the registers on top of the stove, and those registers would be regulated to control the amount of heat reaching the pans.

This was a glimpse of today's kitchen, a century and more ahead of its time. But there was more—what Rumford called the family boiler, his improvement on the steam kitchen. We go back to Rumford's comment about the most common form of cooking, "namely, that almost every kind of food usually prepared for the table in boiling water may be as well cooked, and in many cases better, by means of boiling-hot steam." There were steam kitchens in use at that time, particularly in institutions, but most of them failed Rumford's test of efficiency. "Bare inspection is, indeed, sufficient to show that they cannot be economical," he said, "for the surface of the tin steam-vessel filled with hot steam that is exposed quite naked to the cold air of the atmosphere is so great, that it must necessarily occasion a very considerable loss of heat."

For a foundling hospital he devised a steam kitchen using a large wooden box lined with tin. The box had a wooden cover that was so constructed as to make the box "perfectly steam-tight." He used steam from an existing boiler that was meant for boiling meat, so that "all the steam that is generated in the boiler is forced to pass through the steam-box, and the potatoes, greens, etc., that are in the box are cooked without any additional expense of fuel." Such an apparatus, Rumford said, was also good for large families using a boiler installed for the purpose. The steam box might be divided into two compartments for the preparing of different dishes at the same time.

Besides these various apparatuses for cooking, Rumford devised an array of "culinary inventions," including boilers, stewpans, kettles, and coffeemakers. Rumford had a profound impact on the future of the household, in part because he thought of things that had not occurred to anybody else and partly because he made practical certain ideas that had never been effectively developed. Perhaps as important: by declining patent protection—by "laying before the public complete plans and descriptions of [my] various culinary inventions," allowing them to be replicated without restriction and without any claim to personal profit—he made his new world of wonders immediately and universally available. He was the kind of innovator who would invent a better coffeepot simply because "Nobody, I fancy, can be fonder of coffee than I am."

The Beginnings of Refrigeration

Refrigeration remained primitive throughout the colonial period. There were cold cellars, or root cellars, from the earliest years. A better form of refrigeration was the springhouse, a shelter built over a spring, in which dairy products and other perishable foods could be stored. Going the springhouse one better was the Daniel Boone Homestead, near Birdsboro, Pennsylvania (1730). A log house, it was built over a spring, so that the spring flowed through a small cellar. This provided a source of water as well as a place for keeping food cool. Otherwise many householders preserved food by means of such age-old processes as smoking, salting, drying, fermenting, pickling, spicing, or even freezing (given a cold enough climate).

In keeping with the innovativeness of the times, however, a so-called refrigerator was ostensibly invented in 1803 by a Maryland farmer, Thomas Moore, who claimed to have coined the word, though not the concept. In the age of Rumford, Moore's device stretches the imagination somewhat. It consisted of a box with a coat wrapped in cloth and rabbit fur—obviously an attempt at insulation, but there was nothing to create a cold environment inside the box. Even so, Moore said he built an experimental version that was successful in transporting butter to market a distance of twenty miles—a journey of several hours back then—on a hot day.

Such a primitive device shows how various technologies develop at different rates. Means of refrigeration within the kitchen, even widespread use of the icebox, was still some years away, awaiting the availability of commercial ice.

Icehouses became more common around the turn of the nineteenth century. According to John Watson: "These [icehouses] have all come into use among us [in Philadelphia] since the war of Independence." The icehouse characteristically was a small structure mostly belowground and perhaps double-walled aboveground, where ice was stored after being harvested from ponds and lakes during the winter. The usual insulation material was sawdust, which would be spread 6 to 8 inches thick on the floor. Blocks of ice were placed on this, with additional sawdust between the ice and the walls. The blocks would be piled up to a foot or so from the ceiling, and the remaining space packed with sawdust.

Icehouses were expensive to build and use, and so were found only among the well-to-do. Someone had to be paid to cut the ice, haul it away, and fill the icehouse. In warmer climates it might be possible to buy ice, but the cost was so prohibitive that few people kept icehouses, and ice was used sparingly even in an icebox. An icehouse somewhere on one's property was hardly a kitchen convenience anyway. The icebox came into use only toward the mid-nineteenth century. As of 1805, refrigeration as a kitchen convenience would remain "on ice" until the coming of new technologies.

THE MISSING SINK

Despite the marvelous inventiveness of Rumford and all the other innovators at the beginning of the nineteenth century, there was still something missing from the kitchen—something whose absence today's homemaker would notice immediately. Where did Rumford wash all his stewpans, covered pots, and other culinary inventions? Where was the kitchen sink?

Where indeed? It is a missing link in this chain of development. One of the curiosities in the evolution of household technology is that so simple, so basic, so fundamental a component of the modern kitchen was so slow in arriving and, at that, remained primitive well into the nineteenth century. In curious contrast with his other culinary creations from coffeepot to roaster, Rumford appears not to have thought of a sink as part of the modern kitchen. Few houses of 1805 had them, even those that were otherwise up-to-date. From earliest colonial times, water was hauled into the kitchen in buckets, used in buckets, and then dumped outside from buckets. Somehow this ritual was still followed when other rituals were being put to the test of the "modern."

An early kitchen sink that can still be seen today and that was there in the beginning of the nineteenth century is in the kitchen of the Silas Deane House (1766) in Wethersfield, Connecticut. The sink is located to the right of the kitchen fireplace just below a window. It presumably was added after the house was built, since it bears the date 1771 underneath. It is made of a slab of stone, carefully carved out to create a basin. Roughly 49 by 27 inches, the slab is about 5 inches thick. At the back, just under the window at bottom center of the basin, is a drain hole that extends through the wall of the house. There is no way to run water into the sink, only to drain away what water was used to scrub pots and clean fowl. Water exiting through the drain probably went into a barrel for eventual disposal elsewhere on the property. One wouldn't have wanted the residue of fowl cleaning and similar kitchen chores piling up just outside the kitchen window.

Was the location of the sink chosen because of the window? Most likely not. By the twentieth century, a window location had become the traditional site of a sink both because of the extra light and because the view gives a sense of respite from chores. In the Deane house it was just a convenient site; given the configuration of this particular room, the small space to one side of the fireplace would otherwise have been wasted. Something comparable to the Deane sink was probably the only kind in use at the beginning of the nineteenth century, although there is no way of knowing how many there were. Kitchen technology is particularly fast-changing. When something

LEFT: *Throughout the colonial period and into the nineteenth century, water was usually pumped from an outdoor well, as shown here by Ginny Stromberg, an interpreter at the Bement-Billings Farmstead, Newark Valley, New York.* (Photograph by the author)

BELOW: *The kitchen sink (dated 1771) at the Silas Deane House in Wethersfield, Connecticut. There is still no convenient means of water supply, the use of buckets continuing to suffice.* (Photograph by the author by permission of the Webb-Deane Stevens Museum, Wethersfield, Connecticut)

better comes along, the old is fast discarded. Two sandstone-slab sinks were installed in the basement of Hyde Hall, Cooperstown, New York, in 1820. When more modern sinks were brought in, one of the original found a second life as an outdoor planter, but it has since been restored to the household (see photograph page 166). The sinks were made by John Forester, of New York City, who was primarily hired to carve four marble fireplaces for the house. Presumably Forester knew of, or had carved, similar sinks in New York. The Cooperstown sink is larger than the one at the Deane house; more important, it shows a new stage of development: a circular hole in the bottom for attachment to a drainpipe instead of a spout through the wall. Although no faucet was attached directly to the sink, Hyde Hall had running water, and unquestionably there was a pipe with a faucet adjacent to the sink when it was installed. Thus by 1820 kitchen sinks did have plumbing attached, even if the sinks were decidedly primitive-looking by later standards.

Perhaps the oldest existing kitchen sink in America is this hollowed-out stone slab in the Sisters' House at Ephrata Cloister, Ephrata, Pennsylvania. This and identical ones on two other floors were installed as part of a remodeling in 1745. The stone slab is cantilevered and empties through a drain spout in the wall (sealed with a wood block shown at upper left of the sink). Placement is low by modern standards because this sink was not yet used in the way a modern one is. Washing of dishes and so on was still done using buckets on the floor; the sink was then used for emptying the dishwater, as demonstrated here by guide Nicole Shrom. (**Photograph by the author**)

Furthermore, these conveniences were not used only in the East. There was, for example, a simple kitchen sink with a drain to the out-of-doors in the Menard Home (c. 1802) in Ellis Grove, Illinois.

The earliest existing kitchen sinks in America are probably the three identical examples preserved at Ephrata Cloister in Ephrata, Pennsylvania. They are in the Sisters' House, in kitchens on each of three floors, and were installed as part of a 1745 remodeling of a building constructed two years earlier. Patterned on similar sinks in Germany, each one is a stone basin that drains through the wall, similar to that in the

Silas Deane House but smaller and lower. The Ephrata sinks are little more than knee-high, whereas the Deane sink is roughly waist-high. The reason for this is that the Ephrata sinks were not meant to be used in the same way as later ones (thus even the Deane sink of 1771 shows a degree of evolution). At Ephrata the dishes were washed in wooden buckets on the floor, and the water was then dumped into the sink to drain outdoors. The cloister was founded by German settlers in 1732 and was notable for the austerity of its lifestyle. It thus presents the paradox of having the oldest known examples of one of the most common household conveniences. Schifferstadt in Frederick, Maryland (1756), also built by German settlers, has a kitchen sink that is somewhere between the Ephrata and Deane House sinks.

OTHER WORK FOR BARRELS AND BUCKETS

If refrigeration and sinks were little changed at the dawn of new convenience, laundry was the epitome of non-change. Clothes-washing was done in lakes and streams or in an assortment of tubs, buckets, pails, barrels, and kettles, usually outside, though sometimes in the kitchen. The laundry was then hung or spread on bushes, small trees, grassy areas, or a porch to dry, though it must have been hung inside during bad weather. Such washing as was done by these various means did not necessarily include soap. What soap existed was homemade. With or without it, the technique was the same: twisting, rubbing, and squeezing the clothes to make water penetrate the fabric and wash away dirt; then, if soap was used, rinsing in much the same way. Laundry was probably the most onerous of all household tasks.

THE FUTURE: MORE RECOGNIZABLE 1830

By the third decade of the nineteenth century, the embryonic elements of the modern house could be seen growing into recognizable shapes. Manifestations of comfort at a new and higher level were still rare, to be sure. But in two houses, one in the North and the other in the South, we can find an assortment of conveniences—from water closets to a stall shower, from central heat to a rudimentary refrigerator—that were well ahead of their time.

The Owens-Thomas House in Savannah, Georgia, was completed in 1819; Hyde Hall near Cooperstown, New York, was begun in 1817, first occupied in 1819, and fully completed in 1835, although its significant technology was in place by 1830.

The architect who put the stamp of "modern" on the Owens-Thomas House was William Jay, who arrived in Savannah from England in late December 1817. Only twenty-five, he followed in the footsteps of that other architect-emigré, Benjamin Latrobe, and, like Latrobe, brought with him a keen insight into what made a house not only architecturally modern but comfortably modern. Urbane and affluent Savannah welcomed Jay's refinement of style—he was perhaps the foremost exponent of English Regency architecture in America—and his working knowledge of the technology that made England a leader in household convenience in the early nineteenth century.

Of the several houses Jay designed in Savannah, the best known is the Owens-Thomas House, originally built for Richard Richardson, a banker and cotton mer-

1

Previews of the future. *At Hyde Hall: (1) Still preserved is the set of instructions from J. Bramah & Sons, London, for installation of the water closet. The closet was imported from England in 1827. (2) Artist's conception of the water closet off the main hall. Its location was convenient for guests as well as family. (3) The heating system, dating to 1830. At right is the basement furnace, from which hot air was conveyed through six-inch pipe and thence through heat registers, or "regulators," in the dining and drawing rooms (two each), as well as the rear lobby, water closet, and pantry. At the Owens-Thomas House: (4) A marble bathtub, one of four tubs in the house. (5) The shower stall. It was made of masonry covered by stucco. When in use, a curtain of some sort was presumably drawn across the front. (6) The sink, made of stone, for scullery or laundry purposes. At a time when few kitchens yet had sinks, here was a remarkable instance of the countertop, something that began to define a kitchen sink as modern a century later.* (Bramah water closet **instructions courtesy of Friends of Hyde Hall. Illustrations by Dolores Malecki-Spivack)**

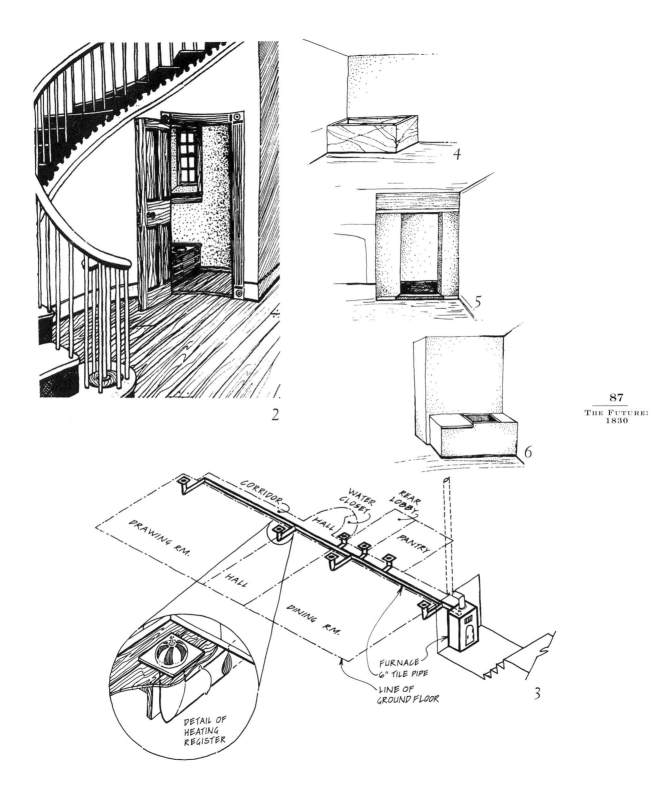

2

4

5

6

DRAWING RM.

CORRIDOR

HALL

WATER CLOSET

HALL

REAR LOBBY

PANTRY

HALL

DINING RM.

DETAIL OF HEATING REGISTER

FURNACE

6" TILE PIPE

LINE OF GROUND FLOOR

3

chant. Jay began designing of the house before he came to America and, once in Savannah, saw it to completion in January 1819.

The most notable thing about Richardson's house was its plumbing. This is the closest we have seen yet to what is taken for granted in modern times. In 1819 this house had water closets upstairs and down, full-size bathtubs with running water, a shower stall, and a scullery sink with running water perhaps also used for laundry. Other features included an ice chamber, a kitchen range, Argand lamps, fireplaces with coal grates, and pivoting windows between rooms for light and ventilation. All in one house!

The sophisticated plumbing system depended on an adequate water supply. Unlike the Waln and Markoe houses in Philadelphia, where city water was available in 1801, Savannah had no water supply system until the 1850s and relied largely on public pumps. Jay solved this problem by equipping Richardson's house with a massive system of indoor cisterns fed by rainwater from the roof. There were three in all: a 2,300-gallon cistern in the attic; a smaller one of 800 gallons between the first and second floors; and a 5,000-gallon tank in the basement. The cisterns supplied a water closet on the second floor, with a sink serving the three bedrooms there; a water closet on the first floor, along with a sink and tub in an adjacent room and a pantry sink; and in the basement, two bathing rooms containing tubs (one containing both a tub and a shower) and a scullery sink with running water adjoining the kitchen (the scullery may have doubled as a basement laundry).

The cisterns on the upper floors were built of wood and lined with lead. The one in the attic furnished water through lead pipes to the second-floor water closet and the basement shower. The between-floors cistern fed the first-floor water closet. The basement cistern occupied an area roughly 15 feet square. It was of masonry construction, covered on top with wood planking. Lead pipe provided water to the tubs and sink. These in turn drained into ceramic conduits built into the basement floor, underneath sandstone paving. The conduits led outside and drained into a rear garden, into either a dry well or a privy vault. Similar ceramic drains served the two water closets and the shower.

The tubs were made of marble slabs joined together. Enough is intact of one of these to see clearly what it looked like. Also largely intact is the shower stall, which was remarkably advanced for its day. It was made of masonry covered with stucco, except for the floor pan, which was stone. Its configuration is almost exactly that of a modern stall shower. The front was open; a curtain probably covered the opening. It was supplied by the cistern in the attic.

The sink that was used for scullery work and laundry is entirely intact, and in its configuration provides an almost eerie look into the future, given the general absence of even primitive kitchen sinks in 1819. It was made of stone, but in its size approximated kitchen sinks of later times; and most interesting of all, it included a countertop (also stone), possibly the earliest known instance in America of something that would not become common until a century later.

The two water closets have entirely disappeared, but enough lead pipe and other evidence remains in place to leave no doubt that they were a part of the original house. Having one on both the first and second floors may also have been precedent-setting in America. They were surely imported from England and may well have been Bramah closets or some other form of valve device, which was the standard of the day.

Adjacent to the cistern in the basement, and at the front of the house, was a two-section ice chamber. One section held the ice; a smaller section, accessible through a hatch, was used for cold storage.

William Jay came to America almost exactly two decades after Latrobe, and the higher level of sophistication that Jay imparted to the Owens-Thomas House provides something of a rough index to the development of household technology in England, especially in plumbing, in just that short a span.

The creative inspiration behind Hyde Hall was Philip Hooker, the leading Albany, New York, architect of the early nineteenth century, working with rough designs furnished by Hyde Hall's first owner, George Clarke. Clarke, the great-grandson of a colonial lieutenant governor of New York, in 1813 married Anne Cary Cooper, the widowed sister-in-law of James Fenimore Cooper. In May 1817 he bought the property near Cooperstown on which Hyde Hall stands, and he set out almost immediately to build a stately country home overlooking Otsego Lake. Enough was complete in 1819 for the Clarkes to move in, although the entire mansion was not complete until 1835, the year of George Clarke's death. Among its features were running water in the kitchen using a lead-pipe gravity flow system from a small nearby reservoir; two limestone kitchen sinks; a wood-burning kitchen range and a cast-iron stove for heating the large entrance hall, the stove being tended not from in front but through an opening to a rear hallway. There was also an unusual auxiliary heating system for the drawing room and dining room consisting of a 6-inch iron pipe running under the floor to circulate fresh outdoor air through air chambers behind the fireplaces (Gauger reinvented once again). The heated air exited through holes on the sides of the chimney breast, creating convection.

The two most significant features are Hyde Hall's water closet and central heating system. The Owens-Thomas House had water closets on both the first and second floors, unusually early for America, but there is nothing left of them except some of the lead pipe. Hyde Hall's single water closet is still largely intact, and as such is perhaps the earliest still in existence in America. A product of Bramah & Sons, it was imported in 1827 and presumably installed that same year. Not only have the basic mechanics of it been preserved, but so have the instructions showing American workmen how to install it. Placed in a small room off the rear hall, it was easily accessible to guests as well as to members of the family (domestic help presumably used an outdoor privy). The water closet drained into a stone cesspool, from which extended three drainpipes that dispersed waste into the ground, well away from the house—something on the order of a modern septic system. Hyde Hall's piped-in water came from a small reservoir built for that purpose on nearby Mount Wellington. This provided enough water to operate the closet.

Hyde Hall's "bathroom" had no sink and no tub. There was a window for ventilation and light. The water closet worked essentially like a modern toilet but much less efficiently.

We can visualize its operation if we look at the instructions for installation, which provide an extraordinarily complete account of how an early water closet worked. The illustration shows only the mechanical structure; it was understood that the bowl and mechanism would be encased in a wooden cabinet with a hole $10\frac{1}{2}$ inches in diameter in the top. At time of use there was apparently a quantity of water in the bowl, or basin, as it was called. After use, the handle at the right of the seat was pulled upward. This simultaneously operated two valves. One was a hinged valve under the bowl, which released the contents. At the same time, by means of a wire, a valve on the cistern, or overhead tank, was opened, causing water to flow down into the bowl to facilitate its emptying. The small box underneath the cistern retained an amount of water equivalent to what was needed to refill the bowl; this reserve continued to flow down once the handle was released and the valves had been closed, thus refilling the bowl for the next use.

Although far less efficient than its modern counterpart, the water closet of the early 1800s, particularly the Bramah, was an improvement over the outdoor privy, but it was definitely a luxury. The Bramah's considerable significance is evident in the fact that its type was still the best indoor plumbing more than a century after it was patented. "There is no water-closet equal to a good valve-closet," wrote British plumbing authority S. Stevens Hellyer in 1887, and "the valve water-closet is practically the Bramah water-closet."

The other significant feature of Hyde Hall is the supplementary central heating system dating to 1830, which worked in conjunction with fireplaces. The system used a soapstone plate stove (the equivalent of what was coming to be called a furnace but was still often referred to as a stove) in a semi-enclosed basement-level room at one end of the house. Hot air was conveyed through a tile pipe running under the floor to "heat regulators" (later known as registers) in the drawing room and dining room (two in each room) and in the rear lobby, water closet, and pantry. Clarke purchased 155 feet of pipe and 28 elbow joints (at a cost of $150.25 including shipment from Albany) for installation of the system, although all of this may not have been used. The stove itself cost $80.00 and eleven heat regulators cost $41.50, transportation included.

One of the net results of this was a heated — or, more accurately, warmed — water closet, a remarkable luxury in 1830.

DR. G. M. STERNBERG'S
ELECTRO-MAGNETIC REGULATOR,
FOR
DAMPERS AND VALVES.

Fig. 1

SECURED BY
LETTERS PATENT,
No. 100,462, No. 105,272 and No. 105,273.

The figure represents the Apparatus applied to the damper of a hot air furnace, and the Regulating Thermometer hanging over the mantle in the sitting-room above. The connecting wires and a battery cup for generating the necessary current of electricity are also shown. The cup is shown below the damper, but it may, of course, be placed in any corner or closet that is convenient.

PART 2

Between Thumb and Finger : 1860

It is a reflection of human nature that one's own time is always considered the pinnacle of achievement. Not even two generations after Latrobe had "perfected" comfort and convenience, a "whole [new] standard of life and comfort" seemed to emerge.

Let us see what that standard was coming to mean in 1860 — what now could be done with thumb and finger? Now one could turn a tap in the kitchen sink and get hot water; strike a match and use it to light a stove, a furnace, or a brightly burning kerosene lamp; drop into a glass of water a shaving of ice from a pantry refrigerator; pull the brass handle of a water closet; or turn a stopcock for a bathtub full of warm water. These, the taken-for-granted of daily life in later times, were giant strides in 1860.

Stoves are a good example. In 1805 heating stoves were rare, and cooking stoves were even more unusual. As late as 1830 only some 25,000 heating and cooking stoves were being manufactured annually in the United States. By 1840, however, there had been a fourfold increase to 100,000, and by 1860 the output was about a million a year, and those million were far more useful and effective than what had existed earlier in the century. Another example was the availability of matches, which were literally a "thumb and finger" convenience. In 1805 they had been a luxury; by 1860 they were being manufactured at a rate of 36 million a day.

While household technology still largely served the well-to-do, it was finding its way into the homes of those of lesser means — not yet such major appliances as water closets and furnaces, perhaps, but simpler conveniences like parlor stoves, iceboxes, lamps, and running water.

The 1860s saw the largest single-decade increase in the number of industrial firms in business in America — a growth rate of 80 percent. With the creation of new jobs came increased spending power, and it was now possible for people to spend that extra money on comfort.

By the 1860s Americans generally regarded their standard of living as superior to that of other societies. England, once the model, was now eclipsed as America set for itself a new standard of comfort and convenience. Anthony Trollope, visiting from England in 1861, could only agree, although he rather overstated his case, especially for the average house:

PREVIOUS PAGE: *Symbolic of thumb-and-finger convenience is this illustration of Dr. G. M. Sternberg's "Electro-Magnetic Regulator" of 1870. This forerunner of the modern thermostat was a battery-operated device that used a hand-set "regulating thermometer" hanging over the mantel in the parlor to operate the damper of a hot-air furnace in the cellar.* (Smithsonian Institution)

In Boston the houses are very spacious and excellent, and they are always furnished with those luxuries which it is so difficult to introduce into an old house. They have hot and cold water pipes into every room, and baths attached to the bed-chambers. It is not only that comfort is increased by such arrangements, but that much labour is saved. In an old English house it will occupy a servant the best part of the day to carry water up and down for a large family. Everything also is spacious, commodious, and well lighted. I certainly think that in house building the Americans have gone beyond us, for even our new houses are not commodious as are theirs.

Another commentary — on how Americans saw their own homes — leaves no doubt to what degree the standard of life and comfort had changed. From a book titled *Eighty Years' Progress of the United States*, a compilation of the reflections of "Eminent Literary Men" published in Hartford, Connecticut, in 1869:

With the improved style of houses there is a constant ambition to occupy a "modern house," or one with the "modern improvements," which may be enumerated as, warming apparatus, whether by hot-air, water, steam, or gas; the water-pipes in all the rooms, connecting with the cooking-range for facility of heating; water-closets and bath-rooms connected with street sewers to carry off the waste water; bells, speaking-tubes, telegraphs, ventilation, burning-gas, dumbwaiters to communicate with different floors, and all the luxury of arrangement and embellishment which makes a modern private dwelling so far in advance even of the fairy palaces in the Arabian Nights' Entertainments.

It may be said that Trollope and some of those Eminent Literary Men were so awed as to exaggerate. So let us see what a real house of 1860 was like — one that incorporated the most up-to-date conveniences of the time and one that real people lived in.

ARCHITECTS, FATHER AND SON

By curious happenstance, it was the ship *Louisiana* that bore James Gallier Sr. from England to America. An Irish-born architect whose talent transcended his recognition in England, he concluded that he "could scarcely fail of success in the United States" and in February 1832, at the age of thirty-three, he departed on a journey that would lead

ABOVE: *New Orleans, a bird's-eye view.* (Lithograph, 1851. Library of Congress)

LEFT: *Portrait of Aglae Gallier (Mrs. James Gallier Jr.)* (Photograph © 1998 by Paul Taylor, courtesy of the Hermann-Grima/Gallier Houses)

BOTTOM: *James Gallier Jr. A portrait by François Bernard.* (Photograph © 1998 by Paul Taylor, courtesy of the Hermann-Grima/ Gallier Houses)

him, in fact, to Louisiana. Before reaching New Orleans in 1834 he worked briefly in partnership with the well-known architect Minard Lafever in New York.

New Orleans in the 1830s was a place of promise. One who arrived in the city about the same time as Gallier was the Irish actor Tyrone Power, there to star in *The Irish Ambassador* at the American Theater. Power had heard much about the city and wrote of "the promise of its future greatness [and] wealth which . . . is on all hands accumulating with a rapidity almost partaking of the marvellous." For an aspiring architect, surely this was a place to find success; and yet not without hesitation, for New Orleans was also a hotbed of yellow fever. Perhaps its most notable victim, from our point of view, was Benjamin Latrobe, who died here of yellow fever in 1820 while working on the design and construction of a waterworks not unlike that which he had created for Philadelphia twenty years earlier.

New Orleans in Latrobe's time was not quite the marvelous place it would become in its Golden Age. "Royal street, towards the swamp," wrote Latrobe in 1819, "retains its old character without variation. The houses are, with hardly a dozen exceptions among many hundred, one-story houses."

It was on this same Royal Street in the French Quarter, no longer in sight of swamp, that Gallier's son, James Gallier Jr. (1827–1868), also an architect, in 1857 began building for himself and his wife, Aglae, and their four children a house that epitomized "modern" for its time.

The Gallier House, built 1860, New Orleans. (Photograph by the author)

Like his father, the younger Gallier wanted the most up-to-date technology: James Senior had supplemented a scant formal education by reading and studying, on his own, whatever was cutting edge in England during his early days as an architect. He later wrote, "I devoted every spare hour to the study of the higher principles of the art of building. I carefully studied the works of Nicholson, Tredgold, and others on the science of construction, the strength of materials, etc.; read all the works I could procure upon engineering, the steam-engine, and machinery."

Evidence of Gallier Senior's success in introducing technology to provide comfort and convenience are the bathing rooms he incorporated into the Saint Charles Hotel in New Orleans, which he designed with Charles Dakin. Opened to guests in 1837, it was perhaps the most sumptuous hotel in the country and among the first with bathing facilities (Boston's Tremont was the first with bathtubs in 1829).

Given his father's fascination with the engineering side of architecture, it is not surprising that Gallier Junior would have a good idea of what made a house modern in his own day. But unlike Latrobe, who designed a house for William Waln in 1805 candidly acknowledging that it was such as he would like to build for himself, we now have an architect actually building his own home — and half a century later, by which time the definition of "comfort" had been considerably expanded.

This house at 1132 Royal Street, on what was once an orchard of the Ursuline Convent — in whose chapel James and Aglae had been married in 1853 — is not unlike many homes of its time. On the first of its two stories are a double parlor, dining room, pantry, storeroom, and kitchen; on the second floor, four bedrooms, a library or general purpose room, a bathroom, and the servants' quarters. The structure is not exceptional until we see how Gallier filled it.

THE VERY MODERN HOUSE, 1860

Let us have a look, beginning with water supply. The New Orleans waterworks that Latrobe had under way at the time of his death were taken over by the city and completed in 1822. The plant continued to operate until about 1840 but was never sufficient for the needs of a growing city, and its unfiltered, muddy product was eventually used primarily for street cleaning. At the time Gallier built his house, many people used wells. But contamination was common, and it was better to have another source. The cleanest, most convenient was rainwater collected in a cistern. This was Gallier's choice — a 5,000-gallon cistern in the backyard, fed from the roof. Coupled with a tank in the attic, filled by pump with water from the cistern, this was the water supply for all indoor needs. The cistern is a circular tank made of cypress, set on a brick base, the hollow core of which also served for cool storage of food. Still another source of drinking water was bottled water, brought in from often distant springs. An advertisement in the New Orleans *Daily Picayune* in 1857 offered water from "Clark & White's Springs, Saratoga," presumably in New York. The Galliers undoubtedly used bottled water as well.

This 5,000-gallon supply of rainwater (and rain is always plentiful in New Orleans) went either directly from the cistern or from the attic storage tank (filled by a force pump) to the kitchen and pantry on the first floor and the bathroom on the second.

The kitchen of the Gallier House. Shown here is a corner including the sink and the copper water boiler attached to the cast-iron range (to left, not shown). The sink receives hot water from the boiler and cold from the cistern in back of the house. (Photograph © 1998 Paul Taylor, courtesy of the Hermann-Grima/Gallier Houses)

Most houses still had no sinks and no running water; the occupants were left to use buckets as they had from time immemorial. If there was something in the nature of a sink, it was merely a place for filling buckets, perhaps with some form of drain.

Gallier, the very up-to-date architect, had a kitchen sink with both hot and cold running water. The sink in the restoration of the Gallier House is copied from another Gallier-designed house. It is lined with copper and has a grooved wooden drainboard. There is also a sink in the pantry, and it was here that tableware was washed (pots and pans were scrubbed in the kitchen). The pantry, which is adjacent to the dining room, also functioned as a serving room.

Hot water was supplied by a copper boiler adjacent to the range. Typical of the time, water was heated in a reservoir behind the range. Water circulated through a copper coil within the boiler to the top, then filled the boiler. Additional water flowed through as hot water was tapped off for use. Pressure created by this system was sufficient to raise hot water to the second floor.

The bathroom was on the second floor, as was becoming usual. That site was near the attic tank or cistern, the most common source of indoor water, and close to the bedrooms, where personal washing was traditionally done. The modern concept of the bathroom as a place for both bathing and elimination was new. Now one room combined both functions, and virtually from the start it was called by that word that is so clearly euphemistic: "bathroom." That was what architect A. J. Downing called it in his *Architecture of Country Houses* in 1850, one of the earliest works showing house plans with tub and water closet in the same room; it is the term Gallier himself used on his own plans in 1857; and that is what the room has been called ever since. The Gallier House bathroom had a water closet and a copper tub in a walnut enclosure with hot and cold water, but there was no sink—not an uncommon situation at the

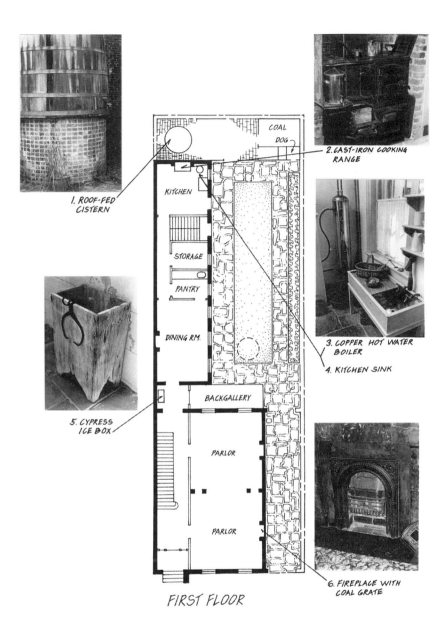

1. ROOF-FED
CISTERN

COAL
DOG

2. CAST-IRON COOKING
RANGE

KITCHEN

3. COPPER HOT WATER
BOILER

STORAGE

PANTRY

4. KITCHEN SINK

DINING RM.

BACKGALLERY

5. CYPRESS
ICE BOX

PARLOR

PARLOR

6. FIREPLACE WITH
COAL GRATE

FIRST FLOOR

THE GALLIER HOUSE, 1860: 1. Roof-fed cistern. *Roughly twice the height suggested by the photograph, with a capacity of 5,000 gallons. Made of cypress (a wood resistant to termites as well as to moisture), it rested on a brick base.* 2. Cast-iron cooking range. *Although not original to house (it was acquired for the restoration) and perhaps not exactly like what was originally here, the significance is the same: as opposed to the open hearth, this was part of what made a kitchen modern in 1860.*
3. Copper water boiler. *Water heated in a reservoir in the range was stored in the boiler, immediately adjacent to the range, from which it was piped to the kitchen sink, the pantry sink, and the bathtub (pressure within the boiler was sufficient to raise water to the second floor). Having hot water presupposed the range to be in operation, a shortcoming of 1860s technology that would be resolved in coming years.*
4. Kitchen sink. *The sink here was copied from the one in another house designed by Gallier. It is copper with a grooved wooden drainboard.*

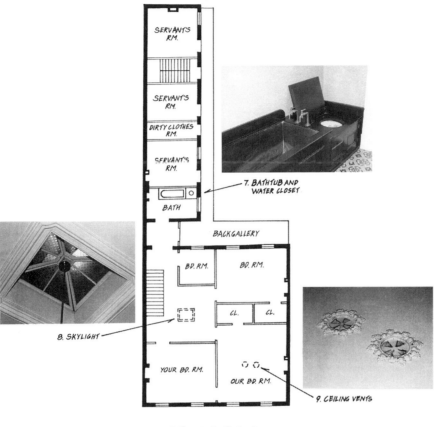

SECOND FLOOR

5. Icebox. *Made of cypress (the top is not shown), this icebox was located in the rear entrance foyer so as to be away from the heat of the stove and to be convenient for delivery of ice. The tongs are for handling the blocks of ice.*

6. Fireplace with coal grate. *One of a number in the house. Partially visible to the right is a toleware scuttle with a removable tin lining used for bringing in coal from the coal shed in back of the house.*

7. Bathtub and water closet. *A conspicuous example of comfort and convenience in 1860. The tub is copper in a walnut enclosure with faucets for both hot and cold water, the cold coming from a cistern in the attic (fed by a force pump from ground level), which also supplied the water closet. The water closet emptied into a cesspool under the rear courtyard (the dotted circle on the first-floor plan).*

8. Skylight. *Panes opened to allow escape of warm air into the attic. In the roof itself is another fixed pane of glass that allowed for light.*

9. Ceiling vents. *Unique for the time, at least in New Orleans. Built into decorative plasterwork in the ceiling of the master bedroom, the vents were opened with a pole.*

(Artwork by Dolores Malecki-Spivack. Photographs of the kitchen sink, copper boiler, and icebox are by Paul Taylor © 1998, courtesy of the Hermann-Grima/Gallier Houses, New Orleans, La. The other photographs are by the author)

ABOVE LEFT: *The bathroom is a conspicuous example of comfort and convenience for 1860. Both hot and cold water were supplied to the tub, which is copper in a walnut enclosure. Cold water for the tub and water closet came from a cistern in the attic, filled by hand pump from the main cistern. Hot water reached the tub by means of pressure generated within the boiler. Typical of the time was the absence of a bathroom sink; the custom of using washbasins in the bedroom still prevailed. The water closet emptied into a cesspool beneath the courtyard (the dotted circle on first-floor plan, page 100).* (Photograph by the author)

ABOVE RIGHT: *Detail of the Gallier House water closet. Although not original to the house it is authentic to the period.* (Photograph by the author)

time. It was during the 1860s, just after Gallier built his house, that the bathroom sink began coming into common use. The Galliers followed the prevailing custom of using washbasins in their bedrooms.

The cold water for the bathroom tub came from the tank in the attic, which was likewise the source for the water closet. By 1860 the water closet was no longer the rarity it had been earlier in the century. There were, for example, more than 10,000 in use in New York and somewhat fewer than that in Boston. The water closet installed as part of the restoration of the Gallier House was typical of the period — a porcelain bowl with a blue transfer-printed pattern set into walnut cabinetry. It emptied into what Gallier's plans labeled a "water closet sink" — a cesspool — beneath a rear courtyard. Such was common where there were not yet sewers. The other amenities of the bathroom were a coal-burning fireplace with a mahogany-framed mirror over the mantel, and a wall-mounted gaslight fixture in the shape of a hand holding a lily.

For refrigeration the Galliers had an icebox in a vestibule off a side entrance, making it accessible for delivery of ice. Here it was also protected from the heat of the kitchen and was convenient to the dining room and parlors for those who wanted ice for drinks. Ice was a luxury in the South at this time, and had to be imported from the North in barges packed with sawdust (ice production did not begin in New Orleans until the late 1860s). The Galliers' icebox, which was simply constructed and made of cypress, was not used for day-to-day storage like a modern-day refrigerator. It was likely filled and used only on special occasions, as for parties or for occasional storage of food in very hot weather. New Orleans being a port city, various meats, seafood, vegetables, fruits, and other foodstuffs were readily available on a daily basis and were bought as needed.

The heating system in the Gallier House suited the climate. Had the house been in a colder region, Gallier undoubtedly would have installed central heating, which was becoming more common by 1860. But central heating of the kind then in use required a cellar, which is impractical to impossible with the high water table of New Orleans, and in any event, moderate temperatures in all but the dead of winter made fireplaces sufficient. There were fireplaces in most rooms, including the bathroom, all of them coal-burning.

Ventilation in New Orleans is a greater concern. Here Gallier used about every technique available at the time, beginning with high ceilings and large windows with shades. In the second-floor ceiling is a skylight that, when opened, allowed heat to escape into the attic. A separate pane of glass in the roof above the skylight admits light. For the master bedroom Gallier created a ventilation system that was unique in New Orleans. It consisted of two air vents built into decorative plasterwork in the ceiling. The vents, which were opened and closed with a pole, allowed air to escape through the attic and thence, apparently, to the outdoors by way of a pipe (this part of the system is no longer extant). How well the vents worked we can only guess. Their effectiveness was probably marginal at best, but the concept was innovative for its day.

New Orleans, in 1824, was among the first cities to have a gas works. Gallier took full advantage. There was gaslight throughout the house, using fixtures of various sorts, including gasoliers—gaslight chandeliers—in the dining room and parlors.

We have seen a remarkably advanced house with the Galliers. Now let us look at the state of technology circa 1860 generally.

Power, Fuel, and Water Supply

Making Giant Strides

Wind and water, the horse, and the human arm were the principal means of power at the opening of the nineteenth century. Steam, to be sure, powered the water supply system of Philadelphia and, more significantly, was the newly evolving motive force in transportation, though only for ships, so far. But steam power in 1800 had direct impact on the lives of few Americans. By 1860 there were few whose lives were not touched.

When it came to technology in the household, the thumbs and fingers turning things on and making things go were still, to be sure, those mostly of people who could afford the convenience. But the impact of the Industrial Revolution was reaching the many — in transportation, in availability of goods, in public water supply. And unknown to those who still read by oil lamps and whose own arms were still their chief source of power, another force, even greater than steam, was around the corner.

THE NEW POWER

Electricity, that sine qua non of the modern house, was largely an abstract idea at the end of the eighteenth century. It had no application in everyday life and would have no impact on the household for most of the nineteenth century. There was, however, at least symbolic early promise when, in 1800, Alessandro Volta created the storage battery—the voltaic pile, as it was known. Before this time an electrical charge had to be produced electrostatically (by friction); Volta's battery made electricity available electrochemically (by chemical means). Charles Coulomb in France in 1785 had demonstrated how opposite electrical charges attract one another and like charges repel. These and other discoveries of the early nineteenth century culminated in Michael Faraday's production of an electric current from a magnetic field.

What this meant (though few could yet appreciate the importance of Faraday's discovery) was that all the essentials were in place for the development of the electric motor—that indispensable element of the modern household. Experimentation with electric motors began with Faraday in England in the 1820s. American ingenuity would contribute to making the motor practical.

Whenever he wasn't in the classroom, Joseph Henry, a professor of mathematics and science at Albany Academy in New York State, was in his laboratory, studying the relationship of electrical fields to magnetism. By 1831 this resulted in the construction of a primitive electric motor. The apparatus, as Henry described it, was roughly 20 inches long and consisted of two permanent magnets standing upright, their north poles at the top. Bridging these and hinged at the center was a bar of iron, wrapped around and around with three strands of copper wire, each strand 25

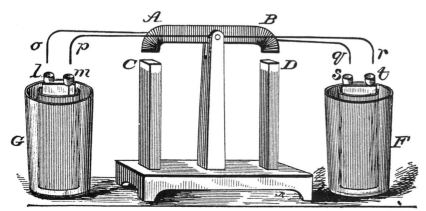

OPPOSITE PAGE:
Joseph Henry. (New York Public Library Picture Collection)

LEFT: *Henry's electric motor. AB is the bar of iron functioning as an electromagnet, C and D are the upright permanent magnets, F and G are the batteries, and l, m, s, and t are the thimbles of mercury.* (Edward Byrn, *Progress of Invention*)

feet long. This was an electromagnet (in effect a temporary magnet), as opposed to the two permanent magnets. It had the properties of a magnet when, but only when, electric current flowed through it. And since it was not a permanent magnet, its poles were not permanently fixed. What was north could become south, and vice versa. Given the fact that likes repel, if the north (let us say right-hand) end were to descend and draw near the north pole of the permanent bar magnet, it would be repelled, the left-hand side (south pole) simultaneously being pulled by the north pole of the other permanent magnet (opposites attracting). If the polarity of the bar, at this point, could be reversed, the left becoming north, it in turn would be repelled, and the right-hand end (now south) attracted. Theoretically this motion should repeat itself over and over again. This is the *principle* behind all electric motors.

But how can the polarity be changed? By reversing the direction in which the current flows through the electromagnet. Volta's battery showed that when two different metals are brought in contact with each other in an acid solution, they react chemically to produce electric current. Henry used copper and zinc. Each battery consisted of a plate of zinc immersed in acid in a copper tumbler. Atop each zinc plate and atop a rim of each copper tumbler was a tiny brass cup, or thimble, filled with mercury. Protruding from either end of the electromagnet were two wires set so as to make contact with the thimbles (the mercury in them facilitated this). As the bar tipped one way, the current flowed from the negative thimble of the battery through the bar and back to the positive thimble of the battery. The bar was now a magnet, having its north pole at the end that was tipped. Since opposites repel, this end was thrust in the opposite direction. When it reached its other extreme, the wires at that end made contact with the mercury in the thimbles at the opposite end, causing the bar to be repelled back where it started. And so on. Henry found that if he added fresh acid from time to time, the device would keep up this back-and-forth motion for an hour or more, at a rate of seventy-five vibrations a minute.

Here, in a primitive stage of development, was the electric motor: motion created by electrically charged opposites repelling one another. It is perhaps the most elementary example of how an electric motor works. A modern electric motor is much more sophisticated and infinitely more efficient, but still a motor only by virtue of what made Henry's apparatus work.

Yet what was Henry's apparatus good for? What could it do besides go back and forth, back and forth?

A MOTOR THAT COULD TURN

Although significant in its own right as the first electric motor in America, Henry's device only established a principle. It remained for another to take electrically generated back-and-forth motion and turn it into rotary motion, which would be more useful. Rotary motion had been demonstrated by Michael Faraday in England in 1821 with a device using a magnet and a movable wire. Yankee ingenuity was not far behind. Thomas Davenport, a Vermont blacksmith, after reading of Henry's work and observing an electromagnet devised by Henry for use at a forge in nearby Crown Point, New York, began experimenting with his own electromagnets and by 1834 developed his own motive device. In 1837 he received the first U.S. patent for an electric motor, a device for "Propelling Machinery by Magnetism and Electro-Magnetism."

Using a single battery with zinc and copper plates in a vessel of diluted acid, Davenport's motor consisted of four electromagnets on opposite spokes of a wheel, revolving horizontally, reacting to two magnets fixed in place. In order to put the machine in motion, explained Davenport, "the galvanic magnet [on spoke] No. 2, being changed by the galvanic current passing from the copper plate of the battery . . . becomes a north pole, while at the same time the magnet [on spoke] No. 4 is changed . . . by current passing from the zinc plate . . . and becomes a south pole." And so on. "In this manner," explained Davenport in

The Davenport motor, the first electric motor to be patented in the United States. (Edward Byrn, **Progress of Invention**)

his patent application, "the operation is continued, producing a rotary motion in the shaft, which motion is conveyed to machinery for the purpose of propelling the same."

And so we have the *practical* electric motor, primitive indeed, but able to do what we expect an electric motor to do — make something work. Davenport built a number of small electric motors, all using galvanic batteries, including one that is said to have powered the printing press he used briefly to print a journal he published in search of support in developing uses for electricity. Few were interested, however. Steam power was well established by now, and the potential of electricity was too indiscernible.

When Davenport died at the age of forty-nine, he was experimenting with an electro-magnetic player piano.

So far we have seen how chemical energy can create mechanical energy — that is, how a chemical reaction can produce the electric current that causes a motor to power a mechanical device. What about the reverse — mechanical energy creating electricity? Faraday, in the early 1830s, while experimenting with magnetism, discovered that moving a permanent magnet through a coil of wire induced an electric current to flow through that wire. Henry, about the same time, came to a similar finding. Here, in embryonic form, was the dynamo, or electric generator.

So there was, in the 1830s in theory, the means of generating electricity and the means of putting it to work operating machinery. Yet nothing came of it in Davenport's time. Electric lighting would not arrive until later in the nineteenth century, and there would be little in the way of electrical appliances until the beginning of the twentieth. The principal obstacle was finding a feasible way of multiplying Henry's little copper and zinc jars, with their brass thimbles, into a dependable and sufficient source of electricity for everyone. The lag between theory and application would leave the house-hold without its sine qua non for the time being.

THE AGE OF COAL

The development of household technology from the early nineteenth century through the beginning of the Civil War parallels the increase in the importance and produc-tion of coal, and central heat is inextricably linked with these changes.

We have a rough idea of the consumption of coal in the colonial period from the few scattered statistics that remain. Prior to the Revolution, for both commercial and house-hold use Americans burned perhaps less than 10,000 tons a year, most of it imported from England, some mined here. (We speak now of short tons — 2,000 pounds.) By the 1790s, it is estimated that 63,000 tons were being produced in Virginia and Pennsylvania. In the early 1800s, with the coming of the Industrial Revolution and the use of steam to power boats and then the railroads, the increasing use of coal was in evidence. Visitors from industrial England often felt quite at home, one observing in 1818 that "the whole town [of Pittsburgh] presents a smoky appearance," giving it promise of becoming "the Birmingham of America." Another visitor was struck by "the smoke of the coals ascend-ing from the glass-works" in Charleston. Production of all types of coal is estimated at just over 100,000 tons in 1800, rising steadily to 20 million tons by the Civil War.

The haze of smoke beginning to hang above cities like Pittsburgh was mostly from commercial use of coal. But coal also facilitated the coming of central heat. Coal burns longer and hotter than wood, so it was practical to have a coal furnace in the cellar, although many furnaces used wood even into the twentieth century. Dr. George Derby, of Boston, writing about coal in 1868, assessed the advantages and disadvantages of wood:

> *Furnaces for burning wood have also many advantages. They are simple in construction, and give an abundance of heat of the most agreeable quality. The expense of fuel, even in Boston, is very little more than that of coal. The disadvantages are, first, the need of abundant cellar or yardroom for the storage of wood; second, the addition of fresh fuel four or five times a day; third, the need of large old-fashioned flues to carry off the smoke, a modern-size flue requiring frequent cleaning; and fourth, the condensation of the products of the distillation of wood, impure acetic acid, in and about the flue and chimney.*

Coal was generally more desirable. While it also consumed a large amount of cellar space for storage, it was longer-burning than wood and required fewer trips up and down the cellar stairs than a wood-burning furnace.

One of the earliest private homes with central heat was Wyck, then the Philadelphia residence of Reuben Haines III, who is known to have hired a workman to install a furnace for burning anthracite coal in the front cellar in 1820.

Here we may further refine our observation that coal facilitated the coming of central heat by looking at the significance of anthracite, which burned hotter and cleaner than bituminous, or soft coal, but was harder to ignite. Anthracite was discovered at Mount Carbon, on the Schuylkill River in central Pennsylvania, in the late 1700s. Attempts to sell it in Philadelphia about 1800 failed. Many believed it wouldn't burn; some disparaged it as "incombustible refuse." Production of anthracite was spurred in part by the War of 1812, which cut off the supply of English coal to American manufacturers. By 1820 anthracite was becoming accepted; and in time, wherever it was readily available, it would be the most popular coal for home use. (According to the August 19, 1865, issue of *The Builder*, an ordinary house used a ton of anthracite roughly every three weeks.) Bituminous and anthracite served as the principal home heating and cooking fuels until the development of the natural gas and heating oil industries in the twentieth century. As of 1860, however, there was not a hint that anything better would ever come along. Samuel G. Goodrich wrote of coal in 1856:

> *Think of the labor that is performed by this mass of matter that had slum-*
> *bered for ages — hidden, senseless, dead, in the bosom of the earth! It now*
> *not only cooks our food and warms our houses so as in winter to give us the*
> *climate of summer, but . . . turns the whizzing wheel of the factory, sends*
> *the screaming locomotive on its way, drives the steamboat foaming*
> *through the waves. This single mineral now performs, every day, the labor*
> *of at least a hundred thousand men!*

OTHER SLUMBERERS

As Goodrich was extolling the virtues of coal, by a curious coincidence its successors were beginning to emerge from their own slumber. In 1859 an unemployed railroad conductor named Edwin L. Drake, after much fruitless digging, struck oil in western Pennsylvania. Its immediate use would be as kerosene, which quickly became cheap enough as a lamp fuel to give almost every family a brighter home. As a fuel for heating, however, oil would not become common until well into the next century.

Gas for heating was likewise still in the future. Manufactured gas was too expensive for heating, though the use of gas as a heating fuel was already being imagined. Dr. George Derby wrote in 1868: "We can see no reason why illuminating gas may not some day be made cheap enough to furnish heat as well as light to our homes. It is possible certainly to imagine that an arrangement of Bunsen burners, easily regulated and graduated according to the weather . . . might be made to supply any amount of heat required for domestic purposes."

The use of gas for heat would have to await the development of the seamless pipe in the 1920s and 1930s. Even so, the first small company to distribute natural gas from a well opened in Fredonia, New York, only nine years after Goodrich wrote his paean to coal.

ILLUMINATING GAS: GOING PUBLIC

The lighting of Peale's Museum in Philadelphia by gas in 1815 gave countless museum goers a preview of things to come in the home. It was certainly the most widely seen display of gaslight in its early days in America. A year later, the smaller Baltimore branch of the museum, run by Rembrandt Peale, also had gaslight. This installation was actually the more significant of the two. As we saw earlier, the Philadelphia museum, under pressure from a nervous city government, disassembled its lighting system in 1820. The museum in Baltimore, however, led to the creation of America's first public gasworks and the first gaslighting of city streets.

In company with some of Baltimore's leading citizens, including the editor of the *Baltimore Gazette* and two bank executives, Rembrandt brought about the organizing of the Gas Light Company of Baltimore in 1816. It was incorporated in February 1817, but a combination of physical obstacles and a downturn in the economy conspired to keep progress slow: by February 1818 only twenty-eight streetlamps were in operation. Another problem was that the gas being used produced

An early gas meter, manufactured by the W. W. Goodwin Co., Philadelphia, c. 1855, painted red, with gilt decoration. (Smithsonian Institution)

a particularly offensive odor. The company hired a new engineer from England to construct a new works to manufacture gas from bituminous coal. By the early 1830s the company had one hundred streetlamps lit and was supplying gas to some three thousand private customers.

New York got its first gasworks in 1823 with the incorporation of the New York Gas Light Company. It had a thirty-year exclusive franchise for laying gas pipe south of Grand Street. The first house to be hooked up and lighted, in September 1823, was at number 7 Cherry Street—the home of Samuel Leggett, the president of New York Gas Light. Gas mains—bored wooden logs, like the ones still being used as water mains—were laid along Broadway from the Battery to Canal Street in 1825. Two years later the company was ready to light streets after replacing existing wooden lampposts with cast-iron ones, and in June 1827 the first of them were lit.

THE AMERICAN WINDMILL

The windmill of the colonial period was a ponderous affair that required the constant attention of an operator to keep it pointed into the wind and to adjust its sails to the wind's velocity. Its use was largely limited to milling grain into meal or flour and, perhaps in a few cases, pumping water for communal purposes. It was not something for the household.

From the mid-nineteenth century on, the mill was smaller, lighter, more efficient,

Before the age of electricity, symbolized by the wires at lower right, this windmill in Brimfield, Massachusetts, supplied the energy by which water from a brook was pumped to the attic cistern of the nearby Wyles-Converse House. From the attic the water flowed by gravity to serve all of the plumbing needs of the house, now the rectory of Saint Christopher's Roman Catholic Church. The windmill is an Eclipse, manufactured from the 1860s to the 1920s (after 1890 by Fairbanks, Morse & Co.). The Eclipse was the creation of the Reverend Leonard R. Wheeler and was similar to, but somewhat simpler than, the Halladay, for which it was the principal competitor. The Brimfield windmill is believed to be one of the earliest Eclipse models. (Photograph by the author)

and, most important, nearly self-regulating. This was the American windmill. It was noticeably smaller and lighter than its predecessor and was also multibladed. The ingenuity behind the first such wind machine to be patented — and to be commercially successful — was that of a Yankee mechanic named Daniel Halladay. Halladay was approached by a pump manufacturer named John Burnham, whose water-powered pumps were selling well wherever water power was sufficient. But what of elsewhere — the Midwest, for example? Burnham asked Halladay if he could improve the windmill enough to make it more generally useful.

The need was for something that would work by itself and also be affordable. Halladay turned for inspiration to a device that James Watt had used to control the speed of the steam engine. This was a centrifugal governor, and Halladay saw its adaptability to controlling the pitch of the blades of a windmill. Instead of the ponderous sails characteristic of a Dutch windmill, Halladay used small wooden blades hinged to a ring around the hub, pivoting forward and backward, in response to the governor, somewhat in the fashion of an umbrella. This allowed the mill to take full advantage of a productive wind and yet be spared the destructive force of a gale. And since the whole of the wind-catching mechanism was now much lighter, it was possible to make it also self-regulating as to direction by means of a wing comparable to that on a weather vane.

The Halladay windmill's principal competitor was the Eclipse, invented in 1866 by the Reverend Leonard R. Wheeler of Wisconsin. It was simpler than the Halladay in that instead of a governor it used a device by which the whole wheel was angled to compensate for the force of the wind. A restored Eclipse windmill in Brimfield, Massachusetts, dating to c. 1880, has seventy-two blades. It is on the property of Saint Christopher's Church and was built originally to pump water from a nearby stream to a third-floor cistern in the Wyles-Converse House, now the church's rectory. At a time when well water and outdoor privies were still common, the windmill made it a very comfortable and convenient house indeed.

USEFUL WORKS CONTINUED

The waterworks that went into operation in Philadelphia in 1801 — the first major use of steam power in America — represented a bold step into the future. Too bold, as it turned out. Within a few years it was replaced by a simpler, cheaper, and more dependable form of technology: waterpower.

There were several reasons. Capital had been hard to raise. Potential investors were skeptical, and in order to generate the necessary capital, management offered to let investors have free water. As a result, two years after opening, the operation was producing only $960 a year in revenue from paying customers — not even 1 percent of the $300,000 it had cost to build the system. On top of this, the engines were subject to frequent breakdowns and were costly to repair, and the system was simply inadequate to keep up with Philadelphia's growing population.

In 1812 the city embarked on construction of a second steam-powered water system, abandoning the original works in 1815 after a total expenditure of $657,398. By now there were some three thousand customers — up from the sixty-eight with which the system started. In 1818 the city concluded that steam was too expensive a source of power and undertook construction of another new works using the waterpower of the Schuylkill River. Frederick Graff, who had been superintendent of the waterworks since 1805, now designed a system consisting of a dam across the river with eight waterwheels from 16 to 18 feet in diameter that pumped water into a reservoir on Fairmount Hill. Construction began in 1819, and the works went into operation in 1822. Water flowed from the hill by gravity to serve the city's needs. Graff remained chief engineer of the Philadelphia waterworks until his death in 1847. He was succeeded by his son, Frederick Graff Jr., a civil engineer.

While visiting Philadelphia in the mid-1820s, author and traveler Anne Royall said there was almost nothing left to see of Latrobe's original project. Technology even then was apt to be replaced quickly: "I saw the old water-works; they were at the centre square of the city; nothing remains of them but a romantic edifice, resembling a temple."

Although steam is particularly well-suited to pumping water (this was its first com-

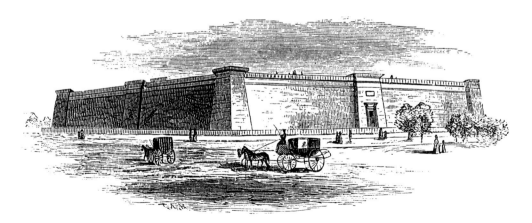

The distributing reservoir for the Croton water supply system, completed in 1842, was at Fifth Avenue and 42nd Street, New York City. Once no longer needed as a reservoir for water, the location became a reservoir of knowledge: the site of the New York Public Library. (**New York Public Library Picture Collection**)

mercial use in America), problems of cost and reliability gave it only a short run initially. The solution in Philadelphia was waterpower—cheap and efficient but also more primitive in technology. And indeed the next major water supply system—and the most important of the century—would be an aqueduct, built on the model of ancient Rome's, a form of supply intended to preclude the need for steam power.

The need for a dependable source of good water was acute by the early nineteenth century. New York, the nation's fastest-growing city, was too densely populated to use well water. There had been a halfhearted attempt to create a water supply system in 1799 with the establishment of the Manhattan Company. But this company made no more than a nominal attempt to furnish water; its real objective was the chartering of a bank, which an innocent-looking clause in its charter permitted. By 1823 it had laid 23 miles of pipe, nearly all wood, and had two small steam pumps as well as a reservoir built by Christopher Colles, who in 1774 had been commissioned to build what might have been the first steam-powered water supply in America—if it had succeeded. The company was thus limited as to how much water it could supply, and what it did supply was of such poor quality that it was used largely for fire protection. Residents who could afford to do so had water brought in hogsheads from the sparsely populated northern reaches of Manhattan.

New York's water had such a bad reputation that ships coming into the harbor brought their own supply from other ports. Much of the city's drinking water was contaminated. Epidemics of yellow fever in 1822 and cholera in 1832 showed that a new, safe source of supply was urgently needed.

As its source New York City chose the Croton River, nearly 40 miles upstate, a tributary of the Hudson. The craggy countryside that forms the watershed has an abundance of springs and streams feeding the Croton River, which Native Americans thought so pure that they called it "the Clear Water." In addition to ensuring water of high quality, the Croton had the virtue of being at such a high elevation that pumping with steam power was unnecessary.

In 1835 the Croton project was approved at a special referendum, and construction began that same year. The project involved construction of a dam across the Croton, creating a sending reservoir roughly 400 acres in area with a capacity of 600 million gallons, estimated to ensure a ninety-day supply even in extreme drought. From the dam was constructed an aqueduct, tracing a 38-mile course into the city. Most of the aqueduct was built into the ground and constructed of masonry. The interior height was 8 feet 5½ inches and the greatest width 7 feet 5 inches. The aqueduct at the sending reservoir was 155 feet above mean high tide in the city. This resulted in an average velocity of a mile and a half an hour. The aqueduct led to a 35-acre receiving reservoir and thence by pipes to the distributing reservoir at Fifth Avenue and Forty-second Street, where the New York Public Library now stands. In the course of its long trip, the water picked up sufficient force to reach all of the densely populated parts of the city. The distributing reservoir, of masonry construction, covered slightly more than four acres and was 45 feet high. From this reservoir, water flowed through a network of mains as large as 36 inches in diameter and pipe as small as 4-inch bore. According to a contemporary account,

> By this means feed-pipes, from half-an-inch to 1 inch bore, are led from the main-pipes into the basement of every house, and in many cases a pipe rises to the bed-rooms, for supplying baths, &c. The mains are also furnished with muzzles, to which the engine-hose of fire-engines can be screwed, for extinguishing fires; and at the harbour pipes are branched out, terminating at the bulwarks, for supplying ships, and filling the water casks on board, by means of a hose.

And so, whereas seamen arriving in port once brought their own water, they now availed themselves of the clear city water. For the privilege of receiving Croton water New Yorkers paid an annual tax of ten dollars for a house of average size (there were more than 33,500 houses in the city at this time), while commercial establishments, including ships in the harbor, paid according to consumption.

When it was completed in 1842, this largest-of-its-kind waterworks in America cost $12.5 million—almost exactly half the federal government's entire operating budget of $25.2 million for the year. And besides a dependable supply of safe drinking water, New Yorkers got additional benefits, including an increase in civic pride. Visiting from England in December 1845, Sir Charles Lyell gave his opinion of the system: "A work more akin in magnificence to the ancient and modern Roman aqueducts has not been achieved in our times. . . . [I observed] with pleasure the new fountains in the midst of the city supplied from the Croton waterworks, finer than any which I remember to have seen in the center of a city since I was last in Rome." There was furthermore considerable benefit in terms of public safety. "The rate of insurance for fire has been lowered," Lyell noted, "and I could not help reflecting as I looked at the moving water, at a season when every pond is covered with ice, how much more security the city must now enjoy than during the great conflagration in the winter of 1835, when there was such a want of water to supply the engines."

Twenty years after Lyell, New York's water supply was still drawing raves from visiting Englishmen. A correspondent for London's *The Builder* wrote of New York in 1865: "The Croton aqueduct, that supplies New York, does its duty magnificently . . . though complaints of waste have obliged the authorities to be somewhat more sparing of the flow than heretofore. London is at present far behind its Yankee rival in this respect."

Boston, which was still relying on wells in the 1830s, began construction of a water system in 1846. It would tap Cochituate Lake, some fifteen miles to the west, using a major reservoir in Brookline and another on Beacon Hill. By 1850 the Boston water system was supplying 11,383 households with piped-in water.

In the years immediately preceding the Civil War, municipal water systems were also established in Cleveland, Detroit, Hartford, Brooklyn (which was not yet a borough of New York City), Jersey City, Louisville, and Cincinnati. By the 1860s all but four of the sixteen largest U.S. cities had municipal water supplies. In the still developing West, water supply was more primitive. Salt Lake City in 1860 ran water in open ditches along the streets. San Francisco pumped water from wells and brooks and had it delivered to homes in carts.

Public water supply did not necessarily mean that people had running water in their homes. Many had only a hydrant in the yard, from which they carried water into the house. This was still better and safer than using a well and a pump, however; at a time of sharply increasing population density, it dependably provided water that was free of pollution from the neighbors' privies.

In some places, at mid-century, there were public hydrants on the streets analogous to the public pumps and wells of earlier times. In other cases, hydrants offering free water to one and all were purposely omitted from plans for a new system. According to an 1850 account in the *American Almanac*, the average bill for water in Boston was a fairly substantial eight dollars a year. For this, customers received "water for all domestic purposes, including private baths, water-closets, &c." But there would be "No public hydrants for the gratuitous supply of water for domestic purposes." In small cities not yet served by public water systems, residents might have recourse to public pumps using common wells. Elsewhere, and particularly in rural areas, individual houses still had their own wells, sometimes with pumps. Undoubtedly there were also those who continued to rely on springs.

Where public water was not yet available, or not yet affordable for many people, public pumps continued to serve many households. (Lithograph by J. B. Lippincott & Co., Philadelphia, 1876. New York Public Library Picture Collection)

But another source of water—virtually one's own miniature waterworks—developed in the late 1700s and has continued in use, in some instances, to the present day. This is the gravity system, which was perhaps most common in New England. This method utilized a miniature aqueduct to connect an upland water supply, commonly a spring, with the house or barn. The conduit was usually wood or terra-cotta pipe connecting with a cistern at the house or a trough near the barn. Depending on individual circumstances, it was sometimes feasible to pipe water directly into the house, where it was available through a simple faucet.

In the 1820s lead pipe was also being used for the conduit. Ichabod Washburn in 1822 advertised that he "continues the manufacturing of Lead Aqueducts, for the conveyance of water . . . free from the trouble of repairing leaky and rotten Logs. . . . Individuals can be furnished with a size sufficient to bring water for the use of their House and Barn."

Some idea of the number of such systems in operation at this time is evident in a sampling of houses, farms, and mills for sale between 1820 and 1840. Roughly 5 to 10 percent of sales notices in the *Barre* (Massachusetts) *Gazette* listed lead-pipe gravity water systems as selling points, so the total number of such water systems (including wood and terra-cotta pipe) was higher than this, perhaps much higher.

The Bryant Homestead in Cummington, Massachusetts, the boyhood home of William Cullen Bryant, had a system consisting of a small spring-fed stone basin on a nearby hillside and pipe, apparently wood, leading to the barn and house. Diary references show there was running water to the barn at least by 1821 and to the house by 1829. Hyde Hall, near Cooperstown, New York, received water by gravity flow through lead pipes from a small private reservoir on nearby Mount Wellington. Water served two kitchen sinks and, after 1827, a water closet. The Park-McCullough House in North Bennington, Vermont, completed in 1865, had a gravity-feed pipeline that supplied the house with water from a spring two miles away.

By the 1860s, especially in cities with public water systems, in-house water supply was well developed. A correspondent for *The Builder* in 1865 described what he saw in America. Closely matching what we saw at the Gallier House, this was state of the art and represents many American households of the time, but certainly nowhere near a majority:

> *The hot-water supply is obtained by a simple apparatus, which seemingly is not known commonly to our [English] plumbers. In describing it, it will be necessary first to remark that all houses have a receiving cistern in the upper part of the building, to render the pressure on the pipes equal, and the supply steady.*
>
> *From this a cold-water pipe descends to the kitchen, beside the range in which the apparatus for heating the water is placed. This consists of a large upright copper cylindrical boiler, generally containing thirty to forty gallons, and sometimes considerably more, the water within which is kept at nearly boiling-point, by being coupled with the fountain, or water-back, at the back of the range. In this upright boiler a coil of pipes is compactly laid against the inner surface, and this coil, connected as it is with the cold-water pipe, receives cold water at the upper end, passes it through the coil to the bottom of the boiler, and then repeating the curve passes it up again in the shape of hot water, ready to be drawn wherever needed, a hot-water pipe connecting this with the bath-room, &c. &c. The water in the coil, by thus slowly circulating, becomes of the same temperature, nearly, as the water within the boiler by which it is surrounded. . . . The cistern being at a proper elevation, the hot water will rise to as high a point as the natural law allows; and the advantage of this simple plan is that, the upright boiler being open, no steam is generated, and there is no danger in its use. This system also gives a large and constant supply of hot water ready to be drawn for domestic use on the spot.*

The boiler is, of course, self-feeding; and it is an excellent feature of the best American cooking-ranges, that they heat this large supply of water without increased consumption of fuel.

For the supply of cold water for drinking purposes, a hydrant is attached . . . connecting with the main, and passing the water through a filtering apparatus, which is generally connected also with the large refrigerator that contains the daily replenished stock of ice; thus giving the luxury of cooled water in abundant flow.

At the other end of the spectrum was the Frame House (1821) in Honolulu, Hawaii, where water was obtained from an outside well using a pump salvaged from a sunken ship.

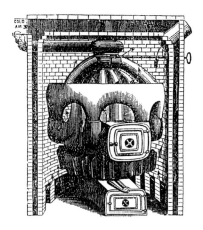

HEATING

KEEPING A WARM HOUSE

Americans are great on heat.
— *THE BUILDER, LONDON, 1865*

The first thing that impressed many a European visitor to America in the 1860s, whether in a private home, a tavern, or even a railway car, was how warm the place was kept. Britons, who liked their open fireplaces and frowned on central heat, were especially struck. Said one observer, writing in *The Builder* in 1865:

> *Much as may be said in favour of the economy of labour from the system of heating their buildings from one apparatus placed in the cellar, the evils are so great and numerous, that on the whole it is conscientiously thought that their houses would be better left unwarmed. Where one is healthily warmed and ventilated, ninety-nine are unbearable. The air is parched and dry, the heat stifling, and the danger from throat afflictions and colds positive. And yet there is much that is very convenient and valuable in some of the systems employed.*

In a few brief lines, that is the story of home heating from the early nineteenth century to the 1860s: a warm house was practical but there was a lingering controversy about whether central heating or even heating stoves were healthy.

As for progress, we have seen central heat reach the household — with the example of Reuben Haines III of Philadelphia, who in 1820 installed central hot-air heat using an anthracite-fired furnace. Haines was one of the first, and perhaps the first documented, to have central heat in a private home, and there were probably few like him in the years immediately following. Haines's brief diary account in November 1820 of hiring a mason to build "a furnace in front cellar for Schuylkill [anthracite] coal" is consistent with Pettibone's description and with later known examples. So it is to be presumed that Haines's system consisted of a brick enclosure (an air chamber) with pipes, probably tin, extending upward to the rooms being heated. Within the air chamber was the furnace — nothing more than a large stove — which could be tended through doors in the brick enclosure. There would have been a duct at floor level to admit outside air, this being warmed in the chamber and then rising through the pipes.

Solomon Willard of Boston, the architect of the Boston Court House of 1832 and the sculptor of the Bunker Hill Monument, was also an inventor who developed a central heating system about 1823. It was a "Hot-air Furnace — placed in the basement of the building, having communication with the external air, and pipes leading to the various apartments to be warmed" — apparently the same as the one Haines had installed, or the one that Pettibone had designed. With Willard, however, there is now evidence that hot-air central heat was catching on; he is said to have had a thousand of these systems manufactured by Daniel Safford of Boston. Not all were for houses, however; a number are known to have been made for churches, including Old South Church and Saint Paul's in Boston, and at least one, and probably more, for a factory. The apparatus was made of sheet iron and used wood as fuel.

In 1825 architect Charles Bulfinch consulted with Willard about a heating system for the U.S. Capitol. In his letter to Willard, Bulfinch allows us insight into just how little was yet understood about furnaces and central heating. Here was one of the most distinguished architects of his time asking questions even a young architect of later times would have known the answers to: "Is it best to admit the warm-air near the floor? . . . Do you find any necessity for ventilators, and how do you construct

PREVIOUS PAGE: *The Boynton hot-air furnace of 1854, in a catalog illustration showing not only the furnace itself but the configuration of a typical air chamber.* (Catalog, Cox, Richardson & Boynton, New York, c. 1854. Smithsonian Institution, Warshaw Collection)

them? . . . What is the difference in size, of furnaces for churches and private houses, and the difference in expense?"

In coming years inventors vied with one another to make furnaces more sophisticated and more efficient. A furnace patented by Gardner Chilson, of Boston, in 1845, had an early version of the humidifier. It was a vessel inserted into the casing of a coal-burning furnace by which "water may be introduced for evaporation in the hot-air chamber." Later furnaces often had the same feature.

The Chilson, also known as the Boston, furnace had a reputation for being a healthier source of heat than its competitors. A. J. Downing, who had a Chilson in his own cellar, flatly declared it "the best air-warming furnace in this country" in his *Architecture of Country Houses*. What made it better than others was that its design prevented it from becoming red hot, which presumably was how a furnace posed a threat to health. Downing talked about this, echoing the fears of many, some of whom preached total abstinence from central heat. Said Downing:

> *Most of the hot-air furnaces hitherto used are open to the strongest objections, on account of their unwholesomeness. They are so constructed as to heat the air by means of a surface of heated iron, raised to a very high temperature—often quite red-hot. Dr. Ure has correctly remarked that, "as cast-iron contains, besides the metal itself, more or less carbon, sulphur, phosphorus, and even arsenic, it is possible that the smell of air passing over it in an incandescent state, may be owing to some of these imperfections; for a quantity of noxious effluvia, inappreciably small, is capable of affecting, not only the olfactory nerves, but the pulmonary organs.*

Chilson's principal contribution was to line the firebox with firebrick to keep the iron casing from becoming too hot and to channel the smoke from the fire through a "heater" of pipe raised well above the fire. The heater was the part of the furnace around which—or through which, in this case—air passed to be heated on its way to the ducts. By having a heater of pipework, Chilson created considerably more radiating surface, adding to the efficiency of the furnace, and minimizing the likelihood of any part becoming red-hot. Downing explained that "the heater, or iron surface which warms the air, is placed high above the fire, and the surface which takes the heat is so extended (by causing the draught to pass through a series of pipes before going into the chimney) that no part of it becomes violently heated."

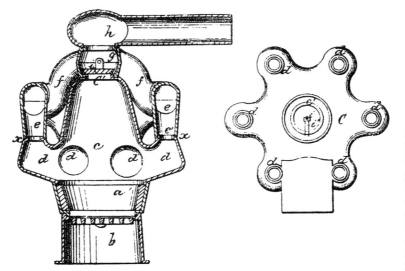

Gervase Wheeler, in Homes for the People (1858), described the firepot of the Boynton hot-air furnace as having "the appearance of a cog-wheel." Shown here: Boynton's patent drawing of 1854, U.S. Patent No. 11,545, Aug. 22, 1854.

By the 1860s, the standard of the day was arguably the Boynton hot-air furnace, manufactured by Richardson & Boynton of New York, which made heating equipment until 1942. The model then in use was patented in 1854. When former president Martin Van Buren installed central heat in his home, Lindenwald, in Kinderhook, New York, he made the Boynton his choice. Richardson and Boynton returned the compliment by supplying a furnace with "Hon. M. Van Buren, Kinderhook, N.Y." cast into the feeder door. The date of installation is not certain; it was sometime between 1854 and Van Buren's death in 1862, probably closer to the former.

Typical of the period, Van Buren's furnace was installed in a brick enclosure, in this case roughly 6½ feet high by 7 feet wide — slightly smaller than the 8-foot-square chamber recommended by Downing for a furnace of moderate size. The feeder door and an ashpit door were inset into the brickwork. From the brick enclosure, ducts ran to the various rooms that were to be heated. This system was the principal means of heating Lindenwald until 1937, and both the furnace and ductwork remain intact.

Richardson and Boyton were the successors to Chilson and Company and in effect refined Chilson's design. The Boynton furnace gained popularity quickly. In *Homes for the People* (1858), Gervase Wheeler said it "must rapidly supersede the older invention. . . . It has a larger amount of effective radiating surface than any other contrivance known; and has a curious, very valuable, and entirely novel feature in the peculiar formation of the firepot . . . the appearance of a cogwheel, by which the power of the furnace is enormously increased." It was also shorter than any other furnace on the market, allowing for greater flexibility in directing the ducts to the rooms above.

Despite the American fondness for heat, it was not always easy to keep a warm house, especially a large house. The fundamental requirement was a large volume of heat, since much of it would be lost because of the lack of insulation and the absence of storm windows. An efficient furnace like the Boynton was thus popular among those who could afford one. Even so, there were probably many who lamented, as did Mrs. Theodore Roosevelt of the family's new home, Sagamore Hill, that trying to keep a house comfortable was like "trying to heat a birdcage."

WARMING WITH PIPES

The factories and workshops are warmed during the winter months by means of pipes connected with the steam-engine.

— BERNARD, DUKE OF SAXE-WEIMAR EISENACH, WRITING OF A VISIT TO
THE HARMONY SOCIETY IN ECONOMY, PENNSYLVANIA, 1826

The Harmonites, followers of religious reformer George Rapp who had emigrated with him from Germany, led a peripatetic life — first the voyage, then settlements in Harmony, Pennsylvania, and New Harmony, Indiana — before returning to Pennsylvania in 1825. Here they built a new community called Economy, in what is now Ambridge, near Pittsburgh; and here they turned to the use of technology, including what was probably the first use of steam heat in America. Although as a "community of equality" Harmonites led an austere life that included practicing celibacy, they by no means renounced all worldly comforts. If their sense of religious and social purpose (which was meant to transcend everyday life) might be furthered by some convenience, it was to be welcomed, not shunned. Hence at Economy the Harmonites turned to steam power to run their cotton mill, and used steam from the same engine to heat their workshops. The date the cotton mill was built is not certain. It may have been 1825; certainly the mill was there by 1826, since a visit was recorded that year by the Duke of Saxe-Weimar Eisenach. In observing that the Harmonites used their steam engine for heat, the Duke documented possibly the first such use in America. Further evidence of early use appears in an inventory of 1833 that recorded, in addition to the engine, "A heating pipe for warming the house 300 feet long." A woolen factory, which came after 1826, was recorded in the same inventory as having "A heating pipe 428 feet long." The steam engines were primarily intended to power the mills, but the existence of a "heating pipe" seems to leave no doubt that they served the additional purpose of providing heat.

As in an orangerie heated by a modern version of the hypocaust of ancient Rome, steam or hot-water heat—in concept, at least—was used for plants before people. An early version of it was proposed by Sir Hugh Plat in *Garden of Eden* in 1653: "To have Roses or Carnations growing in Winter, place them in a roome that may some way be kept warme, either with a dry fire, or with the steam of hot water conveyed by a pipe fastened to the cover of a pot, that is kept seething over some idle fire."

By the late eighteenth century, hot water was often being used to warm greenhouses in England; and in 1782 a physician in Paris, M. Bonnemain, reported to the French Académie des Sciences an invention for circulating hot water through pipes to incubate poultry eggs. The device included a long rod that, as it expanded, closed the flow of air to the fire, thus automatically regulating the heat.

Heating with hot water or steam began to appear soon after this. James Watt experimented at his steam engine factory in 1784, running a steam pipe from a boiler into his office and using a simple tinplate box as a radiator. The results were not satisfactory. His firm, Boulton and Watt, in 1802 installed a steam-heating system in a cotton factory, using only vertical pipes of cast iron. This was also less than satisfactory. Attempts using horizontal pipe coupled to vertical risers—essentially the modern system—proved more successful. Presumably such attempts at steam heat as these in the early 1800s provided the groundwork for the Harmonites' use of steam in 1825 or 1826.

Meanwhile we have inventor Jacob Perkins. A onetime apprentice goldsmith born in Newburyport, Massachusetts, in 1766, he was more intrigued with what he could invent than what he could craft. He first created a machine for cutting and heading nails, then a process for engraving banknotes. Lack of support in the United States for the latter resulted in Perkins's going to England, where, in 1819, he established a factory for making engraving plates and printing banknotes. Within a few years his attention turned—or, more accurately, returned—to heating. In 1815 he had designed and seen to the installation of a hot-air system at the Massachusetts Medical College in Boston. A description written in 1817 by Charles Shaw suggests that it was similar to what Daniel Pettibone had installed in 1810 at Pennsylvania Hospital in Philadelphia. Wrote Shaw of Perkins's system: "The whole building is warmed by a single stove situated in the cellar. . . . The Stove is surrounded by a brick chamber from which a brick flue is carried up to the second storey, communicating by large pipes or apertures with all the principal rooms of the house." Unlike Pettibone, Perkins sought no patent at the time, although later, in England, he did obtain one for a similar heating system.

It is hot-water heating, however, for which Perkins is remembered. When Perkins got to England, low-pressure hot-water heating was already being developed, building on the experimentation of Watt and others. A drawback was that a low-pressure system required a large, awkward pipe. Perkins, working with his son, Angier Marsh Perkins, sought to solve this problem by using a high-pressure system and much smaller pipe, which could be concealed. The first patent was taken out by Angier in England in 1831, and the first installation was at the Guardian Fire Office in London the following year. It consisted of a brick furnace, boiler, and pipe roughly three-quarters of an inch in diameter, about one-fourth the size of the pipe otherwise being used for hot-water heating. The pipe itself, exposed as it was within the rooms to be heated, acted as the radiating surface. One sealed circuit of pipe sufficed. Because the system was sealed, water could be heated to well above the 212°F. boiling point of water, thus building pressure. Perkins intended a normal operating temperature of roughly 350°F., representing about 125 pounds per square inch above atmospheric pressure. But too hot a fire could raise pressure to many times this—in fact to dangerous levels. This drawback led to continued refinement of hot-water heating.

But the Perkins system was quickly embraced, notably by the British Museum, where two Perkins systems were installed in 1835, one for the reading rooms and another for the bird and print rooms. The circuit of pipe for one of these was 700 feet long and, noted the elder Perkins, "not thicker than your little finger."

Jacob Perkins remained in England, as did Angier. A protégé of the Perkinses, also an American, became a principal popularizer of hot-water heating in the United States. Joseph Nason (1815–1872), originally of Boston, Massachusetts, began his career with the Boston Gas Light Company. In 1837, while in England, he became associated with Angier Perkins and acquainted with his heating systems. Nason returned to America in 1841 and went into business with his brother-in-law, James J. Walworth (1808–1896). Their firm, Walworth and Nason, would become the most influential in hot-water heating of the nineteenth century. In 1895 it was said that "For many years every steam-fitting firm in this country could trace its origin to the old shop of Walworth and Nason, through either one or two removes." The two partners set up shop in 1841 in New York and Boston and began to manufacture their own heating system. They installed their first one the following year in Lowell, Massachusetts. Other installations followed, largely in woolen and cotton mills and other large buildings in New England. But the system was used in homes as well. One installed in a home in 1845 was reported to be still going strong in 1892.

Perhaps the most notable Walworth and Nason project was undertaken in 1855—

a new heating and ventilating system for the U.S. Capitol. It was installed as part of construction of the new Senate and House wings, added between 1855 and 1861 (the dome, a part of the same project, was completed in 1863). Up until then the Capitol had relied on hot air, supplied by sixteen separate hot-air furnaces that produced inadequate results.

Nason designed something of a hybrid combining steam and hot air. The basic system was low-pressure steam. For each wing of the Capitol four boilers supplied steam to twenty-two heating coils, each with 1,000 feet of pipe. Coupled to the nests of coils were two huge fans, driven by steam from the same boilers. The larger of the two was 16 feet in diameter. The fans blew across the coils, carrying the heated air through ducts to the rooms to be heated and, in effect, ventilated as well, including all floors of the House of Representatives and the Senate. Complaints about the new system focused not on adequacy of heat (apparently it was sufficient) but on the fact that the new chambers had been designed with no windows. Here was one of the first—perhaps the very first—of that now ubiquitous species of modern building that is sealed off from its outside environment and left entirely dependent on mechanical systems for heat, ventilation, and light. The lack of windows, and hence lack of view, troubled many; Massachusetts Senator Charles Sumner was particularly perplexed because, said he, "there is no public edifice in the world which enjoys the advantages of sight equal to this Capitol" and it was now just a "stone cage."

A similar heating system found its way into houses as well. It was described by A. J. Downing as "Heating by hot water . . . the most healthful and perfect mode of heating buildings [but] costing five times as much as heating by hot air." It consisted of a large coil of pipes connected to a boiler, all within a brick air chamber in the cellar, the type used for hot-air heat. As opposed to the Capitol, with its steam-driven fans, such a household system relied on convection to carry heat to the floors above. The advantage, Downing explained, was that "air which comes from a hot water chamber is always of a mild and gentle heat, since it can never be raised to a high temperature, robbed of moisture, or injured in quality." Purity of air was also a presumption of the Capitol heating system answering criticism of hot-air heat and its alleged spewing of impurities.

Meanwhile, another inventor—another New Englander—was redefining steam heat to help make it popular for the average house. Nason's early steam systems, like those of his mentor, Perkins, used high pressure and, as some bow to safety, relied on the fact that the system was sealed. The pipe itself was the "radiator" emitting heat into the room. What Stephen J. Gold invented was a real, if still primitive, radiator work-

Gold's radiator, patented in 1854. It's hardly a mystery why people called it the mattress radiator. (Stephen J. Gold, *Gold's Patent Low Pressure Self-Regulating Steam Heating Apparatus*, New York, 1868)

ing with a system, the heart of which was a wrought-iron boiler. The radiator consisted of two thin parallel plates of sheet iron fastened together by rivets in a pattern resembling the tufting of a mattress. At one end was a valve to let steam in; at the other, a small cock to let air out as necessary. Steam entered the radiator, circulated through the shell to produce heat by radiation, then condensed, and flowed back down the inlet pipe. This was perhaps the first one-pipe system (as were subsequent steam heating systems, as opposed to hot water heat using a two-pipe system — one pipe in and another pipe out for continuous flow throughout the system). Gold's system also included simple fire and water regulators and a simple safety valve. The radiator drew the most attention because the tuft pattern of its rivets made it look like a mattress, and it quickly became known as the mattress radiator.

Nason now reappeared, offering by 1860 a pipe radiator made up of vertical iron pipes set into a horizontal base. The appearance was much like that of a modern steam or hot-water radiator, except that the openings for the pipes had to be cut and threaded by hand, an expensive process. In 1886 there was introduced a radiator made of vertical sections joined together one after another and supported by end sections resting on the floor. This did away with the need for a base and threaded pipe. It was essentially what the modern radiator looks like, and a design that has never basically been altered.

STOVES: A PLACE IN HISTORY

Despite the emphasis here on central heating, it's important to understand that in the nineteenth century houses with fireplaces and heating stoves far outnumbered those

The variety of stoves available at mid-nineteenth century is evident in this lithograph of Joseph Feinour's stove and hardware store, Philadelphia, c. 1845. (**Smithsonian Institution**)

with central heating systems. The emphasis simply reflects long-term evolution of the household. In our time, almost all homes have central heat.

But we do need to look briefly at the heating stove, even though it does not often serve as a primary source of heat today. Indeed, the nineteenth century was the century of the stove. How much it caught on is evident from the following table:

YEAR	NUMBER OF STOVES MANUFACTURED
1830	25,000
1840	100,000
1850	375,000
1860	1,000,000
1870	2,100,000

These estimated totals were gathered at the first annual meeting of the National Stove Manufacturers Association in 1872. The population of the United States was roughly 13 million in 1830 and 40 million in 1870—a threefold increase. Production (and thus general use of heating stoves) over the same period showed an increase of more than eightyfold.

The stove shared heating responsibility with the kitchen range. The range supplied heat for the kitchen; the parlor stove heated the living space. Bedrooms may also have had stoves, they may have been left unheated, or they may have had simple registers in the floor to admit some little bit of heat from downstairs. Having a stove in every room was rare.

Stoves used both wood and coal, the latter being preferable. Coal made practical the magazine stove, in which a sizable quantity of coal could be placed in a magazine within the stove and fed automatically to the fire below. This was the so-called base-burner stove. The magazine concept first appeared in an English patent of 1770 issued to David Riz. In America one of the earliest and best known base burners was patented in 1833 by Eliphalet Nott, president of Union College in Schenectady, New York. Coal was put in a bin at the top, and was fed to the fire in a receptacle below. A chamber over the flames mixed in air from the room and released it as heated air from the top of the stove. Other improvements included mica windows that made a stove a source of illumination as well as heat (and gave it a slight similarity to the open fireplace). By 1841 the J. L. Mott Company was marketing a self-feeding stove that promised to maintain uniform heat. According to a promotional booklet, "the stove may be left for hours without attendance, having, on return, the same quantity of coal burning."

Stoves would remain the most common form of home heating into the twentieth century, when gradually central heat would supersede them.

All the basics of twentieth-century heating were there by 1860: steam and hot-water heat using room radiators and central hot air. The latter could even be found as forced hot air in the case of the U.S. Capitol, albeit using steam-powered fans. In a sense there was even the heat pump, though still unrecognized, in the basic concept of John Gorrie's ice machine, as we will see when we discuss refrigeration.

LIGHTING

TURNING UP THE LIGHT

The nineteenth century was something of a rheostat in time—an unparalleled turning up of the light in the American home. From parlor to bedchamber, from front hall to kitchen, from cellar to attic, there was a gradual but clearly discernible transition from darkness and shadow to brightness and clarity. It is nearly impossible for us to appreciate this transition from a vantage point lighted with fluorescent tubes and halogen bulbs. It is seen more easily through eyes that watched it happen. Writing some years afterward, Harry J. Thorne, of Evanston, Illinois, by then in his seventies, reflected on a life that had begun in candlelight:

> *In our homes, each carried his candle in its candlestick to his bedroom. In many homes this was the only means of illumination. Those who were better equipped used oil lamps in the living room, but for the bedroom the lone candle sufficed.*
>
> *Candles were an important part of the grocer's stock. No order was complete without this necessary article.*
>
> *In addition to the candles, especially in the country, fish oil was in*

*general use. In the city, coal oil [kerosene produced from coal] began
to be used.*

*When I began work for my uncle in his brick store facing the town
hall, I was attracted by huge vats arranged along the wall containing oils.
There were the linseed oils used by painters; also three kinds of illuminating oil. They were labeled in large letters, "Whale Oil," "Seal Oil," and
"Fish Oil." The first two were used . . . for illumination, and the latter for
general use on harness, boots, et cetera, and was a general mixture of
second-class fish oil of various kinds.*

*Our store was lighted with lamps burning whale or seal oil, and so
continued to be until the advent of coal oil which replaced the fish oils.*

*We were now waiting for the coming of gas which was being used in
the larger cities—waiting for enterprising citizens to form a local company
to erect the works and lay the pipes. That came in good time and I remember the excitement when we looked into the trenches being laid in our
main street for the pipes.*

OPPOSITE PAGE: *Truesdell's Illuminating Heater, c. 1870, promised to provide light as well as heat. It used kerosene
and was intended primarily as a heater for parlor or drawing room.* (Smithsonian Institution)

ABOVE: *A panoply of lighting fixtures, from the colonial period through the nineteenth century. From left to right:
Brass candlestick, late sixteenth or early seventeenth century, probably French. Wrought-iron crusie, Scottish, eighteenth century or earlier; the wick lay in the nozzle of the upper receptacle. Brass whale oil lamp, c. 1815, a popular
type in the early 1800s. Gas burner, c. 1860, consisting of a perforated ring using the principle of an Argand lamp with
its tubular wick; a glass chimney was intended to be fitted into the upright wires. Burning-fluid lamp, pewter, date
uncertain, probably mid-nineteenth century. Lard lamp, brass, 1842 patent; as the lard burned, the tubular part was
pushed down to force lard up into the wicks. Kerosene lamp, pressed glass, c. 1870, missing its glass chimney, which was
meant to be placed within the upright clips.* (Smithsonian Institution)

*It was a great event when in my uncle's store, the gas took the place of
the oil lamps. How eagerly I watched the workmen as they did their work,
and the flashing of the new light as the gas was turned on. It was goodbye
to candles, to fish and mineral [coal] oils. We had arrived. It was the sum-
mit. Nothing could excel the new light. No longer the snuffing of candles,
the cleaning and filling of oil lamps. We had but to turn the button, to
apply the match, and behold the glory of the new wonder.*

For most families, until the coming of inexpensive kerosene in the 1860s, home
lighting was little changed from what it had been in the eighteenth century — candles
and simple oil lamps. Candles continued in common use. The only significant difference is that they were now frequently store-bought, sparing many a family the bother-
some chore of making them. Most oil lamps were still primitive enough to give candles
the advantage.

The Argand lamp was an improvement, but it lighted relatively few households
because of its high initial cost and the ever increasing price of its principal fuel, whale
oil. A cheap and abundant alternative could be found in lard oil, but it was too viscous
to flow through the complex burner of an Argand lamp.

One development was the solar lamp of the 1840s and 1850s. In this lamp the fuel
reservoir was wrapped around the burner, so that the heat from the burner kept the lard
oil fluid. The lamp's name was apparently meant to suggest that its light would be as
bright as the sun.

Another drawback to the Argand was that when its reservoir was to one side and
just above the burner, as it was originally, it cast a shadow. The astral lamp, patented
in France in 1809, sought to minimize this with a circular, or annular, reservoir that
diffused the shadow. Its name derives from the notion that its light, coming unhindered
from above, was starlike, hence "astral." A variation in etymology equally as fanciful
was the sinumbra lamp (from the Latin *sine umbra* by way of the French, *sinombre*)
which simply meant "without shadow." Popular in the 1820s and 1830s, it was of the
same basic concept as the astral lamp.

With the price of whale oil continually going up, was there some other less expensive fuel that could satisfy the need for ever brighter light in simple lamps other than
Argands? Indeed. It was discovered in the late 1820s that if one mixed camphene
(freshly distilled turpentine) with alcohol, the result was a fluid that was cheap (like
lard oil), free-flowing (unlike lard oil), and clean-burning. It was also clean and simple

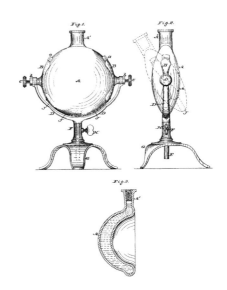

ABOVE LEFT: *A nineteenth-century whale-oil peg lamp designed to be inserted into a candleholder.* (Museum Village, Monroe, New York. Photograph by the author)

LEFT: *The nineteenth century's determination to turn up the light often produced curiously simple results. This "refracting apparatus," patented in 1881, was a water-filled lens designed to augment the illuminating power of whatever light source it was set in front of.* (Photograph by the author, Museum Village, Monroe, New York)

ABOVE RIGHT: *As the refracting apparatus looked in the original patent drawing.* (U.S. Patent No. 244,798, July 26, 1881)

in name: "burning fluid." By the late 1850s, when whale oil cost more than $1.50 a gallon, burning fluid could be had for less than half that price. And how popular was it? By 1857 more than one million gallons a year were being manufactured in Philadelphia alone, at a retail cost of about 60 cents a gallon. All in all, burning fluid looked like the solution to cheap lighting fuel, except for one major drawback: it was dangerously explosive. In that same year *Godey's Lady's Book* advised that it was not merely dangerous but "suicidal to have camphene lamps in the house." *Scientific American* in 1860 went further by reporting some actual statistics: in the past year alone, at least 83 persons had been killed and 106 seriously injured by the use of burning fluid; and in the 1850s there were 424 deaths and 623 serious injuries. Said

Scientific American bluntly: "We long ago ordered this stuff out of our house, and we advise all our readers to do the same thing. Use coal oil, tallow candles, pine knots, anything rather than hazard life, limb, and property."

What happened next was a blessing not only to humans but also to whales.

A GOOD TIME FOR WHALES

On the eve of 1860, the sleepy little farming village of Titusville, Pennsylvania, was suddenly transformed into what one observer thought was another San Francisco in the making, what with all the speculators and miners pouring in and houses of all description shooting up like weeds. Within five or six months, the population of Titusville had nearly quadrupled. The town now had a newspaper, and a hotel was in the works. One of the biggest businesses in town was a cooperage that was turning out two hundred or so iron-hooped barrels a day. And this boom was the result of what was going into those barrels — oil.

Said one observer who saw in Titusville the glitter of Gold Rush San Francisco: "As an illuminating oil it excels everything yet produced. . . . In fact it possesses twenty-five percent more illuminating power than the best coal oil, and from the fact that it does not chill in the cold is far superior to the best sperm oil. . . . Soon the poor whale will be followed only for his bones. . . . [There's] a good time coming for whales."

The oil was already known as kerosene. It was named (from the Greek *keros,* "wax") by a Canadian geologist, Abraham Gesner, who as early as 1846 had demonstrated that a lamp fuel could be distilled from coal. In 1854 and 1855, he received four U.S. patents for the process. Kerosene was a better lamp fuel than whale oil, sperm oil (the most expensive, from the sperm whale), lard oil, rapeseed oil, rosin oil, burning fluid, and other lamp fuels. Yet while Gesner's patented distilling process provided a means of supplying it, coal-based kerosene was expensive to produce and thus limited to those who could afford it. In less than two decades, however, as a result of the discovery of oil at Titusville, oil-based kerosene was cheap enough, and available enough, to light nearly every American household. By the late 1870s, kerosene lamps were considered so much a necessity of life as to be found in almost every house. Even where there was gaslight, at least one kerosene lamp was usually kept on hand — just in case.

GASLIGHT: FROM CONCERN TO CONVENIENCE

Occasional public displays of gaslight, such as those at Peale's Museum in Philadelphia and its branch in Baltimore, gave people a preview of what would someday brighten

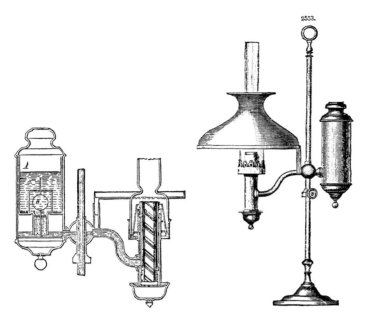

2553.

A popular type of kerosene lamp— and one that was widely replicated as an electrical fixture—is the so-called student lamp, first devised in 1863. The oil reservoir is placed so as to avoid casting a shadow on the work area, a common failing of other designs. (**New York Public Library Picture Collection**)

their homes. But the prospect of immediate acceptance was considerably less bright. There was no commercial gas supply in America until 1817, and only a small number of connections to residences in the years following. And at this time no other David Melvilles, so far as is known, chose to build their own personal gasworks.

There was also the question of safety. Gas was still a vague and mysterious something to most people, and they were reluctant to set a match to it, even outdoors. When Westminster Bridge in London was fitted with gas, the lamplighters at first refused to light the lamps, fearing for their safety. In 1815 the London Fire Insurance Companies declined to insure buildings lighted with gas. Samuel Clegg, engineer of the London Chartered Gaslight and Coke Company, sought to give reassurance by having the underwriters visit the gasworks. He explained the process of making gas and storing it in a gasometer. Thereupon he took a pick and made a hole in the top of the gasometer and lighted the escaping gas. There was no explosion. The gas burned harmlessly. Others also tried to reassure the public. Fredrick Accum, a chemist and also an engineer for Chartered Gaslight, stated flatly that

> *no danger can arise from the application of gas-lights in any way, but what is common to candle-light, and lamps of all kinds, and is the fault of none of them. Even in this case the gas-lights are less hazardous. There is no risk of those accidents which often happen from the guttering or burn-*

ing down of candles, or from carelessly snuffing them. The gas-light lamps and burners must necessarily be fixed to one place, and therefore cannot fall, or otherwise become deranged, without being immediately extinguished. Besides, the gas-light flames emit no sparks, nor are any embers detached from them. As a proof of the comparative safety of the gas-lights, it need only be stated, that the Fire-offices engage themselves to insure cotton-mills, and other public works, at a less premium, where gas-lights are used, than in the case of other lights.

Concern over safety quickly gave way to the promise of convenience for those who could afford gaslight when it became available. In New York, where home gaslighting had begun in 1823 at the home of New York Gas Light Company president Samuel Leggett, a second company, the Manhattan Gas Company, was incorporated in 1830; a third, the Metropolitan, was established in 1853. Sometimes a house being built was piped for gas even though the mains had not yet reached its part of town. Number 29 East Fourth Street in New York, for example, was built in 1832 within the operating territory of Manhattan Gas, but in an area not yet serviced. Nevertheless, it was built with gaslight in mind. House-hunting in 1835,

The coming of modern comfort and convenience in the home had its countereffect in a landscape forever changed. Later in time that change would be manifest in huge electric generating stations and millions of miles of overhead wires crisscrossing the country. By the mid-nineteenth century scenes like this— the Philadelphia gasworks—were becoming common. (Gleason's Pictorial Drawing-Room Companion, *1853. Library of Congress, Prints and Photographs)*

hardware merchant Seabury Tredwell seems to have taken into consideration the fact that the house was fully piped on two floors. Having seen gaslight in use farther downtown, he bought it; and when Manhattan ran its mains north to Fourth Street, Tredwell made his house probably the first in the neighborhood to be gaslit. (The house is preserved as the Merchant's House Museum.)

In addition to improving on the illuminating power of candles and lamps, gaslight allowed for new possibilities in lighting the average house. Candles and lamps lit relatively small areas — tables, chairs, and so on. Chandeliers using candles and oil lamps could light larger areas, but they were too expensive to be practical for most people. The gasolier — a chandelier using gaslight — on the other hand, made room lighting practical for the first time for the average house.

By 1855 there were 297 companies in the United States selling manufactured gas to more than a quarter-million customers. By the outbreak of the Civil War, gas was available in 381 cities and towns, of which 44 were in the South.

Public gasworks supplied most of the gas that was in use, but they were not the only source. Many households outside of supply areas made their own illuminating gas, and so perhaps did some within such areas, preferring not to be dependent. "Every House Occupant His Own Gas Manufacturer," advised the catalog of one firm supplying gas-generation equipment. A Boston firm, the Portable Oil Gas Company, in 1855 offered what was probably a state-of-the-art apparatus to be installed in the basement. It included various tanks connected by pipes and was in fact just a somewhat more sophisticated version of what David Melville had in his own home at the dawn of the gaslight era: a retort to heat the fuel (in the case of Portable Oil Gas, rosin oil instead of coal), a purifying chamber (analogous to Melville's lime water), a condensing box, and a storage tank (or gas holder), which optionally might be installed at some other location. All this, the company promised, could be operated with "perfect safety. . . . To work the apparatus, no more than ordinary skill is required, and the care of it may be safely intrusted to a domestic."

Skill aside, ordinary or not, being one's "own gas manufacturer" cost money. This was hardly an inexpensive substitute to being hooked up to a public gasworks. A complete apparatus for family use as supplied by the Portable Oil Gas Company cost $350. And on top of the purchase cost, there was the expense of the rosin oil — for "an ordinary family," about $24 a year. Thus the rosin oil alone equaled one-tenth of the annual wages of a low-level industrial worker, and the complete

Although still essentially what David Melville used in 1806, equipment for producing illuminating gas in the home was a luxury few could afford. Shown here: a Standard Gas Machine, c. 1892. (**Smithsonian Institution**)

installation represented more than his whole year's wages. Gaslight by home manufacture was clearly for the well-to-do, and even then, the gasworks in the cellar was not necessarily in use all the time. Sometimes it was turned on only in advance of special occasions, so as to have the gas lamps and gasoliers all aglow for guests. And when the duly impressed visitors had left, the family perhaps went back to using kerosene lamps.

THE BATHROOM

A ROOM OF ITS OWN

There is no evidence that any bathroom in the modern sense — that is, a single room containing a toilet, tub, and sink — existed in America in 1805. One washed here, took a bath there, and attended to nature's needs somewhere else entirely. By 1860 bathing and elimination occurred in a place known even then as the bath room. To be sure, there were not many in 1860. And the relative few that existed often did not yet have a sink. The tradition of washing in one's room persisted somewhat longer, whereas the desire for privacy while using a tub or a water closet made a separate room more important for these functions.

Even so, just combining a bathtub and water closet in the same room was a significant event in the evolution of the house. What brought about consolidation was simple practicality. To have a water closet, it was necessary to install a pipe to conduct water to the device and another drainpipe to empty it; a tub likewise, except that in a really up-to-date house in 1860 there were two pipes leading in, one for hot water and one for cold. It was as obvious then as it is in retrospect: run all those pipes into and out of the same common room. And so the creation of the bathroom.

That the room, from the start, was known as the bathroom is evident from house plans of the day, notably those provided by A. J. Downing in *Architecture of Country Houses,* 1850. A somewhat later confirmation of that term can be found in the 1884 catalog of the J. L. Mott Iron Works. It is titled *The Bath Room Illustrated* and includes water closets, bathtubs, sinks, and assorted accessories. Mott was one of the principal manufacturers (and trendsetters) of the day. The company's use of "bath room" in the title should dispel any doubt that "bathroom" (before there were yet a great many of them) had precisely the same meaning in the later nineteenth century as it does at the end of the twentieth century.

Evolving along with the whole were its parts.

An Increasing Sense of Necessity

A water-closet, or its equivalent, is an absolute necessity in any house that is proposed to be a convenient and agreeable residence.

—Calvert Vaux, 1857

The curious thing about the water closet is that it took so long to come into general use — not occurring universally until the twentieth century. The water closet, after all, requires no fuel, electricity, or any form of power, let alone computerization. All that is needed to make it work has been around since the beginning of time in greater abundance than any other substance on earth: water — and only a couple of gallons at that.

Yet even as architect Calvert Vaux was decreeing the "absolute necessity" of water closets, the ranks of those heeding his advice were still few. All of New York City that year had only some 10,500 water closets for a population of approximately 650,000, or 1 for every 62 people. Ratios for other cities for which statistics are available ran from roughly 1 for 19 (Boston) to 1 for 400 (Albany).

There are some good reasons why water closets in 1857 were relatively few in number. One reason was that they were still expensive. This would change in the years ahead as industrialization made water closets cheaper, a process hastened by health codes requiring them and thus spurring production.

Infrastructure was still another hurdle. A water closet, especially in the city, required adequate water supply and sewerage. New York's acceptance of the water closet reflected the completion of the Croton Aqueduct in 1842. But even though fresh

Previous Page: *Water closets of the nineteenth century are commonly shown apparatus only. It was understood they would be enclosed in a wooden cabinet. From the 1866 catalog of Hayden, Gere & Co.: a valve closet.* (**Library of Congress**)

water was now available to the city in great quantities, most individual houses were not yet equipped with internal plumbing to convey water throughout the house, nor was adequate sewerage available. On top of this, plumbing was a new field, in which hardly anyone was trained. According to one estimate, there were barely a half-dozen plumbers in the entire city of New York in the 1840s. Furthermore, whatever in the way of crude fittings they installed they largely had to fashion for themselves in their own workshops. The first plumbing supply factories were just beginning to meet the challenge (and seize the business opportunity) of all that water coming daily from Croton.

The slow acceptance of water closets is not entirely attributable to water supply, cost, or availability of plumbers and plumbing supplies, however. People were also suspicious of this would-be successor to the privy, which had always served humankind *outside* the house. Many people didn't trust water closets; many regarded them as unwholesome and offensive. And in fact there was still much to be improved. At the time of Calvert Vaux's admonition, the water closet was still going through a process of much-needed improvement.

The first patents for water closets in America were issued in 1833 and 1835, both for what were described in records as "portable" water closets. No drawings or specifications remain. (Most early patent records were destroyed by a fire at the U.S. Patent Office in 1836.) It can only be assumed that the patents of 1833 and 1835 were for portable closets similar to devices made in England, which from their "lightness, and small size" were "well calculated for travelling, for camps, and for ships." Probably very few such devices were made, either in England or America, and they have little significance to the evolution of the bathroom in the home.

No further patents were issued until January 1847, when a so-called pan-type

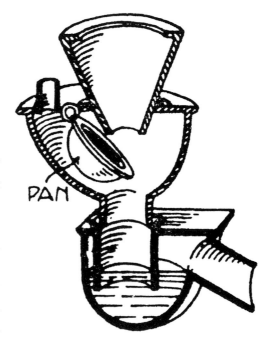

The pan-type water closet was literally that, having a hinged pan, usually copper, that tipped when flushed. In its closed position, the pan acted as a seal to prevent a backup of sewer gas and to ensure that a quantity of water remained in the bowl. When flushed, the pan tipped and the contents of the bowl passed into a cast-iron receptacle underneath and thence into the soil pipe. Inevitably, both pan and receptacle accumulated excessive filth. (**Banister Flight Fletcher**, *The English Home*, London, 1910)

closet was registered. This suggests that no water closets were manufactured in America until the late 1840s, which was about the earliest that their use can be described as anything but very sporadic.

Water closets in use in America prior to the late 1840s probably were imported — all, or nearly all, of them from England. We have seen a typical one at Hyde Hall — the Bramah closet shipped to the home of George Clarke near Cooperstown, New York, in 1827. Bramah was state of the art in the late eighteenth and early nineteenth centuries, and indeed the basic design of the Bramah, with some refinements, remained so until the later 1800s. It may be that the Bramah was the most common type in use in America in the early nineteenth century; and if not the Bramah, likely some comparable closet, which is to say, a device with a valve mechanism.

But another design was also in use, and it was called the pan type. It was probably the most common variety used at midcentury in America. This was the type for which the first patent for a "permanent" water closet was issued in 1847. As a broad generalization, it is probable that most of the water closets in use in 1860 were of the pan type.

The pan type was actually a step backward. It was a simpler and cheaper device; hence it lent itself more readily to proliferation than the more expensive, more sophisticated valve closet — but at the cost of meeting with almost universal disfavor among experts in sanitation. The essential feature was a hinged pan, commonly of copper, that, when in its horizontal position, formed a water seal to prevent backup of sewer gas and also ensured that a quantity of water would remain in the bowl. When the closet was flushed, the pan tipped, and the contents of the bowl passed into the receiver — a cast-iron receptacle underneath — and thence into the waste pipe.

The pan closet was popular at midcentury and continued so for a number of years. It was not considered second-rate by virtue of being cheaper; some such closets could be made quite elegant. One that was installed in 1850 at Lindenwald — the home of Martin Van Buren in Kinderhook, New York, after he left the presidency — remains in its original location and virtually its original condition. It has a white Wedgwood bowl with a blue transfer-printed floral pattern. The closet itself is installed in a wooden case within a small alcove in a room also containing a tub and sink.

Wedgewood or not, pan closets had one disadvantage: filth inevitably accumulated in the receptacle underneath. According to British authority S. Stevens Hellyer, "The filth, splashed about over the receiver and copper-pan, is left to corrode, and to be added to by each usage of the closet, for it is impossible to get at it to clear it away [except] to take it to pieces and burn off the corrosion over a fire. . . . It has always been a puzzle to me," Hellyer went on, "to understand how such a water-closet as a pan-closet should become so great a favourite with architects, plumbers, and the public. The only bliss that the public can have about so foul a thing is ignorance of its nature."

In the United States at about the same time, Glenn Brown, an architect and authority on water closets, said, "Sanitary authorities agree, without an exception, that pan-closets should never be used." Yet used they were, in great numbers, until the coming of a new generation of water closets—substantially the equivalent of the present-day apparatus—in the 1890s.

While the pan closet was the most common at midcentury, and valve closets on the order of the Bramah continued in use, other types came into use in the later 1800s, including a modern version of the plunger closet—the type used at Governor Horatio Sharpe's Whitehall c. 1765 and dating back to the early 1700s in England.

The popularization of the water closet was tied in closely with development of public sewer systems. Until the coming of sewers, water closets emptied much as priv-ies did, indeed often into a privy pit. The Gallier water closet emptied into a cesspit in the side yard (a separate outdoor privy for servants at the far back of the property had its own cesspit). On Gallier's plans the pit is labeled "Water Closet Sink." This now largely forgotten term was commonly used to denote the pit for a simple privy or for a water closet.

Emptying a water closet into an existing privy pit or one dug for the purpose posed a problem at mid-nineteenth century. The water closet was a long-term blessing in terms of public health. The vast increase in population in the United States in the later nineteenth and early twentieth centuries would have posed an insuperable burden without sewers and water closets, the latter eventually being required universally by public health codes. Yet in its earlier days the water closet itself often posed a public health risk. The amount of water needed to flush it was often more than a privy pit could handle, and the result was overflow. Where early sewers did exist they were fre-quently too primitive to cope with the gallonage. The result was sometimes a greater threat to public health than the privy or chamber pot. Improper plumbing that allowed sewer gas to escape also posed a risk to those living in the house. Pioneer sanitary engi-neer George E. Waring in 1876 quoted the medical officer for Edinburgh, Scotland, as reporting in 1872 that wherever water closets were introduced, deaths from typhoid and similar diseases doubled in one year. Sewer systems of adequate capacity, coupled with sewage treatment, would effectively end that threat.

The periodic emptying of privy vaults, commonly required by law in cities, was done by "night soil" workers using shovels and buckets until the late nineteenth century. Using a pump and 4-inch-diameter rubber hose, this truck of the late 1870s could do the job faster and in a more sanitary way. Its capacity was 600 gallons. Except for the lack of a power-operated pump, it was essentially the equivalent of a modern septic service truck. (Brochure, late 1870s, Matthewman & Johnson Pump Co., New Haven, CT. Smithsonian Institution)

Privies, or outhouses, meanwhile continued to serve a majority of the population through the nineteenth century. They were not maintenance-free, and must have suffered considerable neglect. It was commonly understood—and required by law in many places—that the privy pit, or vault, or sink in contemporary parlance, should be emptied out periodically. This was customarily done and the contents carted away at night, leading to the common term of "night soil" for what was emptied out. This was done for many years by laborers using shovels and carts, but by the late 1870s the process had been modernized and was done with wagons using hoses and pumps. Although it was not a motor vehicle, this was virtually the same as today's septic system cleaning truck.

The cleaning of privies in the country was less of a public health concern. Cities, by virtue of the concentration of population, had to be more zealous. There survives in the archives of the John Jay Homestead a reminder of this from the old days in New York:

NOTICE

To Owner, Lessee, or Occupant of House No. 3 Third Avenue. You are required to have your sink [privy pit] emptied on or before the 4-Day of April [1845]. N.B. Scavengers [to do the work] may always be obtained by applying at the City Inspector's Office, No. 1 City Hall, between the hours of 9 A.M. and 1 P.M. By order of the City Inspector. Zachary Peck Health Warden.

Also surviving is proof that the occupant of No. 3 Third Avenue was faithful to his civic duty, even if just within the deadline—a receipt from one Francis Dolly dated April 4 and showing payment of $8.00 for emptying the privy pit.

If country privies were less hazardous to public health and, the country being what it is, less subject to the scrutiny of health wardens, they were by no means hazard-free. Their threat—if not necessarily to health, at least to comfort and dignity—was to those who had to use them. A reflection on this as pungent as its subject is included here for the sheer purpose of communicating to a later generation the reality of life before the modern bathroom. The squeamish may skip to the following paragraph:

I know of nothing more disgusting to sight and smell, more nauseating to the stomach or more dangerous to health, than a typical country privy, with its quivering, reeking stalagmite of excrement under each seat, resting on a bed of filth indescribable. I feel as if it devolved upon me to ask pardon of the reader for even mentioning such a nightmare horror; but the writer upon such subjects must not stop to choose his words when attacking an evil so serious as this. Such privies as I have described are by no means exceptional. One may find them peering over the lilacs or hiding in conscious shame behind the grape arbors close beside an unfortunately large percentage of country houses occupied by people who, in all other matters, live decently and comfortably.

An alternative to both the water closet and the privy—the earth closet—appeared in 1860. It was the invention of an English clergyman, Henry Moule, and gained some small measure of popularity in America in part because of the advocacy of Catharine Beecher and Harriet Beecher Stowe in *The American Woman's Home* (1869). Its chief advantages, according to Waring in 1870, were its "complete suppression of the odors

An earth closet (seat lid down). The hopper in back contained the mix of earth and ashes. The door below the seat was for emptying the tray. A lever (not shown here) was commonly provided for releasing earth and ashes onto the waste. In some models a spring-loaded mechanism was built into the seat, so that when the user stood up, the earth release was activated automatically. One model had a small placard advising the user to "get up quick."
(**George E. Waring Jr.**, *Earth Closets*, 1868)

which, despite the comfort and elegance of modern living, still hang about our cess-pools and privy-vaults" as well as its nondependence on water at a time when only major cities had public water supplies.

The earth closet looked like a water closet except that it had a tank or hopper full of coarsely sifted sun-dried earth or a mixture of two parts earth to one part finely sifted ashes, but never sand. There was a simple wooden seat, and underneath it a box. After each use, the person pulled a lever, which released sufficient earth to cover the waste. After a number of uses, the box could be taken out and dumped in a cesspit, or the contents could be used as manure in one's own garden—and this was still being suggested into the 1890s. In time, of course, the pernicious effects of human waste were understood so as to preclude its use in the garden; in the meantime there had been relatively little use of the earth closet anyway. Given the limited means of disposing of its contents, the earth closet's days were numbered from the start.

BATHING ON THE INCREASE

When George Read II slipped into the warm water of his bathtub and stretched out in its 7½-foot length, he was bathing himself in luxury.

That was in 1811 and was not merely an exception to the rule but an exception to exceptions. Read's bathtub was spacious when most people had to settle for a small portable tub (some were not much more than oversize buckets) set up in the kitchen and using water heated in the fireplace, and Read's was on the second floor, with its particular privacy, and had piped-in hot water, as we saw earlier. While there were other bathtubs, George Read's was remarkable for its unusual comfort. We can look to

Philadelphia about this same time for some actual data on the number of bathtubs. According to the annual report of the Watering Committee for 1815, there were 228 houses with baths (out of 2,883 receiving piped-in water) and out of an overall population of roughly 100,000. By 1823 the total number of tubs had increased to 401, representing a rate of increase somewhat greater than that for the population (the census of 1820 recorded 108,116).

The growing number of tubs says something significant about bathing generally. More people were starting to do it. As the facilities for bathing had been expanding, so had ideas about the need to bathe. For a considerable part of the population, it made little difference. Particularly for the poor in cities — those still getting their drinking water from public pumps — bathing was of questionable value and was not done simply for the sake of cleanliness. In hot weather, bathing was also a way of keeping cool.

For the masses, however, a bath was often only to be wished. Writing just after completion of the Croton Aqueduct in 1842, author Lydia Maria Child observed of New York that

> We not only have the three large fountains, to refresh us with their graceful motions and cooling sound, but in various gardens and inclosures, public and private, little marble nymphs, tritons, and dolphins, are playing prettily with finely spun showers. [But] we have no free public baths. The wealthy can introduce water into their chambers, or float on the bosom of the tide, in the pleasant baths at the Battery; but for the innumerable poor, this is a luxury that can seldom, if ever, be enjoyed. Open bathing around the wharves is of course prohibited; and the labouring man has to walk three or four miles to obtain a privilage so necessary to health.

Actually, public baths had begun to appear in the 1790s, and they became increasingly common in the nineteenth century and the early twentieth. But they were rarely free.

Many people had their first opportunity to bathe in a real tub, in a private bathing room, when they visited a hotel. Boston's Tremont Hotel, which opened in 1829, was the first to have bathtubs as well as water closets.

For those who could afford to install their own bathing facilities at home, the increasing availability of public water supply made it more practical. Boston by 1860 had 3,910 tubs. Given a population of 177,902, that represents a ratio of 1 to 45, compared with roughly 1 to 450 for Philadelphia in 1815 — a revealing index to the degree of change taking place. We can assume that these tubs were of the kind that the Gallier family had — wooden vessels with a lining of tin or copper. The more modern tub — a self-contained unit without wooden cabinetry — began to come into use after the Civil War and shows up in catalogs of the 1870s. A typical one in the 1878 catalog of the J. L. Mott Iron Works was cast iron with a plain, galvanized, or enameled finish. Unlike the old wood-enclosed tubs with external water taps, faucets now were set into the tub itself. There were feet to raise it a few inches off the floor; and it could be 54 inches or 60 inches long — a good deal shorter than George Read's custom-made tub. The standard width was 23½ inches.

The remaining fixture in the typical bathroom — the sink, or lavatory — was slower to become standard and was still relatively rare in 1860. Gallier, in that year, for example, had none. Personal washing does not require the privacy expected when using a bathtub or shower; it could continue to be done in the bedroom. So it was, with little thought to the contrary.

Whether one was washing one's face with water at a bedroom washstand or bathing one's whole body in a tub in the bathroom, the ablutions were not necessarily, or even commonly, done with soap. There was plenty of soap around; you could make it yourself or buy it. But soap back then was tough stuff meant for washing clothes. For personal washing of a gentler kind, there was toilet soap, but it was expensive and generally used only by the well-to-do. Only during the post–Civil War period, with the gathering proliferation of bathtubs and the coming of the bathroom sink, did soap for personal washing become common. A landmark was Procter and Gamble's introduction, in 1882, of Ivory soap, with its familiar notch around the middle. The purpose of the notch was well advertised. Used full size, the bar of soap was just right for the laundry; broken into two by pulling a stout thread around the notch, it became two small bars of soap "pure and pleasant" for personal use.

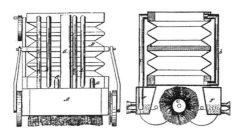

APPLIANCES

CATCHING UP WITH THE FUTURE

*Visited a Machine at Doctr. Franklins (called a mangle) for pressing, in place of Ironing,
clothes from the wash. Which Machine from the facility with which it dispatches business
is well calculated for Table cloths & such Articles as have not pleats & irregular foldings
and would be very useful in all large families.*

—GEORGE WASHINGTON, 1787

We haven't discussed appliances until now because of the absence in the colonial and early Federal periods, generally speaking, of anything that we would call an appliance.

To be sure, there was no shortage of gadgets and clever devices. The likes of Benjamin Franklin's mangle, almost always imported, could be found here and there.

A mangle was a device with a roller, used for pressing fabric. In one form it consisted of an oblong wooden box filled with stones so as to make it press firmly on the cloth. Mangles of a primitive kind were in use at least by 1600; one "of new construction" was patented in England in 1774. Perhaps it was one of these that Franklin owned.

For whatever labor it might have saved as opposed to ironing of the traditional kind, the mangle was still hand-operated. The essential quality of the modern appliance is that

151

it saves labor by using an independent power source — usually electricity, sometimes gas.

Yet even before electricity, the concept was at work, if on a primitive scale. The prime example is the clockwork mechanism. A useful form in the colonial period was the clock jack, which kept meat rotating on a spit for even cooking when being roasted at the hearth. There was one at the Silas Deane House in Wethersfield, Connecticut. Although what is there today is not original, it is authentic to the period. It looks something like a grandfather clock without its case, except that there is a wall-mounted pulley to allow the weight to be placed outside the cooking area. Otherwise it is essentially the same as a clock: as the weight winds down, the mechanism turns, revolving the meat over the fire. There is also a reproduction clock jack at the Governor's Palace in Williamsburg, Virginia. Decidedly high-tech for its time was the steam jack patented by John Bailey of Boston in 1792. It worked like a clock jack but was powered by a miniature steam turbine. Its use was undoubtedly very rare.

In the eighteenth century and into the nineteenth where such luxury was possible, the clock jack was an effective mechanism. In theory a clockwork could do other things — like run an automatic fan. Patented in 1830 and probably never produced, this contraption must have set some kind of record for the maximum of contrivance for a minimum of comfort. Another automatic fan, patented in 1868, used a mainspring like the ones commonly found in spring-wound clocks. This worked through gearing, to make the fan blades (quaintly fringed) spin at least fast enough to create the illusion of a breeze. It was a small device that could be placed on a tabletop or suspended from the ceiling to stir the air over a bed, crib, cradle, settee, or chair.

THE MECHANIZATION OF MONDAY

In the spirit of the age, the nineteenth century was a marvelously inventive time in America. From the truly ingenious to the absurdly impractical, inventors generated a vast assortment of devices intended to make home life easier.

If the number of patents is indicative, doing the laundry was the most onerous household task of the nineteenth century. Some two thousand patents were issued by the 1870s for washing machines of every description, most of which never got beyond the drawing board.

Laundry day was traditionally Monday, even through the mid-twentieth century, when the automatic washer came into use. Having a designated day owed in large part

PREVIOUS PAGE: *A preview of the vacuum cleaner, 1860: a carpet sweeper with a bellows mechanism to suck up dirt.* (U.S. Patent No. 29,077, July 10, 1860)

This washing machine dating to perhaps the 1840s is an exhibit at the Bement-Billings Farmstead in Newark Valley, New York. Its rounded bottom shows its method of operation, as demonstrated here by guide Ginny Stromberg. In addition to clothes, water, and soap, it is commonly supposed that rocks were put in to add to the effect of the rocking action. There is a drain hole at one end. (**Photograph by the author**)

to the fact that the vast majority of homes of the nineteenth century still did not have running water, so pumping enough water from a well or carrying enough from a stream was chore enough to start with. Then the water had to be heated on the kitchen stove. Laundry tubs might be placed in the kitchen or on the back porch. The principal instrument was the washboard, originally just a wooden board with grooves cut into it; in its later state it had metal or glass corrugation that made the task of rubbing a little more efficient and at the same time reduced the likelihood of splinters. Clothes were rubbed against the board, over and over again, item by item. Then each item had to be rinsed. Drying was normally done outside, and was often nothing more sophisticated than draping wet clothes over bushes or laying them out on the grass in the sun. If Monday was a rainy day, then there was the need to improvise inside. By the later nineteenth century folding racks were becoming common for indoor drying.

The first washing machine was patented in 1797, and within fifty years there were U.S. patents on nearly three hundred such devices. They came in many shapes and sizes, and in many degrees of usefulness. There were nearly as many ideas as to how the machine should work and what it should look like as there were inventors. Some early washers looked like wooden barrels set horizontally in simple wooden frames; hand-powered cranks created the rotary motion to perform some semblance of washing action inside. Many apparatuses replicated the back-and-forth action of the human arm in washing clothes; and while such a device may have provided a degree of

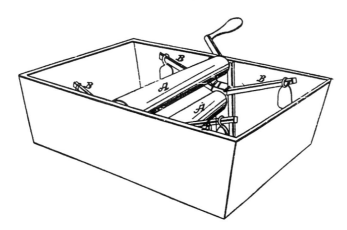

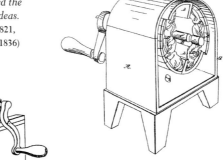

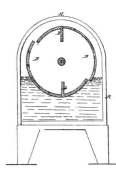

The nineteenth century's quest for a practical and efficient washing machine inspired the best (or often the worst) of inventors' ideas. (U. S. Patents [no numbers] dated Dec. 7, 1821, March 28, 1828, Oct. 14, 1830, and Jan. 6, 1836)

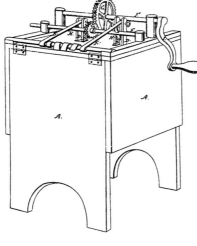

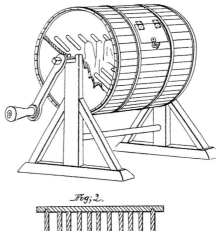

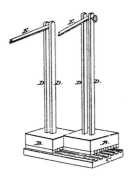

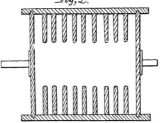

leverage to the task, it was still the back-and-forth motion of the human arm that powered the apparatus. This was a virtually universal shortcoming of the ostensibly labor-saving machines of the time: the labor needed to operate them often equaled or even exceeded the labor required to do the job the old-fashioned way.

By 1869 the device had been refined basically to what the washing machine is today: a tub with a gyrator. But until the coming of the compact electric motor all such devices had limited usefulness.

Early machines duplicated the rubbing action of the washboard, but they created the effect in different ways. One machine might be a simple washboard suspended in a tub, against which clothes are rubbed by a sliding frame operated by a handle. In another an agitator might be turned by a crank, forcing the clothes against the corrugated sides of a round tub. Later the tub became a drum inside a horizontal cylinder; in some washing machines by the 1850s the apparatus was constructed so that the drum, as it was turned, automatically reversed direction from time to time.

Something of a breakthrough was King's Washing Apparatus of 1851, invented by James T. King of Baltimore. It not only eliminated the washboard effect but also heated its own water. The machine consisted essentially of a cylinder revolving over a small steam boiler. The clothes were placed in the cylinder, which was revolved by a small handle. As King explained its operation,

> [the] difference between this Apparatus and all other washing machines which have been invented is that they are all rubbing machines [and] rubbing the dirt from clothing by force must, to some extent, injure the fabric and destroy the buttons. . . . [With this apparatus] the clothes, while undergoing the process, are alternately in steam and suds; the steam being saturated with alkaline properties, penetrates the fabric and neutralizes the grease, while the suds removes the dirt; this accounts for the rapidity with which clothing is washed by the machine.

Not yet the modern washer, but clearly a step in that direction. In 1860 some twenty-nine small factories in ten states were manufacturing mechanical washing machines and wringers. Many of these were for commercial use, some for use in the home. For most households, however, Monday was still Monday.

OTHER PREVIEWS

Three other important appliances were making their appearance at midcentury. Inherently similar to the clothes washer was a machine that has come to be a common part of the modern kitchen — the dishwasher. The incubation of the mechanical dishwasher goes back almost as far as the washing machine, but its actual appearance in the kitchen would not come until the 1920s. Nevertheless, the first one that was patented in 1863 is recognizable: a large tub with a wire rack inside to hold plates and dishes, much like a modern dishwasher. Like the clothes washers of the day, it was operated with a crank using hand power. As the crank was turned, the sudsy water was forced through the slats of the rack and dashed against the plates and dishes. There is no record of such a dishwasher being produced; a few may have been specially made, but the dishwasher remained only a concept for now.

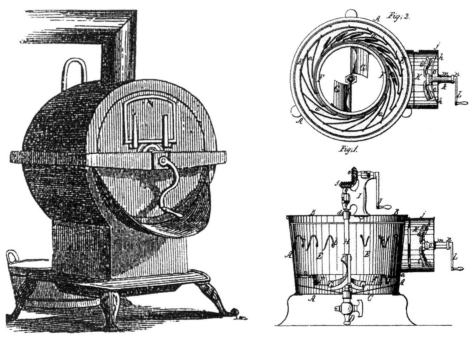

RIGHT: *Dishwasher, 1863.* (U.S. Patent No. 40, 280, Oct. 13, 1863)

LEFT: *The state-of-the-art washer at mid-nineteenth century was James T. King's steam washing machine. This one sold for $50; a slightly larger model was priced at $75. Its essential feature was a cylinder 18 inches in both diameter and length. A wood-fired steam boiler was underneath. The cylinder was half filled with water and soap. Once steam was being generated, the clothes were put in, a gasket was inserted in the opening, and the door was screwed on tight. When the clothes were washed about five minutes, they had to be rinsed in a separate tub, once in warm water and again in cold, while another load used the same sudsy water in the machine.* (American Steam Washing Machine Manufacturing Co., New York, 1855, *Description and Philosophy of James T. King's Patent Washing and Drying Apparatus.* Smithsonian Institution Archives. Warshaw Collection)

Carpet sweeper, 1858. As this sweeper was pushed, the brushes revolved, sweeping dirt into a small pan. (U. S. Patent No. 21,233, Aug. 17, 1858)

With increasing use of carpeting in the nineteenth century, in contrast to the bare floors of the colonial period and the early 1800s, came the need for something better than the customary cleaning method: taking the carpet outside and beating it. The first solution was a device similar to what was coming into use for the cleaning of streets. Mechanization of street sweeping, heretofore delegated to squads of men wielding brooms, came in the 1840s, beginning with a mechanized sweeper patented in England in 1842. The sweeper consisted of a series of small brooms affixed to a circular chain. As the apparatus was pulled along the street, the chain turned, causing one brush after another to sweep the pavement, carrying the dirt onto a conveyer belt that dumped it into a container. The first U.S. patent for a carpet sweeper applied the same principle, greatly simplified. One circular brush was connected to a pair of driving wheels. As the sweeper was pushed, the brush revolved, and the dirt went into a pan that was part of the device. This was the mechanical carpet sweeper, essentially what is still in use today.

But was there not a better method of cleaning carpets than sweeping dirt into a container? The real predecessor of the vacuum cleaner was a device using a bellows. A bellows can work both ways: to force air out, as for example to pump up a fire, or suck air in. The latter was the mode of a bellows sweeper devised in 1860. Here the turning of the wheels of the apparatus, as it was pushed, served to operate a bellows to suck up the dirt. Obviously this is an analogue of the vacuum cleaner, though considerably less efficient. But what to do with the dirt? The inventor explained: "The nature of my invention consists in drawing fine dust and dirt through the machine by means of a draft of air and forcing the same into water." And indeed this is what he did, using a water-filled apparatus attached to the bellows. He suggested, besides water, "anything else which will retain the dust." By the early twentieth century there would be not just

In less than two decades, the sewing machine was recognizably modern and well on its way to becoming a household fixture. (Broadside, 1869. United States Sewing Machine Company. Library of Congress, Prints and Photographs Division)

a bellows to do the sucking up but a machine to produce a vacuum effect; and not merely a water chamber to receive the dirt but an "anything-else" in the form of an airtight bag to be dumped and reattached (and later a disposable one to be discarded).

In this age of imaginative and uninhibited inventiveness, sometimes primitive concepts were catching up with the future.

The mid-nineteenth century also gave birth to the sewing machine. Although several patents were issued to other inventors earlier, it was Elias

The original Singer sewing machine of 1851.
(Edward Byrn, *Progress of Invention*)

Howe's patent in 1846 that effectively launched the sewing machine. Hundreds of thousands were produced during the 1850s and 1860s, and by the 1870s there were more than two hundred American firms in business.

THE KITCHEN

THE EVOLVING KITCHEN

The kitchen was still an inchoate place in 1805, a holdout in the coming of a new age of comfort and convenience. The house of the early nineteenth century, though much changed elsewhere, still largely retained its eighteenth-century kitchen.

Yet hiding in obscurity, the modern kitchen was there. It could be previewed, for example, by those who chanced upon it either in person or in *Rural Economy* by Stephen William Johnson: "[My] kitchen, with these conveniencies, now contains the pump [inside the kitchen], waste-water tub, sink, boiler, and perpetual oven; there is no necessity for going out for cold water nor hot, neither to throw waste water away . . ."

In Johnson's description we have the kitchen emerging in recognizably modern form. There was no need to haul water into the kitchen in buckets; the pump made it available at the sink. And no need to dump water outside in buckets; the sink had a drain of some sort. And there was both hot and cold water. The sink itself had ledges around it, perhaps like the countertop of later times. And the sophisticated cooking center included an oven, a simple steam kitchen, and a water boiler, all working from the same central fire. And this was not some abstract notion; this, said Johnson, was his own kitchen. Of the plumbing facilities, he took pride in observing that "By these arrangements much labour may be saved, and that nasty appearance which is too frequently seen, where all the dirty water of the kitchen is thrown out at the door, to escape into the atmosphere, or form a mire for hogs and poultry to paddle in, avoided."

The cooking center was a model of efficiency for its time: "With . . . a few coals of wood, charcoal, pit coal, or peat, victuals may be cooked, and all the conveniencies of a family, requiring the agency of fire, be answered. They may be fixed so that by drawing a damper either of them will heat by the fire that is used in common."

A very convenient kitchen — one more representative of 1860 than to 1806.

SUCCESSORS TO THE DANCING FLAMES

Even in 1860, kitchens like that of the Galliers, with its big efficient range, or that of Stephen W. Johnson, with its cooking center, were far from universal. For many there was still the "great open kitchen fire with . . . its roaring, hilarious voice of invitation, its dancing tongue of flames," to quote a contemporary observation of Harriet Beecher Stowe.

Yet welcoming though the fireplace might have been to one who was there to be warmed or to take a meal, it was anything but convenient for the poor housewife who had to stoop, bend, reach, and lean to get her pots and kettles, usually of iron, into and out of the flames. It would seem that anything offering even faint promise of lightening these burdens ought to have immediate success. But it was not so. It was not that simple.

OPPOSITE PAGE: *The cooking center of the very modern kitchen of 1806 described by Stephen W. Johnson. At left is the cast-iron boiler for hot water; at right is the oven, also cast-iron. Both are heated by the central fire, the grate of which afforded additional means of cooking. The boiler could also provide steam for steam cooking.* (Johnson, **Rural Economy**, 1806)

LEFT: *The open hearth: the romance of its "dancing tongue of flames" was offset by its heat and the often oppressive weight of cast-iron pots and kettles.* (**Harper's Magazine**, October 1871)

There had been some use of stoves for cooking in the eighteenth century, but such use remained rare until the second decade of the nineteenth century. The cookstove era is generally considered to have begun in 1815, the year of the James stove. Designed by William T. James and manufactured in Troy, New York, this was the first really successful stove for cooking. It had a good-size oven as well as folding doors that, when opened, allowed one to see the fire — not quite like a fireplace, but a semblance of a tradition that was perhaps more difficult to let go of than anything else related to domestic technology. Furthermore these doors, once opened, provided a place to broil or roast meat — like the open hearth and unlike early stoves generally. Semicircular extensions on either side of the stove gave it its nickname, "saddlebags stove," and provided a place to set kettles and heat water.

This ability to perform a variety of functions would be typical of the kitchen range of the future. Yet the James and other stoves of the early nineteenth century, like all new technology, were expensive. The James stove came in eight different sizes that, in the 1820s, sold for $15 to $50. Ruth Henshaw Bascom, whose husband was a Congregational minister in Massachusetts, recorded in her diary that the $30 they paid for a cookstove in 1819 represented roughly 15 percent of their household budget for the year. For them it was affordable, but not without sacrifice. In any case, James sold some 5,000 of his stoves by 1823.

Perhaps the most significant feature of the cookstove for the housewife was its height. Even the heating stoves of the late 1600s had a certain ergonomic efficiency to them. Unlike a fireplace, a cookstove was of a height suited to the physical realities of those using it. The average stove, for heating or cooking, of the early nineteenth century was less than waist-high; the housewife who had been stretching to hoist an iron pot into an open hearth now needed to lift only so far. The height of the stove would increase in time until stove, sink, and dishwasher would all be the same height. By which time, mercifully, most pots and pans would also be lighter.

In the 1830s, of course, the stove could more readily be made lower because it had far fewer features than its modern counterpart. Yet there was clearly consumer awareness on the part of stove manufacturers then. What might make a particular stove more attractive? An example is the stove that Henry Stanley patented in 1832. It had a rotary top, with potholes, that could be turned so as to allow for heating directly over or away from the fire, in effect providing a form of heat regulation.

And stoves were far more economical of fuel than the notoriously wasteful fireplace. The ovens of early stoves, however, were often too small to be of practical use, fre-

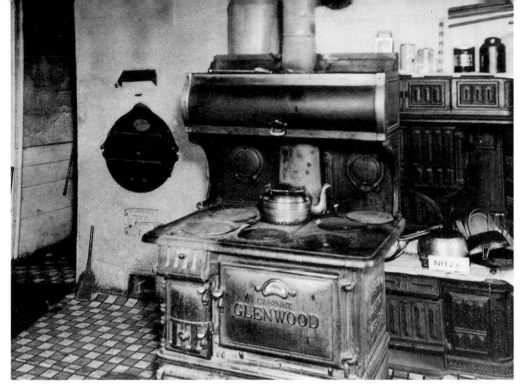

The kitchen of the Captain Barnes House, Portsmouth, New Hampshire: a Rumford roaster (circular door at left) remained as a relic of the past, succeeded by one cooking stove (rear, partly obscured) and then another. When this photograph was taken in 1936, the later of the two stoves was apparently still in use. (Historic American Buildings Survey)

quently requiring housewives to continue using their brick ovens for baking. Cooks also complained about stoves heating things unevenly. As Harriet Connor Brown of Athens, Ohio, recalled, "When we went to keeping house in 1845, Dan'l and I, he bought me a little iron stove, a new thing in those days. It was no good, and would only bake things on one side. I soon went back to cooking at an open fireplace."

John Jay Janney of Loudoun County, Virginia, had a different recollection of his youth in the 1820s:

> We had the first cooking stove ever seen in the neighborhood, which the women soon learned to love. It took much less wood than the fireplace, did the cooking just as well, and with much less discomfort, but it had one discomfort for me. We had no means of starting a fire in the morning, if it had gone out during the night; and it was soon found out there was no person about the house could cover the fire in it to "keep" all night but myself, so I had to stay up till all were ready for bed. I have many times gone to a neighbor's house for fire in the morning, ours having gone out, and sometimes have gone to more than one before I could get it.

By 1845 cookstoves were beginning to improve. Advances in iron manufacture made possible larger stoves with larger ovens. By 1850 the typical cookstove had evolved into a device with four to six boiling holes and an oven that extended virtually the full length of the stove.

By now the range had also come into use, though it was expensive and mostly to be found in the homes of the well-to-do. The range was larger and had multiple fireboxes that allowed for different types of cooking at the same time. The range also was advantageous in summer in that the use of one firebox might suffice whereas with a cookstove the whole stove had to be heated even for a small task.

By 1860 cookstoves frequently had a built-in reservoir to supply a constant source of hot water. It was a considerable convenience.

Convenience was pivotal to general acceptance of stoves. Many people still lamented the passing of the open fireplace — the hearth with its warmth and serenity, its supposed bonding of family, and its representation of old values. The open fireplace was also considered the only proper place to make a succulent roast of beef. A stove could cook or bake. But could it roast? And did it matter all that much? Ann Howe wrote in 1867 that "meat is better roasted than baked; but in these days of cooking stoves, the latter mode of cooking is generally the most convenient."

Even before this time there had been experimentation with electricity for cooking as well as for heating. An "electro-heater" was patented in 1859 by George B. Simpson of Washington, D.C. Intended for both cooking and heating, it was an 8-inch-square block of inch-thick soapstone on the face of which were cut parallel grooves as close together as would accommodate the insertion of a continuous coil of wire. Except for the density of the grooves, it was much like the inside of a toaster of later times. In a toaster, a couple of coils are sufficient to brown a piece of bread. On the electro-heater, twenty-one coils spaced close together on an 8-inch block would have scorched a slice of bread. At the same time, the device was clearly inadequate for heating a room. And it had another drawback in that electricity in 1859 was available only from batteries. Yet in its essentials, here were the electric hot plate and the electric space heater of the twentieth century. It was a preview of kitchen technology to come.

Another modern convenience, the gas stove, was less a dream but still only a limited reality in 1860. An early example was announced in *Godey's Lady's Book*, January 1866:

NOTES AND NOTICES
THE GAS-CONSUMING COOKING STOVE

We know, from our own observation, the excellence of this gas-consuming
stove, which has neither smoke nor dust, and saves both time and fuel.

James Spear of Philadelphia was by now manufacturing and selling one of the earliest gas stoves. Whether it saved time was arguable, while the alleged saving of fuel was likely so much advertising talk. Illuminating gas from the local gasworks was all that would have been available at the time, and in the quantity needed for cooking its cost would have been considerable. The gas stove might have been a reality, but as a significant part of household life, it was still something for the future.

Already at hand was the easing of one traditional burden of the kitchen — a gradual introduction of tin cookware, beginning in the 1850s. Tinware was lighter and easier to use than copper or iron, but it was also more expensive and less durable.

THE NO LONGER MISSING SINK

What few sinks there were in 1805 were usually slabs of stone that drained through a pipe in the wall and lacked running water. Most kitchens probably had no sinks at all; the use of buckets likely continued — perhaps on the floor, perhaps at a dry sink that had neither running water nor a drain.

By the second decade of the nineteenth century somewhat more sophisticated sinks began to come into use. Hyde Hall near Cooperstown, New York, in 1820 had two sandstone slab sinks made by John Forester, who had been hired to carve four marble fireplaces for the house. Forester had come from New York City and presumably drew on his knowledge of a sink of this sort there (though no trace remains of an early 1800s sink in the city itself). One of the original sinks preserved at Hyde Hall shows a degree of evolution in that there is a hole at the bottom that was obviously part of a plumbed drainpipe, as opposed to a simple pipe through the wall. Furthermore, Hyde Hall had running water piped into the house from a reservoir constructed on a nearby hill, so there was almost certainly a faucet at the sink.

Hyde Hall's sink, like the prototypes that must have existed in New York and elsewhere, was a functioning kitchen sink; but its darkish sandstone makes it look primitive by later standards.

Restored houses like Hyde Hall provide insight into what was once state of the art.

LEFT: *The evolution of the kitchen sink: the limestone sink at Hyde Hall, c. 1820. While similar in appearance to the 1771 sink at the Silas Deane House (see page 82), which emptied through a drain in the wall, this one took a step forward by virtue of being attached to a drainpipe set into the sink itself. A faucet was mounted separately in the wall.* (Photograph by the author)

RIGHT: *By the 1880s the kitchen sink was recognizably modern—and yet of obvious parentage. This sink is from an 1884 catalog. It is porcelain-coated cast iron with a brass plug and a nickel-plated strainer. It was available in lengths from 30 to 48 inches and was 7 inches deep. Faucets were still often wall-mounted.* (J. L. Mott Iron Works, New York. Catalog D. 1884)

An example from three decades later is the house in Kinderhook, New York, in which Martin Van Buren lived after he left the White House. When his son agreed to join him there in 1849 and manage his 220-acre estate, Van Buren hired architect Richard Upjohn to enlarge and remodel the house. This was also an opportunity to install the most modern of technology.

For the kitchen this meant a metal sink set into a wooden cabinet. The original sink is still there; the cabinet is a reconstruction. A faucet (cold water only) was set in the wall over the sink. Here was the modern kitchen sink at midcentury.

The 1849–1850 remodeling also meant a new and up-to-date water-supply system. The pump supplying it was immediately adjacent to the kitchen sink. Drawing from an outside well, the pump supplied a 90-gallon cistern located over the first-floor bathroom, a short distance away. The cistern provided water for the

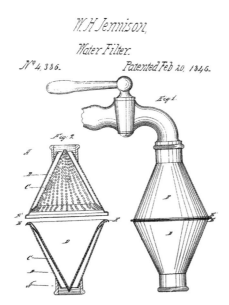

Household water filter, patent drawing of 1846. Designed to be attached to an ordinary faucet, this device consisted of interlocking cones made of perforated tin with felt as the filtering medium. (U.S. Patent No. 4,386, William H. Jennison, Feb. 20, 1846)

kitchen sink as well as the bathroom. A small overflow pipe from the cistern back to the kitchen sink told whoever was pumping when the cistern was full. The kitchen sink apparently drained into a dry well.

Only a decade passed between Van Buren's remodeling and the building of the Gallier House, but there was progress to see. The Gallier sink, a copper shell in a wooden cabinet, was basically the same as Van Buren's, but now it had hot and cold running water, the hot being furnished by the copper boiler attached to the range.

Stone sinks had not yet been entirely displaced. When the Bishop William White House in Philadelphia was remodeled in 1858, there was no need to skimp, and yet the homeowner chose a sink of stone. Over the ensuing years, however, metal was clearly more popular. The catalog of the very fashionable Hayden, Gere & Company in 1866 offered copper sinks in nine sizes, ranging from 12 by 20 inches to 18 by 30 inches. Cast iron was also coming into use and was the choice for the Park-McCullough House in North Bennington, Vermont, in 1865, which had both hot and cold running water. Regardless of type, it was still customary for the faucets to protrude from the wall over the basin rather than to be a part of the sink itself.

AN AMERICAN INSTITUTION

Ice is an American institution—the use of it an American luxury—the abuse of it an American failing.
—DE BOW'S REVIEW, 1855

In 1803 Maryland farmer Thomas Moore called his insulated box of cloth and rabbit fur a refrigerator. By latter-day definition it was not really a refrigerator, since no true refrigeration was involved—that is, no cold environment was being created. On the other hand if he had put a block of ice inside his cloth and fur wrapping, he would actually have had refrigeration in the form of an icebox. Mary Randolph described just such a device in 1825. Here now was actual refrigeration as well as insulation. The device Randolph described was 4 feet long and 3 feet high and was actually a box within a box. The 4-inch space between the two boxes was filled with powdered charcoal. In the center of the inner box was a canister to be filled with chunks of ice. The canister rested in a tub that received the meltwater. This essentially was the icebox.

So-called refrigerators combining her description with Thomas Moore's name for them were actually on sale at this time, as is evident in this 1826 advertisement in Boston:

REFRIGERATORS, *manufactured under the direction of the subscriber,
and for sale at his counting house in Sea Street, Wheeler's Point. The principal use of these articles is for the preservation of Meat, Butter, Milk, &c.
and for cooling Wines and other liquors. Their excellence consists in the
great power of the non-conductor [insulation], together with the mode of
diffusing coldness in them [ice]. A small quantity of ice is sufficient to produce a uniform and powerful effect. A large assortment constantly on
hand, which are offered at reasonable prices.*

In the coming years the icebox (it was commonly called a refrigerator then but will
be called an icebox here to avoid confusion with the mechanical refrigerator of later times)
gradually came into use. But its utility was hindered by a scarcity of ice. Many trying out
these early iceboxes were so concerned with conserving their ice that they improvised
insulation, usually in the form of a blanket, to keep it from melting too fast. In *The House
Book*, E. Leslie recommended blankets. In reality, of course, such attempts at conserving
the ice made the device inefficient, undoubtedly causing some to wonder if the icebox
was a passing curiosity rather than a permanent and useful addition to the household.
Used properly, even at this stage of development, the icebox was indeed a practical new
appliance — one that struck some as already nearly perfect in its development. A particularly good account of the early icebox is found in the *New-York Mirror* in 1838:

*The refrigerator is a double box, the outside of mahogany or other wood,
and the inside of sheet-zinc [or tin], the space between being three or four
inches. By filling this space with finely powdered charcoal, well packed
together, the box is rendered almost heat-proof, so that a lump of ice
weighing five or six pounds, may be kept twenty-four or thirty-six hours, or
even more, if the box is not opened too often, so as to admit the hot air
from without. Of course while it is kept closed the air contained within it,
being in contact with the ice, is reduced to nearly the same temperature;
and meat is preserved perfectly sweet and good, the same as in winter. The
interiour of the refrigerator is provided with shelves for the reception of
dishes, bottles, pitchers, etc.; and thus, by a very simple contrivance, joints
of meat are kept good for several days, wine is cooled, butter hardened,
milk saved from "turning," and a supply of ice kept always on hand for the
more direct use of the table.*

In a typical icebox of this period, the receptacle for the ice was normally at the bottom. The bottom made for easier drainage of meltwater, but the ice also melted more slowly here than at the top. The next step in evolution was to move the ice to the top. This enhanced its cooling effect and also created circulation of air—the denser cool air descending to the bottom and displacing the lighter, warmer air, which rose to the top. Meltwater was easily drained off through a pipe. Although the earlier style remained in common use for many years, the newer configuration eventually superseded it and remained in use into the twentieth century.

But it was the almost simultaneous commercialization of ice cutting that made the icebox practical, particularly for city dwellers, who had no access to a pond or lake for cutting their own ice. And even for country dwellers this was practical only if they had a place to store the ice. Commercial ice changed all this. By 1850 ice cutting had become so efficient that ice was being shipped throughout the country and even exported to the Caribbean. Though it was expensive, ice was readily available in the South. Dr. Thomas Low Nichols, of New Hampshire, wrote of Memphis, Tennessee, at midcentury:

> *In the long and almost perpetual summers of the South, ice is a luxury of the first order. Every morning the ice-cart comes round as regularly as milkman or baker: ice is on every table at every meal. Stored in great warehouses, built with double walls, filled in with spent tanbark or sawdust, it is made to last from year to year, even in a climate where the thermometer ranges for weeks at nearly a hundred degrees. But whence comes the ice? A thousand miles up the [Mississippi] river the winters are long and cold. The ice, two feet in thickness, is cut out in blocks, and stored up for the opening of navigation. Loaded in immense flat-boats or rafts of boards, it floats down with the current to Memphis.*

By the late 1850s New York City was using 100,000 tons of ice annually, though this estimate includes both domestic and commercial use. Boston in 1860 used 85,000 tons, the delivery of which to the city and its environs required the services of more than 90 wagons and 150 horses. There was substantial use even in the Deep South, where the retail cost was higher because of the greater cost of shipping. For example, New Orleans in 1860 used an estimated 24,000 tons a year. In some places ice was popular in drinking water; chilled water was thought good for medicinal purposes.

The American diet at this time was dominated by bread and salted meat; fresh meat, fish, fruits, and vegetables were a less significant part of the diet, except where there was proximity to source. By 1860 the coming of the icebox and the availability of affordable ice to fill it had influenced the diet. A growing number of city dwellers were using iceboxes not only for the ice itself but for preserving fresh meat, fish, butter, and other perishables.

Of course, as a change in the way of life this was gradual. Both iceboxes and ice continued to be expensive and hence those who could afford them were few in number. Yet as a manifestation of major change, the evolution of the icebox, particularly in the period before 1860, ranks as one of the more significant.

For the time being, however, for probably the majority of households, food preservation remained little changed through most of the nineteenth century. Smoked, dried, salted, fermented, pickled, and spiced foods were staples, supplemented by what was available from one's garden in season and what the housewife could preserve and store in the cellar.

At the same time, an entirely new means of refrigeration was almost around the corner. Medical doctor John Gorrie, a native of Charleston, South Carolina, after

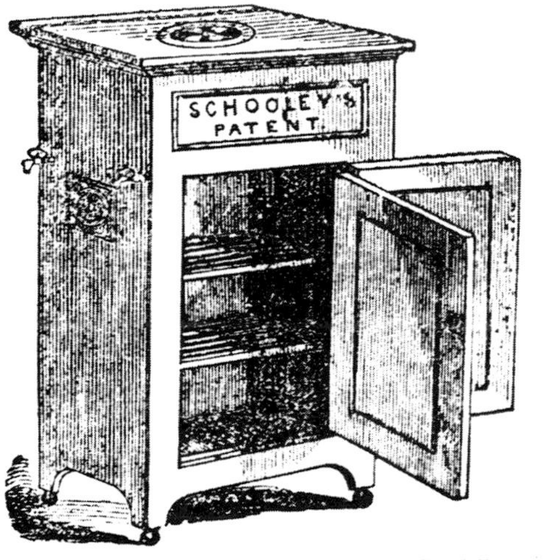

SCHOOLEY'S MEAT, PROVISION AND FRUIT PRESERVER,

IN which is introduced his patent process of producing a *dry, cold current of air from ice.* **The inside of this PRESERVER, intended for household purposes, is warranted to be dry—consequently free from moisture, mould, must, or impure flavor.**

Pamphlets giving full description of the different applications of the process, and all information respecting the purchase of manufacturing rights, can be had by addressing JOHN C. SCHOOLEY, ***Patentee.***
june 16 Cincinnati, Ohio.

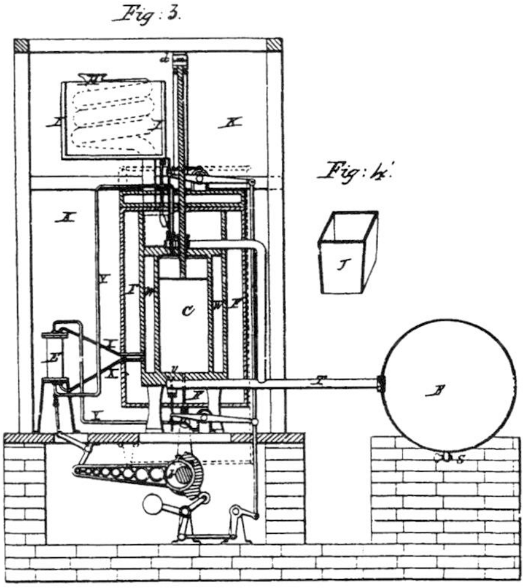

ABOVE: *Gorrie's "Ice Machine," 1851.* (U.S. Patent Collection, May 6, 1851)

LEFT: *Schooley's "meat, provision and fruit preserver," 1855: one of many attempts to improve efficiency during the "ice age" of refrigeration.* (Library of Congress, Prints and Photographs Division)

graduation from the College of Physicians and Surgeons in New York City, now part of Columbia University, had settled in the cotton port of Apalachicola, Florida. Practicing medicine there he was frequently confronted with cases of tropical fever. Could he ease the fever-racked suffering of his patients by making their sickrooms cooler, a consideration more important than usual on the notoriously sultry and humid Gulf coast of Florida? Gorrie's preparation for a career in medicine included sufficient training in science to know that when air is compressed, it gets hot; when it expands, it cools off. Was it possible to create a machine to make use of this principle and mechanically generate cool air to make patients' rooms more comfortable and speed their recovery from fever?

Gorrie in 1844 devised (and patented in 1851) an ice machine that used a force pump to compress air, thus creating heat; by then allowing the air to expand, to cool down, and to pass around a vessel of water, the machine could turn the water to ice. Or instead, Gorrie reasoned, he could let the expanding air pass through a tube and into the room. So dispersed, it would hardly be enough to freeze anything, but it might be enough to cool the room, he thought.

Gorrie's machine resembled a modern refrigerator or air conditioner. Yet it had no significant immediate impact even on the medical treatment of tropical fever. Only in retrospect can we see that it was the effective beginning of mechanical refrigeration in America.

Experimentation with refrigeration was going on in Europe as well, notably in France with Ferdinand Carré, who produced the first successful commercial freezing machine in 1860. This and its immediate successors in both Europe and America were too large to be useful in the kitchen, however, and it was not until the twentieth century that a unit compact enough to be practical would be mass-produced.

The Future: More Recognizable 1900

Most houses built before 1900 contained little if anything of twentieth-century technology. Well into the twentieth century many of these houses relied on kitchen and parlor stoves for heat, kerosene lamps for light, portable tubs for bathing and laundering, and outdoor privies for use as bathrooms. For the vast majority of homes at the turn of the century modernization came gradually as technology developed; as electricity, water, and sewerage became available; and particularly as people could afford to install these sometimes expensive creature comforts.

Because it is similar to so many homes throughout the country, and because there is a well-preserved record of what was added and when, a very good example is the house that David and Ida Eisenhower bought in Abilene, Kansas, in 1898.

Abilene had always been something more than a dusty dot on the Great Plains. After the Civil War, as the terminus of the Kansas Pacific Railroad (later absorbed by the Union Pacific), the town was known variously as the End of the Chisholm Trail and the Cow Capital of the World. Cattlemen from as far away as Texas drove their clattering herds to Abilene to be shipped to the East. As the destination of hungry, thirsty, trail-weary cowhands, it abounded with places to eat, drink, and find female companionship. As a result, it earned a reputation as the toughest, meanest, most murderous town in the Kansas Territory, its notorious Texas Street "a glowing thoroughfare which led from the dreariness of the open prairies into the delight of hell itself."

After the railroad was extended westward, and new capitals emerged, Abilene settled down and became more respectable — if perhaps duller. Churches, seven by the late nineteenth century, replaced the saloons, and incivility gave way to civic pride. By the 1890s there was talk of Abilene becoming the capital of Kansas, though it never did. But a touch of the old glitter remained in Abilene's being the home of the C. W. Parker Carnival and the site of its merry-go-round factory. It was to this Abilene that a deeply religious David Eisenhower, who liked to read the Bible in Greek, settled with his family.

David Jacob Eisenhower was born in Elizabethville, Pennsylvania, north of Harrisburg, in 1863, and was a teenager when his family, like many others, migrated to Kansas in the late 1870s. Ida Elizabeth Stover, originally of Staunton, Virginia, went there with her older brothers in 1883. David and Ida met at Lane University in Lecompton, Kansas — a small institution with some two hundred students, only a few of them girls — operated by the United Brethren Church. They married in 1885, and seven children followed, all sons: Arthur, born in 1886; Edgar, 1889; Dwight, 1890; Roy, 1892; Paul, 1894; Earl, 1898; and Milton, 1899.* The family's first home in Abilene was on Second Street. It was a tiny house, with just a patch of land for a front yard. Largely taken up by a coal and wood shed and surrounded by wooden fences, the backyard, recalled son Dwight later, was just large enough "to swing a cat in, if it were a small one."

It was certainly not a big enough place for a family of eight. The Eisenhowers moved in 1898 to Fourth Street, taking advantage of the opportunity to buy the house of David's brother, Abraham Lincoln Eisenhower, a veterinarian and also, for a time, a part owner with David in a store in Abilene; Uncle Abe had decided to move farther west. The new place struck the boys as *very* impressive: unlike their one-story cottage on Second Street, this was a *two-story* house. And yet of small proportions. "I don't know yet how my mother jammed us all in," Dwight recalled later. "A quick calculation on a scratch pad reveals that her domain — for living, sleeping, working — totaled 818 square feet for a household of eight."

It was 818 square feet of pretty basic living space. The house as built, and as the Eisenhowers moved into it, was six rooms with only the most fundamental of

---

*Arthur became executive vice president of the Commerce Trust Company in Kansas City, Missouri; Edgar, a lawyer in Tacoma, Washington; Dwight, general of the army, president of Columbia University, and president of the United States; Roy, a pharmacist; Earl, a newspaper executive and state legislator; and Milton, president of Kansas State, Penn State, and Johns Hopkins Universities. Paul died in infancy.

conveniences. Water from the well was supplemented by a roofed cistern. The combination kitchen–dining room was heated by a woodburning stove on which Ida also did the cooking. A potbellied stove on the first floor supplied a little warmth to the second through a register in the floor. "Before that little potbellied stove had cooked up a full head of steam on winter mornings," remembered Edgar, "it was rugged getting out of bed. We avoided cold air as much as possible by putting on our clothes under the covers."

There appears to have been a root cellar in the basement for cool storage of fall crops, and there may have been an icebox, though no evidence remains. Light was provided by kerosene lamps. For bathing, a galvanized steel washtub was set up in the kitchen. "There was always a scramble to see who got to go first," said Edgar. "The water had to be heated on the kitchen stove, and to save time all around, several of us often shared the same bathwater." The privy was out back.

Yet, recalled Dwight later, this "was a step up in the world! A two-story step, for the new house seemed a mansion with its upstairs bedrooms." There were two bedrooms of average size and one not much bigger than a large closet. Given the size of the family, this meant a lot of doubling up. After grandfather Jacob Eisenhower came to live with the family, there was no choice but to build a two-room addition to the first floor. The upstairs was never materially changed.

Housework was divided up among the boys. As Dwight recalled:

> *Some mornings were worse than others. On washdays, all white clothes were boiled to kill germs. While one of us [boys] turned the washing machine, the others brought in water for heating in the reservoir, a tank holding five gallons, built as an integral part of a cookstove.*
>
> *She [mother] rotated our duties; helping with the cooking, dishwashing, laundry (she never had reason to miss the assistance usually provided by daughters); pruning the orchard, harvesting the fruit and storing it for the winter; hoeing the corn and weeding the vegetable garden; putting up the hay in our immense barn; feeding the chickens and milking the cow. By rotating chores weekly, each son learned all the responsibilities of running the house and none felt discriminated against.*

About 1900, a year or so after buying the house on Fourth Street, modern convenience began to arrive in the form of central heating: a woodburning hot-air furnace in the basement. Since a woodburning cast-iron stove remained in use in the kitchen, formerly the source of heat there, furnace heat may have been provided only to the other rooms, and not necessarily all of them.

By 1904 electricity had reached the Eisenhowers' part of Abilene, and the family was quick to take advantage of it. Father, with the help of the four older boys, ranging in age from twelve to eighteen, wired the house himself. Electric light now replaced the kerosene lamps, though if the Eisenhowers were like most families, they probably held on to their lamps and kept a supply of kerosene on hand, just in case.

The family reached another milestone about 1908 — running water. City water was now available, and this meant it was now practical to have a kitchen sink, though for the next ten years it would give forth only cold water; water still had to be heated on the woodstove. But perhaps even more convenient than the kitchen sink was the indoor bathroom installed in a first-floor room that had previously served as a small bedroom (the usual place, second-floor or first, for a bathroom added to an older house). Now there was no need for that nuisance of a trip to the privy, so awkward in the dark, so particularly vexatious in deep winter. And no more baths in that galvanized washtub, although for a time it was still the kitchen stove that supplied the hot water for the bath.

THE INCORPORATION OF COMFORT AND
CONVENIENCE IN THE EISENHOWER HOUSEHOLD

| 1898 | c.1900 | 1904 | 1908 | 1913 | 1919 | 1920s | 1930s |

THE DAVID AND IDA
EISENHOWER HOUSE

Abilene, Kansas. Built 1887, purchased by the Eisenhowers 1898

c. 1900	Hot-Air Furnace
1904	Electric Light
1908	Kitchen Sink, Water Closet, Bathtub
1913	Telephone
1919	Gas Hot Water Heater, Gas Range
1920s	Electric Refrigerator, Washing Machine
1930s	Vacuum Cleaner, Electric Coffee Percolator,
	Electric Toaster

From records preserved by the National Archives and Records
Administration. Images based on surviving artifacts or on comparable
appliances as illustrated in the Sears, Roebuck catalog for the year
acquired.

Illustrations by Dolores Malecki-Spivack

In 1913 the installation of a telephone signaled the continuation of convenience, and fortuitously so, once long-distance service became available. The older boys, Arthur and Edgar, were in their mid-twenties now and off on their own, and Dwight was at West Point. (The local phone company was called United, and subsequently expanded to include telephone and utility companies from the Rockies to the Alleghenies; it later became a part of United Telecommunications, and eventually Sprint Communications, serving the entire country.)

One of United's subsidiaries was the Abilene Gas Company, which by 1919 was supplying Abilene with natural gas. Now there would be hot water at the Eisenhower house, using a gas water heater in the basement; and a modern gas range to replace that old wood burning stove. A Norge Rollator refrigerator followed in the 1920s, along with a Maytag electric washing machine and a Conlon-Chicago ironer. And in the 1930s came a Hoover upright vacuum cleaner, an electric percolator, and a Toastmaster. David and Ida were on their own now, though the sons and their families came back frequently to visit. The home that they made ever more convenient, step by step, gave them a comfortable place to spend their retirement years. David was nearly eighty when he died in 1942, his life having spanned the period from the Civil War to World War II. Ida died in 1946 at the age of eighty-four.

David and Ida Eisenhower in their seventies in 1935, on the porch of the family home. (Courtesy of the Dwight D. Eisenhower Library, Abilene, Kansas)

Marvels *of the* Electric Home

How New Inventions Utilize Electric Light, Heat, and Power in Every Room of the House

ELECTRICITY is changing our homes so swiftly and yet so smoothly that the younger generation today can scarcely conceive of homes as they were thirty years ago.

One marvelous device after another has been imagined, invented and perfected. One irksome household task after another has been lightened or eliminated. The electric washer and ironer are producing a new race of laundry-girls—young, trim, girls who "wash by machine only." The vacuum cleaner has brought order out of the annual chaos of spring housecleaning. The electric refrigerator promises to make the iceman a picturesque memory. Electricity cools us, warms us, and cooks our food.

Every nation has its ideal home. In the electrical home, it seems, America has found its own ideal. Partly responsible for this is our lack of groove-bound traditions; partly, the activity of our scientists, electrical men and inventors. At least the ideal we are offering the world is something entirely new—that of a home beautiful and comfortable, but, above all, easy to run.

It is not often given to inventors and scientists to see the direct fruits of their labors so strikingly benefiting their own generation. Even more inspiring is the thought that there are countless electrical inventions yet to be made

ELECTRIC TOYS

HAIR DRYER

IMMERSION HEATER

FAN

CURLING IRON

IRON

SEWING MACHINE

VENTILATOR

HEATER

RADIO

VACUUM CLEANER

THERMOSTAT

REFRIGERATOR

DISH WASHER

KITCHEN UNIT
CAKE MIXER,
SLICER, CHOPPER,
COFFEE GRINDER,
EGG-BEATER ETC.

ELECTRIC STOVE

PERCOLATOR   GRILL   TOASTER

IRONER

BLOWER for OIL-BURNING FURNACE

WASHING MACHINE

In the picture, our artist has suggested a few of the ways that electrical invention is changing traditional methods of doing household tasks. Even the children play with electric toys, while the housewife vacuum-cleans to radio music. Every room has benefited by electricity's service of light, heat and power

PART 3

THE PERFECTING
of COMFORT:
THE 1920s
TO THE PRESENT

It is to the changing concept of comfort that we owe the development of our homes. . . .
It remained for our own era to bring comfort up to perfection.
—HOUSE & GARDEN, 1926

America's preeminence in household convenience was officially recognized in 1926 in the form of the "most unusual American ambassador" ever sent abroad. This unusual envoy was a house.

It was a typical American dwelling, a "two-story, shingle house [in which] only Colonial and early American furnishings and decorations are used," according to a contemporary account. The house was designed in America and assembled in Brooklyn, New York. In late 1925, under the auspices of the French government, it was taken apart and shipped to France for reassembly and exhibit in Paris, "complete with running hot and cold water, gas and electric service, and a place for every labor-saving and comfort-providing device used in American homes throughout the country." The occasion was an International Exhibition of Household Appliances and Labor-Saving Devices, and the American house was the centerpiece.

The house's furnishings were copies of pieces at New York's Metropolitan Museum of Art. Its mission was to show how America had "mastered the art of getting household and office work done with a minimum of human drudgery."

So said Albert Broisat, France's general commissioner for the exhibit. "The French people [and thus the world's people] know that you Americans have mastered the art," continued Broisat, in announcing the exhibit, but

> *they do not know how you manage this. The French housewife who still does her washing, ironing, cooking, sewing, scrubbing and cleaning with her own hands [and for whom electricity was used almost exclusively for lighting] has much to learn from the American woman who uses little electrical servants for such work. . . . The kitchen and laundry will undoubtedly make the French women rub their eyes in amazement. For this model home will introduce to French women devices which are rarely seen or heard of in France, such as the vacuum-cleaner, washing and ironing machines, fireless cookers, electrical refrigerator, and numerous other labor-saving devices.*

Indeed, allowed Broisat, the American house might well cause another French Revolution—"a revolution in the French household." There had already been a revo-

PREVIOUS PAGE: *From* Popular Science Monthly, *March 1926: the complete modern home of the 1920s. The emphasis here is on the marvels of electricity, but the whole range of household technology is on display. There has been much perfecting since then, but the American house at the turn of the twenty-first century is clearly recognizable here. Note the telephone in the kitchen, an early instance.* (**Courtesy of** Popular Science Monthly)

lution of sorts in America. By 1926 the American home was recognizably modern. With a few exceptions, like air conditioning and microwave ovens, most of what constitutes the modern house was there, and it has been mostly a matter of perfecting since then.

In the 1920s, a housing boom gave impetus to the forward evolution of the American home. The same decade marked the beginning of the proliferation of the motorcar and thus the birth of suburbs. With all this house building, there was chance to modernize on a wide scale. Architecture was changing apace. Gone now were Victorian styles. In their place came new conceptions, including avant-garde images of a wholly new style of living.

Perhaps the most dramatic evidence of change was the arrival of all those new servants, electrical and otherwise, that so amazed Albert Broisat. They hardly reached into every household yet, but the transformation had begun. These various devices and systems, from a furnace in the cellar to a portable heater for the bathroom, had not only been brought to a significant state of development, they made technology itself available to a far greater part of the population than ever before. And this accessibility, as much as technological refinement, was the "revolution" in the American household.

A look at Sears, Roebuck catalogs for 1926–1927 makes this clearer. A vast number of big and little helpers were now available, including electric vacuum cleaners, from $19.95 to $37.30 with a complete set of attachments; washing machines, from the basic hand-powered Quick and Easy for as little $4.95 to the electric Water Witch with "vibrator propeller action" for $92; an electric ironer for $91.25; a "fireless cooker" (electric range) finished in porcelain enamel, complete with combination oven-broiler for $79.50, or a compact rangette with oven for only $48.50.

Many of these new "servants" were no more affordable to the family of modest means than live servants. But there were economical alternatives. The ironer, or mangle, a device heated by gas or electricity and employing a roller to make ironing semi-automatic, was a luxury; a simple electric iron could be bought for as little as $1.89. Options were available in between the old-fashioned Quick and Easy washer and the top-of-the-line Water Witch — for example, a hand-powered High Speed Wizard for $15.95 or the Allen Washer, which was electric but less fancy than the Witch at $79. And instead of an electric vacuum cleaner costing from $19.95 to $37.30, one might settle for a Bissell carpet sweeper for $3.95, or for Sears's house brand for $2.47. A furnace costing $75 (average among those offered) put central heat within the means of more people than ever before.

Another significant factor in the proliferation of household conveniences was installment buying. An estimated 15 percent of all goods were now being bought on the installment plan. That pricey $92 Water Witch could be had for as little as $5 down and payments of $7 a month. The $75 furnace was available with a down payment of $10 plus $10 a month. For a basic electric vacuum cleaner with all the attachments, the terms were $2 down and $2.50 a month. Of course, even with buying made so seemingly easy, there were a great many Americans for whom modern life was no different than it was for the French housewife who still did all of her chores by hand, and this was particularly so with the onset of the Great Depression. But the cumulative effect was of an ever increasing attainability of household comfort and convenience.

THE MODERN HOUSE OF THE 1920s

Comfort is relative, yet there are basic standards by which to measure progress. In observing that "we owe the development of our homes . . . to a changing concept of comfort," *House & Garden* in the mid-1920s recognized what vast progress there was for the measuring. And what was modern then remains essentially modern today. To be sure, there has been much perfecting. But the meaning of "modern" as defined in the 1920s has changed very little since then. Let us take a brief look at what could be found in the 1920s.

Notably transformed was the kitchen. With the exception of a microwave oven, here was most of what constitutes the modern kitchen, albeit at a simpler stage of development: electric or gas range, electric refrigerator, sink, dishwasher, cabinets, a ventilating fan to exhaust hot air and cooking odors, even a roll of paper towels on the wall. Components were being grouped so as to create an efficient working space. Appliances were even available in different colors; one manufacturer was offering refrigerators in ivory, gray, blue, and green.

A conspicuous if expensive proclamation of modernity was the dishwasher. "There is probably no machine in the entire galaxy of electric household devices that comes nearer to the feminine heart than the dish washer," said one woman. "For, while most women have the choice of patronizing a commercial laundry or having their own things done at home, dish washing is something that is thrust upon them, with little hope of escape, since dishes cannot be sent around to the corner laundry."

Other electrically powered kitchen conveniences included toasters, percolators, griddles, waffle irons, hot plates, mixers, grinders, cutters, slicers, choppers, beaters, and polishers. A sensation of the day was the "kitchen aid" (or "kitchen unit") that packed an assortment of these functions into one large cabinet using one electric

Comforts and conveniences of 1926–1927:

1. Leader gas range with four burners, an oven, and a broiler.

2. The Allen electric washing machine took much of the work out of washing but still required the use of a wringer.

3. Quick and Easy washer, priced at $5.25 for the die-hard traditionalist or the family on a really tight budget. This was 1840s technology in the 1920s.

4. Liberty gas or electric ironer with a 26-inch roller. Best for sheets, bedspreads, tablecloths, and other linens.

5. Challenge vacuum cleaner. Attachments included an 8-foot rubber hose, a 5-inch steel tube, and brushes. The dust bag was permanent; throwaways were still well in the future.

6. A so-called refrigerator, but an icebox by later definition. Mechanical refrigerators were still rare. This one had an ice capacity of 75 pounds and was one of the first to have a finish of white enamel instead of wood.

7. Hercules hot-air furnace burned hard or soft coal or wood.

8. The mid-priced Iroquois bathroom contained a bathtub, a sink, and a siphon jet bowl toilet in white only.

9. Elmwood kitchen sink with a double drain board. A swing-spout faucet with soapdish was available for a nominal additional charge.

10. This "kitchen cabinet" was available in wood finish or white or gray enamel. A central work station with "a place for everything."

11. Paper towels had 150 sheets to the roll.

(Reproduced from 1926–1927 Sears, Roebuck catalogs by permission of Sears, Roebuck and Co.)

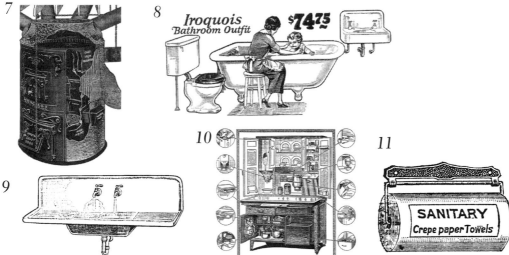

1805

OCCUPATION AND	LABORER	SHOEMAKER	CARPENTER
ANNUAL WAGES	$256	$296	$312
Bathtub, $27	11%*	9%	9%
Kitchen Stove, $120	48%	41%	38%
Water Closet, $104	41%	35%	33%
As installed (est. $208)	82%	70%	66%

1860

OCCUPATION AND	LABORER	SHOEMAKER	CARPENTER
ANNUAL WAGES	$312	$530	$633
Water Closet, $22	7%	4%	3%
As installed (est. $55)	18%	10%	9%
Washing Machine, $50	16%	9%	8%
Hot-Air Furnace, $90	29%	17%	14%
As installed (est. $270)	87%	51%	43%

1927

OCCUPATION AND	LABORER	MACHINIST	AUTO WORKER
ANNUAL WAGES	$1,042	$1,771	$1,812
Water Closet, $21	2%	1%	1%
As installed (est. $52)	5%	3%	3%
Washing Machine, $79	8%	4%	4%
Hot-Air Furnace, $75	7%	4%	4%
As installed (est. $225)	22%	13%	12%
Gas Range, $78	7%	4%	4%
Vacuum Cleaner, $20	2%	1%	1%

*Percent of Income (**Illustrations by Dolores Matecki-Spivack**)

motor with various interchangeable attachments. It struck one observer as "bewildering and overwhelming" that one machine could beat, mix, mash, whip, chop, grind, slice, strain, and even peel potatoes. One awed housewife insisted that hers could do anything but talk.

For those who didn't want to send clothes around the corner, there was the electric washing machine, and where electricity was not yet available, a washer could be had with a one- or two-cylinder gasoline engine. By the mid-1920s there were some forty manufacturers of electric laundry equipment, their products varying in design and features. For clothes-cleaning short of washing or dry cleaning, there was an electric clothes brush — basically a miniature vacuum cleaner for removing dust from garments.

The bathroom by now had its full complement of tub, toilet, and sink, all looking and working as they would in later times. The tub had lost its old familiar claw feet and was a simple-looking thing now. Occasionally it was recessed into a tiled alcove. Showers were not as common as they are today, and those that did exist were apt to look rather makeshift, with tubing holding up a shower curtain around the bather. But if a recessed tub was equipped with a shower, it might have all of the convenience and sense of permanency of a shower stall or tub shower today. A new convenience was the mixer faucet, a single lever that could be set for just the right mix of hot and cold water. The toilet was still formally called a water closet though its more familiar name was coming into use as well. Sometimes an electric bathroom heater provided additional warmth on getting out of the tub.

Even the bedroom had some modern technology. One contemporary account mentioned "the small electric hair dryer, designed for home use, in which heat as well as breeze is electrically derived." The same writer spoke of "the electric heating pad, that very soothing and comfortable substitute for a hot-water bag. . . . [If used as] a pad under bed clothing, after the bed becomes once thoroughly warm, the user will generally slip the switch to medium or low." This was a forerunner of the electric blanket, which would not appear until the late 1940s.

Speaking of heat, much of what was modern was in the cellar, out of sight. Heat was more often than not hot air, with new devices—the blower, the stoker, and the thermostat—to make the central system more efficient and more convenient. The blower marked the beginning of forced hot-air heating. The mechanical stoker (or "electrical furnace man") automatically fed coal into the furnace by means of a screw conveyor. And all of this could be regulated by a thermostat. Said one contemporary observer,

> Indeed, it is really unnecessary for the housewife even to turn the switch to
> set the blower going, for these are usually installed with a system of thermo-
> static control, by which a fall in temperature in the house automatically
> closes the switch and sets the blower to work. This thermostatic arrange-
> ment, however, must be turned off at night, lest the cooling off of the house
> during sleeping hours automatically start the blower, and thus cause the
> waste of fuel during the night season. It is, though, a very simple matter to
> turn the thermostat off at the last firing of the furnace and on again the
> first thing in the morning, since the control button may be placed entirely
> at the operator's convenience—at his bedside, indeed, if he so prefer.

POWER, FUEL, AND
INFRASTRUCTURE

THE AGE OF TAMED LIGHTNING

An electrical switch at one's bedside. At his home in Philadelphia, after his
return from France in 1785, Benjamin Franklin installed a device by which,
using cables and pulleys, he could unlock his bedroom door without getting out of bed.
Likely never in his slumber did he dream that someday it would be possible, figura-
tively speaking, to light fireplaces all over the house while still in bed.

Franklin himself had given only a hint of the impact of electricity on everyday life,
suggesting a turkey be roasted with the help of an electrical jack. Nearly a century later,
the significance of electricity was more discernible. Thomas Davenport sensed the
future when he stood in an iron works in 1833 and watched with amazement as three
pounds of iron and copper wire, working as an electromagnet, lifted anvils that
weighed up to three hundred pounds. Of that moment he wrote, "Like a flash of lightning the thought occurred to me that here was an available power which was within
the reach of man . . . [the] lightning of Heaven will soon be tamed and become the
servant of mankind."

In the twentieth century the lightning of heaven was not only tamed but capable of doing vast service to humankind beyond the mere lifting of anvils. This was the age of electricity—an age not foreseen in 1860. So this is a good time to look back and see the giant strides that have been made since thumb and finger began transforming everyday life.

The 1860s and the decades that followed were still part of the age of steam, as was America's first great celebration of technology, the Philadelphia Centennial of 1876. The exposition's Machinery Hall offered an unprecedented display of all that was new in science and technology. It was here that the public first saw such marvelous things as the telephone and the typewriter. But it was steam that made the fair, and modern life, work. Everything at the fair was powered by a single enormous steam engine—the "Eighth Wonder of the World," some claimed—estimated to weigh 700 tons. Its flywheel was an astonishing thirty feet in diameter. The assembling of the engine prior to the opening of the fair was exhibit-worthy in its own right. As reported by the *New York Times*, "The great engine erected by the Corliss firm of New York City is being built up with great rapidity, and the enormous fragments of the huge driving wheel are generally surrounded by little groups of open-mouthed admirers."

Less than twenty years later America's next great world's fair, the World's Columbian Exposition of 1893, opened in Chicago with President Grover Cleveland throwing a switch that activated not a steam engine but electrical power. It provided light (8,000 arc lamps and 250,000 incandescent bulbs) and powered an array of attractions. Particularly popular were the Tower of Light, an 80-foot spire capped by a giant replica

OPPOSITE PAGE: *Thomas Davenport*
(National Cyclopaedia of American Biography)

LEFT: *Before the taming: Benjamin Franklin and his kite experiment, 1752.* (Guillaume Louis Figuier, *Les merveilles de la science*, Paris, 1866–1869)

An early demonstration of electric light—arc light, in this case—on a levee at night in New Orleans, 1883.
(**Harper's Weekly**, March 3, 1883)

of an Edison lightbulb, and the Electricity Building, containing the greatest concentration of electric light at the fair. One newspaper account went so far as to say that "With the lights exhibited by other exhibitors and the thousands of incandescent lamps employed by the management, the illumination in Electricity Building will rival in brilliancy the sun itself." The Columbian Exposition followed by a decade the effective beginning of the age of electric light. Until the 1880s, electricity was merely scientific theory. It meant little to the general population until the coming of the incandescent lightbulb and the electric streetcar.

We will discuss the development of electric light in a later section. Suffice it here to say that a peripheral benefit of electric lighting was to create a delivery system for electricity. Once that system was in place, uses for electricity multiplied exponentially.

There were, of course, the usual perils of progress. In Philadelphia in February 1882, when the Brush Electric Light Company tried stretching wires over the roofs of several houses to get from Chestnut Street to Market Street, there was a public outcry. The American Fire Insurance Company gave immediate notice of cancellation of policies unless the wires were removed.

Yet progress prevailed. The first central distributing system, Edison's Pearl Street Station in New York City, went into operation on September 4, 1882, supplying electric current for 2,323 lamps. One newspaper account the next day began, "Edison's central station, at No. 257 Pearl Street, was yesterday one of the busiest places down town, and Mr. Edison was by far the busiest man in the station. The giant dynamos were started up at three o'clock in the afternoon, and, according to Mr. Edison, they will go on forever unless stopped by an earthquake."

Here now was Davenport's "bolt of lightning," sufficiently tamed to be sent over a wire right into one's house. The electric motor, as conceived by Davenport and others, was slower-moving. By the 1880s it had evolved dramatically from four electromagnets on the spokes of a wheel, but its use-fulness was relative to its size. To be practical, it had to be too large for use in the household in all those myriad ways that make the electric motor a part of modern life. Its chief use in the 1880s was one in which its bulk was of no consequence: powering the street-cars, otherwise horse-drawn, that had become an essential part of daily life in every major city in Europe and America. The German firm of Siemens & Halske demonstrated an experimental electric streetcar line at the Berlin Industrial Exhibition of 1879, and Edison also experimented with streetcars at Menlo Park about this same time. The first complete electric street railway in America fol-

The "Little Wonder" that was too little too late: the water motor was soon forgotten in the age of electricity. (Advertisement in Scientific American, March 19, 1904)

lowed in Richmond, Virginia, in 1888—a twelve-mile system that was built by Frank J. Sprague, a protégé of Edison. By 1902 the United States had nearly 23,000 miles of streetcar track. "The most important application of the electric motor," wrote Edward Byrn in 1900, "is for streetcar operation."

Very simple motors were also coming into use in the household, but only for very simple tasks. By the end of the nineteenth century, such motors could be found in Sears catalogs for uncomplicated operations like powering small fans. The 1897 cata-log had four sizes ranging from one-twentieth to one-sixth horsepower, all battery-powered. The smallest was advertised as being appropriate for mechanical toys; one rated at one-fifteenth horsepower was said to be able to run a fan.

Analogous to the miniature electric motor of the day was the water motor. A tiny device that could be attached to the faucet in the sink, its mechanism revolved as water flowed through it—the greater the pressure the faster the speed. It was claimed to be handy for sharpening knives and scissors.

The electric motor as first conceived and as developed through the streetcar lines of the 1880s was DC, or direct current. This is the type of current produced by a battery, and also by the early dynamos supplying the network of lines required for a streetcar system. The DC motor was, and is, good for use in transportation. Besides being rugged, the motor is easily regulated: it can be speeded up, slowed down, stopped, and reversed with simple controls. But the DC motor requires a high degree of maintenance—not a useful quality for household appliances.

Credit for development of a smaller, more simplified electric motor usually goes to Nikola Tesla, a native of Croatia of Serbian descent, who had arrived in America in 1884 armed with a letter of introduction to Thomas A. Edison attesting to his experimental work with motors in Europe. He outlined his new way of thinking in a paper, which he read before the American Institute of Electrical Engineers in 1888:

> *In our dynamo machines, it is well known, we generate alternate currents which we direct by means of a commutator, a complicated device and, it may be justly said, the source of most of the troubles experienced in the operation of the machines. . . . The function of the commutator is entirely external, and in no way does it affect the internal workings of the machines. In reality, therefore, all machines are alternate current machines. . . . In view simply of this fact, alternate currents would demand themselves as a more direct application of electrical energy.*

Hence the coming of the alternating current (AC) induction motor. It can be built in a vast range of sizes and speeds and made nearly maintenance-free. Since Tesla's time the AC electric motor has undergone little change, and today runs so much of the household—from refrigerator compressor to hair dryer, from VCR to air conditioner—that its absence would have had a profound effect on comfort and convenience.

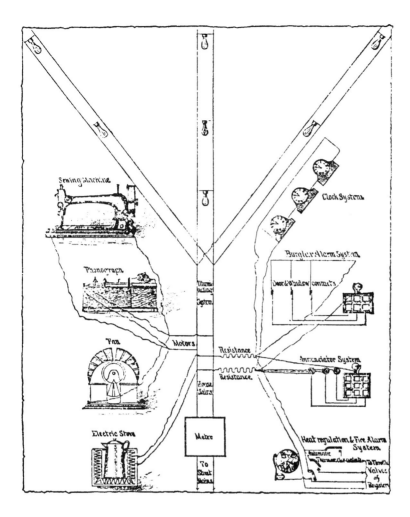

A LOOK BACK AT THE FUTURE

Even in Tesla's time, a grand vision of the modern electric household was coming into focus. Against the background of the gaslit 1890s, it was a rather remarkable vision: "We find, in fact, that the adoption of electrical household appliances is daily becoming more widespread, here adding a utility, and there an ornament, until in the near future we may anticipate a period when its presence in the homestead will be indispensable."

The future, according to A. E. Kennelly, writing in 1890, included winter comfort with thermostatically controlled central heat; summer comfort using ice-cooled air pumped to various rooms by an electric blower; electric fire alarms and burglar alarms; electric water pumps; electric motors to power carpet sweepers, lawn mowers, and shoe polishers; electric coffeemakers; electric sewing machines; and electric door openers. In some form or another, all eventually became a part of household life.

Kennelly spoke of the convenience of modern heating:

> *In winter time, whether a house be warmed by water, hot air, or steam, it is only necessary to place in each room an automatic thermometer which makes a contact as soon as the temperature reaches a desired point, and to arrange that the contact so made shall electro-magnetically cut off the supply of heat from that chamber. . . . The parlor thermostat can therefore be set at 70° while that in the hall is fixed for 60°.*

He also mentioned central air, before modern air conditioning had been invented: "In the same way, during the summer months, this thermostat can, by an additional contact, control the supply of fresh or, if possible, ice-cooled air, so as to maintain a pleasant temperature within doors." On the other hand, pretty fanciful was his description of a "miniature railroad track [that] runs round the [dining room] table within easy reach of each guest. [On it run] little trucks fitted with tiny motors [that] are started out from the pantry to the dinner-table. They stop automatically before each guest, who, after assisting himself, presses a button at his side and so gives the car the impetus and right of way to his next neighbor."

THE POWERING OF COMFORT

All those visions of the future were wondrous—as long as the electric power supply could keep pace. And clearly it could. Not only was the American house an exemplar of comfort to the world, so was its electric power industry the world's model by the late 1920s. Production of electricity for public use in 1928 was estimated at 88 billion kilowatt hours—an output equal to the rest of the world combined. Just within the previous seven years, the overall output of energy had doubled and more than 10 million new customers had gone on line—1.4 million during 1928 alone—for a total of 23 million customers, 19 million of them households. Production of electrical power was running way ahead of population growth, and use of electricity in the home was leading the way. Between 1912 and 1927, while the nation's population rose 24 percent, the population living in houses served by electricity soared 520 percent.

Clearly American families liked all those new things running on electricity. Yet many still had to do without them. Only roughly two-thirds of American homes had electricity in the late 1920s. And the same proportion would hold through the mid-1930s when the slowest sector—rural America, and farms in particular—began to catch up after the creation of the Rural Electrification Administration. When the REA was established in 1935, roughly 10 percent of farm households were wired. By the mid-1990s, when the REA had become the Rural Utilities Service, nearly all farms had electricity and, of course, nearly all nonfarm households as well. By now overall production of electricity was 3,000 billion kilowatt hours.

When Edison opened his central station on Pearl Street in New York, electricity was used entirely for lighting, but other uses quickly caught on—electric fans at first and then other simple appliances. General Electric in 1907 had some three dozen appliances for cooking or heating on the market, including commercial as well as household models.

Standardization of voltages, which had varied considerably at the beginning, aided development of the power industry and allowed for forming power pools. The standard home voltages today are 220 and 110 volts. Similarly standard is alternating current, which makes transmission over long distances practical by allowing for the use of very high voltage (up to 500,000 volts). The effect of adoption of AC over direct current (DC) was to make distribution of electricity easier over a broader geographic area, and thus more readily available to more homes.

Means of producing electricity changed with development of the steam turbine early in the twentieth century. The turbine, which replaced the reciprocating steam engine that had been the force behind the earliest electric power, turned larger dynamos more cheaply, making electricity more economical. Conventional steam power remains the primary means of producing electricity, accounting for two-thirds. But the bulk of this (roughly 55 percent of all electricity produced) comes from the use of coal.

With continuing construction of new pipeline, however, natural gas has become the fuel of chioce wherever possible for power plants being built, and "combined-cycle" the method of choice for producing electricity. With combined-cycle, a gas turbine (much like the jet engine of an aircraft) directly drives one generator while its hot exhaust vapors are harnessed to produce the steam that powers a steam-turbine generator. This new method is more efficient and results in emission of fewer pollutants than past methods using fossil fuel (a depletable resource).

Hydroelectric power came into use at virtually the same time as the first steam-powered dynamos, and has been an important source of power ever since. It has the advantage of being a renewable source of energy but is most suitable to geographic areas with sufficient water resources—the Northwest, for example, where it has been the primary source of electric power.

Nuclear power came into use early in the atomic age. In the 1990s it accounted for roughly 20 percent of overall output. As of 1996 there were 110 nuclear generating stations operating in the United States.

An emerging source is geothermal energy, which is still of barely marginal significance, statistically speaking (less than half of one percent of electric power production), yet it holds promise because it uses a renewable resource: the heat in the interior of the earth. A geothermal power plant, instead of burning coal to run the steam turbine that generates electricity, simply taps natural underground steam.

If geothermal energy is one of our newest hopes, one of the oldest is that first source of power we saw in the colonial period: wind. It was then used chiefly for grinding grain. Almost at the beginning of the age of electricity wind came into use for generating power. A windmill erected in 1888 generated power on the estate of electrical pioneer Charles F. Brush in Cleveland, Ohio. It chiefly supplied the power for daily use of some one hundred incandescent lights, and remained in operation for twenty years.

As a result of development of the airfoil propeller for aircraft in the 1920s a small, typically three-bladed propeller came into use for a wind-driven device known as the windcharger, which was used for generating electric power and was ideally suited to the individual household. Many of these were in use in the 1930s where electric power was otherwise not yet available. Windchargers were effective for small devices like lamps and radios but usually not for major appliances. The coming of the REA largely, although not entirely, ended the use of wind for individual power needs.

Today the use of wind for power is almost entirely commercial, usually available from wind farms that concentrate numerous wind machines in favorable locations. An exception was built at Medicine Bow, Wyoming, in 1982 as a project of the Federal Bureau of Reclamation. Whereas most windmills had been getting smaller over the years, this one was intended to see how much electricity could be produced from one large machine. Along with another slightly smaller unit, the answer was enough power to supply 1,600 customers—when everything was working right, which was only periodically. The propeller of the largest mill measured 257 feet from tip to tip, and when winds reached between 40 and 60 miles per hour, the tips of the propeller sliced through the air at a velocity of nearly 180 miles per hour. But whereas the windmill built in John Winthrop's Massachusetts Bay colony in 1632 suffered from too little wind, it was too much wind that got the better of the one at Medicine Bow one day in

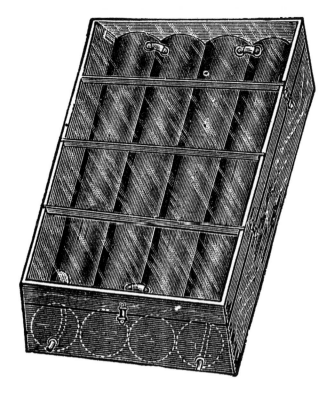

Solar heating—that is, the production of heat from light without its first being converted into electricity—is not new. For example, Scientific American *in 1893 reported on a rooftop solar panel for heating water. It consisted of a wooden framework containing four galvanized iron cylinders covered with a pane of glass and connected by pipe to a bathtub in the house. According to* Scientific American, *the device was "said to work so successfully in practice that the water was sometimes made almost boiling hot."* (Scientific American, September 1893)

January 1994. The windmill blew apart, leaving splinters, stubs, and assorted parts of machinery scattered about the countryside.

Wind power was a significant source of household technology in the later nineteenth and early twentieth centuries. It remains a source of electricity for the household, but for only a relatively small number of homes.

The most fundamental source of heat, indeed of energy, remains the sun; yet its power remains little utilized in the household. Of 106 million year-round homes counted in the 1990 census, only 20,000 used solar energy as their source of heat—a total barely worthy of a footnote. Slightly more common was the use of solar energy to heat water; here the total was 258,000—still substantially less than one percent.

Despite its lack of popularity, there are signs of a brighter future for solar energy. Probably the chief obstacle has been cost. Converting sunlight into electricity has never been seen as cost-effective. In 1996 the average cost of electricity from solar power was about thirty cents per kilowatt-hour (figuring in the cost of installing the system) whereas the average household paid eight cents for utility-supplied electricity.

By the late 1990s engineers were producing more efficient, and thus more cost-effective, solar cells and were seeking to bring down the overall cost by incorporating them directly into building materials. Instead of using ordinary shingles on the roof, for example, one might use photovoltaic panels. Whereas in the past one built a roof of the usual kind and then covered it with solar panels, now the panels *are* the roof. Similarly, photovoltaic cells can be built into exterior wall cladding and even windows and skylights.

Strictly speaking, solar energy is the conversion of light into electricity. When sunlight strikes a photovoltaic, or solar, cell, the cell frees electrons, generating electric current that can power electric lights and other devices.

Solar *heating* is the production of heat from light without the solar energy first being converted into electricity. This is an earlier and simpler form of technology. Devices using solar heat for hot water were around in the late nineteenth century, and a primitive device of this sort is said to have been built by the Swiss scientist Horace Bénédict de Saussure in 1767.

FUEL: CHANGING PREFERENCES

The American home of the 1920s relied heavily on coal. An average house used up to 30 tons during the heating season. Oil was becoming increasingly popular and, by January 1926, was heating an estimated 600,000 households.

Times change. At the beginning of the twenty-first century the American home depends most heavily on natural gas for heating and on electricity for cooking. Use of heating oil, though still significant, has declined. Coal, once the mainstay of domestic heating and cooking, has almost disappeared for domestic purposes. Wood continues to have some use for heating but virtually none for cooking.

Since it is the most widely used fuel for heating, let us look first at gas—and particularly natural gas, since we have already considered manufactured gas, which was intended primarily for lighting.

Even with electric light rapidly coming into use, gas continued to be in high demand in the early 1900s. But sensing that electricity would sooner or later supersede gas for lighting, gas manufacturers began promoting other uses in the household, including gas heating stoves—room heaters, for now, as opposed to furnaces—as well as gas ranges, gas water heaters, and gas-fired hot plates.

Gas, which was ideally suited for all these uses, still included coal gas, that old mainstay going back to 1817 in Baltimore. Although the production process had changed, the product was essentially the same. Gas was also made from petroleum, waste fats and oils, and even from gasoline.

All of these were manufactured gases. What really made gas useful in the household, especially for heating, was natural gas, which was effectively just coming into use.
It was explained in 1906 that natural gas "will develop more heat per cubic foot in burning than any other kind of gas except acetylene," and highly explosive acetylene was
hardly suited for the household. Over and above its high heat value, piped-in natural
gas had the advantage of taking up no space in the cellar (as did coal) and of not requiring deliveries (as did both oil and coal). Yet of modern household fuels, natural gas was
the slowest to gain wide use, and for good reason.

Actually, there was nothing new about natural gas. It had been observed from time
to time over the centuries. But there was no attempt to use natural gas as a fuel until
1821 when a well being dug for water in Fredonia, New York, produced gas, which was
then piped to a few nearby buildings and used for lighting. In 1865, as was mentioned
earlier, the first company to distribute natural gas was formed, also in Fredonia. There
was little attempt to develop natural gas resources in the following years because of the
rush to exploit the discovery of oil in Titusville, Pennsylvania. Oil for lighting also had
the advantage of being easily sold and distributed in barrels and bottles whereas natural gas required piping. The coming of electric light a few years later further pre-
cluded serious consideration of natural gas for a while.

In the early 1900s, however, the discovery of vast gas reserves in Texas, Louisiana,
and Oklahoma caused renewed interest in natural gas, and the industry was reporting
steady growth by the 1920s. Some 250,000 households switched to natural gas in 1927,
bringing the overall total to nearly 4 million domestic customers. Use of manufactured
gas still predominated, however, with an aggregate total of nearly 12 million customers,
industrial and commercial as well as domestic.

Improvements in pipeline technology spurred development of the natural gas
industry. At first the pipe was of small diameter and joined with screw couplings. This
was expensive to install and was generally economical only for transmission routes of
250 to 300 miles. By the early 1930s, joints were being welded, and seamless pipe of
large diameter and high strength was coming into use; by now, also, there was mechanization of the process of digging the trenches in which the pipe was laid. As a result,
piping gas a thousand miles or more was economical. The feasibility of long-distance,
large-diameter pipe was firmly established during World War II when the federal government constructed the "Big Inch" (a pipeline 24 inches in diameter) and the "Little
Big Inch" (20 inches) to ensure a dependable flow of crude oil from Texas to war plants
in the East. In postwar years similar pipelines were built for natural gas, and today we

have nearly a million miles of pipeline of various sizes to collect and distribute natural gas throughout the country.

The ascendancy of natural gas and the use of electricity for lighting eventually eclipsed the use of manufactured illuminating gas. In retrospect, though, it was the simple, short-haul wooden mains of early systems like Baltimore's that were the prototypes of the Big Inch.

For homes beyond the practical service area of piped-in natural gas, the recourse has long been bottled gas, which works just like natural gas but requires truck delivery and on-site storage. It is much less common for heating than for cooking.

Fuel oil for heating became popular in the 1920s; by 1926, an estimated 600,000 American households had converted. A clear advantage over coal was that oil required no large bins in the basement. More to the point was what one observer noted: ". . . women have found no magic words that will serve unfailingly to coax the head of the household away from his evening paper or radio and into the coal bin. . . . Out of these dislikes, as common as human nature, has developed the domestic oil-burner." By 1950, fuel oil accounted for roughly 23 percent of households—very nearly the same as natural gas (27 percent). Then oil use declined while gas steadily gained in popularity. Gas allows for a simpler burner and does not require on-site storage. In many places, however—particularly in rural areas—natural gas is not available, and oil remains the common fuel for heating.

Coal was still the most common home heating fuel in 1950, with roughly 35 percent of the market. Electricity that same year was statistically negligible at 0.7 percent. By the end of the century electricity was preeminent for cooking (60 percent) and common for heating (27 percent). Coal (including coke) by this time represented only 0.3 percent for heating and about the same for cooking.

INFRASTRUCTURE: WATER AND SEWERAGE

A fast-multiplying population in the second half of the nineteenth century made water supply a critical need. Public health was an obvious reason. So was fire protection for cities of ever increasing density. It was not entirely coincidental that a dramatic increase in waterworks construction came during the 1870s—from 243 plants in 1870 to 598 in 1880. The Great Chicago Fire had occurred in 1871.

Public water supply generally kept up with population growth. In 1900 public supply was furnishing 3 billion gallons a day. That had more than doubled to 7 billion by the mid-1920s, a demand for water that now reflected increased use in the home for showers as well as tubs, for water closets instead of outdoor privies. By the late 1990s the daily total was roughly 34 billion.

Besides having to meet a continually higher demand, modern water supply must also meet continually higher standards — both for safety (absence of harmful bacteria, pathogens, and other disease-causing organisms) and for quality (taste, color, and odor).

Rural areas continue to rely on wells and pumps, as in days gone by, but today they use electrically driven pumps and pressure tanks, and often water softeners, all of which ensure a supply of water as dependable and as safe (given environmental regulations) as the water in cities.

Though no less essential to public health, sewer systems lagged somewhat behind water supply in the nineteenth century. Their contribution to public health was compromised by the fact that the usual recourse was to take what was collected and dump it in the river. The solution to this came in the development of sewage treatment plants in the late nineteenth and early twentieth centuries. An early model was built in Worcester, Massachusetts, in 1890, using six 60- by 100-foot settling tanks to treat raw sewage with lime. The effluent, after settling, was pumped into lagoons. By the early twentieth century bacterial decomposition began to come into use; the first major treatment plant was opened in Manchester, England, in 1914.

Heating and Air Conditioning

From Central Sun to Central Heat

As of the 1860s, we may recall, the principal means of heat was the heating stove, and that continued so over the coming decades with little change. The Central Sun, Art Garland, Radiant Sunshine, and other stoves with fanciful names continued to warm American parlors, and often other rooms as well, into the new century—frequently many years into it. But we discussed the heating stove in Part 2, and there is nothing of significance to add here. Now we must trace central heat, for that is what will bring us up to the present.

And to follow central heat is chiefly to trace the hot-air furnace, which heats the majority of modern American homes. In the 1860s the hot-air furnace was still basically a big iron stove in a little brick chamber—the same configuration that had been the principal form of central heat in the home since before 1820. But that would soon change. By the 1880s the self-contained furnace was beginning to take over, soon to make quaint that brick enclosure known as an air chamber. The new furnace substituted a sheet-metal jacket for the old enclosure. Air was admitted through a duct from outside, heated as it circulated around the hot stove (still so called in *Scientific American Home-Owners Handbook* in 1924) and then allowed to rise through ducts to the rooms above. The same stove could also be used with a brick enclosure, but the new self-contained type saved space. Gradually the jacketed furnace superseded the air chamber altogether. By 1901 it was the only type illustrated in a review of heating and ventilating in *Domestic Engineering* magazine, although the writer allowed that some traditionalists might still favor brick:

> In construction a furnace is a large stove with a combustion chamber of ample size over the fire; the whole being enclosed in a casing of sheet iron or brick. The bottom of the casing is provided with a cold-air inlet, and at the top are pipes which connect with registers placed in the various rooms to be heated. Cold fresh air is brought from out of doors through a pipe or duct called the cold-air box; this air enters the space between the casing

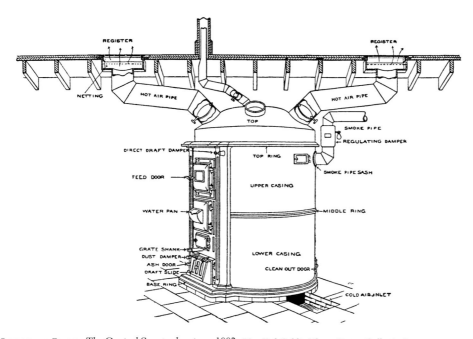

OPPOSITE PAGE: *The Central Sun parlor stove, 1882.* (New York Public Library Picture Collection)

ABOVE: *By the beginning of the twentieth century, as central heating became more and more common, the self-contained hot-air furnace was predominant. The old masonry air chamber was largely a thing of the past. The self-enclosed furnace shown here continued in use until after midcentury. Then the hot-air furnace began to take on a whole new appearance — an entirely different configuration: a simple boxlike structure not unlike a large filing cabinet. This reflected the transition to a gas or oil burner, a much smaller device than the firebox of a coal- or woodburning furnace, and the use of an efficient modern blower to create forced-air heating.* (Domestic Engineering, April 15, 1901)

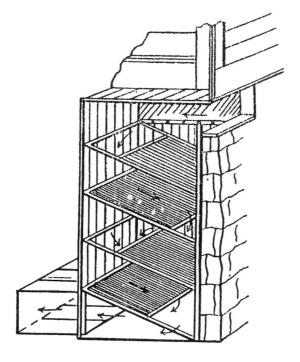

One important feature of a modern warm-air heating system began appearing surprisingly early, albeit in relatively few homes. This filter system, which was in use in 1909, consisted of a series of screens that could be removed for cleaning.
(Federal Furnace League, *The Warm Air Furnace* [Albany, N.Y., 1909])

and the furnace near the bottom and in passing over the hot surfaces of the fire pot and combustion chamber becomes heated. It then rises through the warm air pipes at the top of the casing and is discharged through the registers in the rooms above.

The interesting thing about this quote is that it comes close to being a paraphrase of Daniel Pettibone's account of the use of central heat in America in 1810 (*Description . . . of the Rarifying Air-Stove*). Except for the use of a casing supplanting the brickwork, the model furnace of 1901 was not fundamentally different from Pettibone's stove of 1810. And yet that is not to say that there had been no progress. The design of the stove itself had undergone a certain degree of transformation to make it more efficient. And then there was that twentieth-century convenience, taken for granted in modern times, the thermostat. It was not, to be sure, very common when it was introduced in 1870 as the electromagnetic regulator. And there was the paradox of its anticipating twentieth-century convenience even while delivering heat by nineteeth-century standards.

The device consisted of a regulating thermometer — what would come to be called a thermostat — hanging in the living quarters. Wires connected it to the furnace by way of a battery. When the temperature reached a preset point, an electrical circuit was completed, resulting in an electromagnetic device opening or closing a damper on the furnace. *Scientific American* on August 27, 1870, thought it an ingenious thing that had possibilities beyond just home heating: "In fact its possible and useful applications are almost beyond enumeration." A pamphlet published by the inventor Dr. G. M. Sternberg of New York offered the observation that "The regulative function of electricity over mechanical movements has not hitherto had the attention it deserves." Indeed. This was 1870, and the generating of electric power was still more than a decade away.

By 1927, with electrical power now common, the heating thermostat was frequently to be found regulating an improved furnace, whether hot-air, hot-water, or steam. And regardless of the type of heat, the most common fuel was coal. The backbreaking job of shoveling it every time the furnace needed to be refilled was eased by the development of the electrically operated automatic stoker. Stokers had been in use for industrial applications since early in the century, but only in the mid-1920s did they begin to appear in American households. The stoker was installed next to the furnace and connected to it by a conveyor belt, which carried coal automatically into the firebox as needed. Stokers became relatively common toward midcentury — about the time oil and gas began to supersede coal as the primary heating fuels.

A new and significant improvement was the coming of the blower, which made possible modern forced-air heating. The effec-

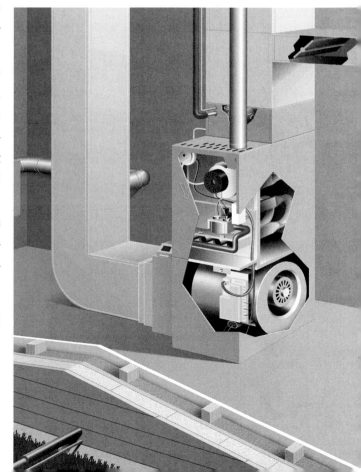

Today's warm-air heating system has a range of features never dreamed of in the early days of central heating, among them computerized controls and electronic air filtration. Warm-air heat remains the most widely used heating system in part because its ducts can also be used for central air conditioning. (**Courtesy of York International Corporation**)

tive beginning of this, so far as residential heating goes, can be found in the early 1920s as the aerofan, designed to boost the circulation of air through a hot-air system. An aerofan described in *Scientific American's Home-Owners Handbook* (1924) used a motor 4 inches wide (so as not to restrict flow of air through a duct) coupled to a fan installed within the heating system, usually in the cold-air duct, thus forcing circulation of air before its actual heating. But small aerofans could also be installed within individual risers where a boost was needed. The aerofan was thermostatically controlled.

The aerofan eventually led to the modern blower, which produces a more effective and more powerful thrust. This, however, required redesign of the furnace. It coincided more or less with adoption of the more efficient oil-gas burner, which was also more compact than the firebox of a coal furnace. The result was the compact furnace that could be found by 1940, especially in new homes just being built.

At the beginning of the twenty-first century the essential configuration of a hot-air furnace remains little changed from 1940, but it works with considerably greater efficiency, comes with computerized controls and an electronic air cleaner, and can be provided with motorized dampers that give it zone control, allowing it to heat only certain sections of the house at a given time. This feature, in the past, was a selling point of hot-water heat as opposed to hot air.

The typical turn-of-the-century radiator was this cast-iron sectional unit that could be made in any size.
(*Domestic Engineering*, April 15, 1901)

Hot-air heat was the first type of central heat to become common in America, and it has remained the most popular ever since. It is the simplest type of central heating system and the least expensive to install, and the heat comes up quickly. It occupies no space in the room being heated, the registers being flush with the floor or wall, unlike the radiators used for steam or hot-water heat. It is also easily adaptable to central air conditioning, since all the ducts are in place. And whereas earlier hot-air systems sometimes spread dust and even finely powdered ash throughout the house, modern filtration is effective in preventing this. Hot-air heating is most effective when used in a relatively compact structure, thus making it ideal for the average-size house.

The hot-air furnace, which is used in 54 percent of American homes, is clearly the favorite system. Add in systems that use hot air (floor, wall, or other units without ducts) and the total comes to 59 percent. Steam and hot water, by comparison, account for only 14 percent, while heat pumps, a comparatively recent development, claim 10 percent and built-in electric heating 7 percent. The remainder includes portable heaters, room heaters, stoves, and fireplaces.

Radiator heating—steam or hot water—was coming into use even before the first hot-air systems were installed. And almost from the start, the consensus has been that hot water is considered the more desirable of the two.

Steam heat uses a one-pipe system. Water is heated in a boiler to at least 212°F. and the resulting steam rises through a pipe to a radiator above. As the radiator gives off heat, the steam condenses and passes back down the same pipe.

Hot water uses a two-pipe system, the heated water ascending to the radiator by one pipe and returning to the boiler by another. From its earliest days and well into the twentieth century, this was a gravity flow system: the water, as it was heated in the boiler, expanded and grew lighter, thus rising up the pipe; cooling, it became heavier and descended back to the boiler by another pipe. By 1940 the forced-circulation system using a pump (comparable to the blower in the hot-air system) was coming into use, and this is standard today. Pump-driven hot water does not heat as quickly as hot air, but it maintains room heat longer, since the radiator remains hot even after the water begins to cool, whereas when the hot-air blower stops, so does the heat. Modern hot-water systems usually use baseboard radiators that are inconspicuous and take up only a few inches of space. "Hot-water heat is generally recognized as the most satisfactory kind of heat where expense is not the main consideration," said *Scientific American's Home-Owners Handbook* in 1924, even before the circulating pump was introduced. Most heating experts would probably still say the same.

Although hot-air and radiator heating are the most common, other forms have also been used—the heat pump, for example, which came into use for the household in the 1950s. The heat pump is sometimes thought of as a reverse air conditioner; and indeed an early one marketed by Carrier Corporation was literally that—a portable window unit that worked as an air conditioner and then, explained a brochure, "At the first hint of cool weather, reverse the Portable in the window and, like magic, comfortable warm air starts to circulate."

Carrier explained the operation of the heat pump this way:

Think of it in terms of an ordinary household refrigerator [which] removes heat from the interior of the box and discharges it out the back—warmth you can feel by putting your hand behind the refrigerator in your own kitchen. Now if we were to take the refrigerator, remove the door and push the open side through a hole cut into the outside wall of the house, the machine would take heat from the outdoor air, absorb it in the cooling chamber, then pass it through the hot condensor coils to the inside of the house.

Modern heat pumps operate in just this way, except that some, instead of extracting heat from the air, suck heat from the ground. Generally speaking, heat pumps work well in moderate climates, where summers are long and winters are mild. Even so, they are more expensive than conventional heating systems, and a ground extraction system is considerably more costly.

Still other modern forms of heating are the radiant electric or hot-water systems. Radiant systems with hot water flowing through pipes embedded in concrete slab floors were used beginning in the late 1930s—for example, in Frank Lloyd Wright's Pope-Leighy House in Falls Church, Virginia, built 1939–1941. Such systems provide well-distributed heat but take longer to generate warmth than conventional heating systems. Radiant electric heating uses cable installed in the floor or ceiling or along the baseboard.

The secret of modern comfort goes beyond the heating system: the house itself has been made more heat-tight—or cold-proof, depending on one's perspective. Use of insulation accounts for a substantial part of this, as do improved windows. Prefabricated units that combine thermal glass with an airtight assembly prevent heat from escaping. In earlier times, keeping the windows from admitting cold air required the use of storm windows. Although they were largely a twentieth-century development, the idea was there well before. In 1856 Henry W. Cleaveland, Willard Backus, and Samuel Backus, in their book *Village and Farm Cottages*, advised that "windows be doubled. . . . Put another thin glass before, or behind it, so that the air between, no matter how narrow the space, shall be tightly inclosed, and the remedy is perfect." Just what Count Rumford had in mind very early in the nineteenth century, when he suggested the use of "double windows" for the same purpose.

INVENTIONS FOR COOLING

The technology of keeping cool lagged well behind that of keeping warm. Not until the mid nineteenth century was there anything worthy of being called cooling technology — and that first device was only a simple electric fan. The earliest motorized fan was patented in 1854, long before modern electric supply would make such devices really practical. What Louis Stein, of New York, designed nevertheless foreshadowed the future. It was a two-bladed ceiling fan run by a primitive battery-powered electric motor. It was a relatively sophisticated device in that its mechanism caused the blades not only to revolve but also to flap. Given a dependable electric supply, it might have been surprisingly effective for its time, but battery power was still crude, expensive, and rarely accessible. The first permanent central generating station was opened in New York in 1882. With the coming of electric power for lighting there quickly developed other uses for electric power. A desk fan that used commercial current was devised that same year of 1882, and others followed.

But fans were only simple devices for doing what servants had done for their royal masters in ancient Egypt. Modern society expects machines to do the work. Long before Stein, the Reverend Manasseh Cutler, a Massachusetts clergyman, had noted in his diary that on a visit to Philadelphia in July 1787 Benjamin Franklin "showed us . . . his great armed chair, with rockers, and a large fan placed over it, with which he fans himself, keeps off flies, etc., while he sits reading, with only a small motion of his foot."

By the mid-nineteenth century, as ice became more readily available, it was increasingly seen as the practical as well as logical means of creating a cooling effect.

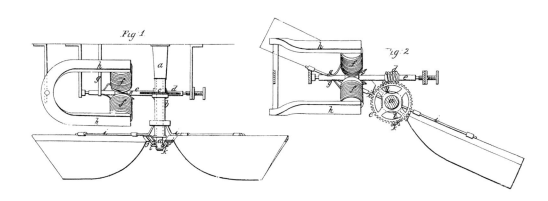

Louis Stein's first-of-a-kind electric fan, 1854. (U.S. Patent 12,106, December 19, 1854)

The Manufacturer's Depot of Philadelphia in 1859 announced that it had on sale "Kahnweiler's Patent Ventilating Rocking Chair." It went Franklin one better by having an ice chest beneath its seat. This meant, according to the manufacturer, that for, "say, two cents worth of ice per day, the luxury of pure air may be fully enjoyed within doors, and the heat of the summer, or the vitiated atmosphere of a closed apartment, defied."

Until the perfecting of mechanical air conditioning in the twentieth century, ice continued to be the principal means of cooling. It was also the basis of an early device approximating modern air conditioning, improvised jointly by U.S. Navy engineers, a professor, an inventor, and an army doctor tending to the mortally wounded President James A. Garfield in the summer of 1881. Garfield had been shot on July 2 and was confined to the White House, his condition continually deteriorating. Those attending him sought to ease his discomfort with some measure of relief from Washington's oppressive heat.

The system was built around an "air-cooling apparatus" patented in 1881 by inventor Ralph S. Jennings of Baltimore. Although intended as a means of refrigeration for the food industry, it could also be used to cool a room. Jennings's device consisted of an iron case containing thirty-six wire cylinders wrapped in terry cloth. Overhead was a perforated iron pipe, fed from a cistern filled with water and shaved ice, that kept the terry cloth saturated. At one end was a battery-powered electric blower that forced air through the case, thus cooling it.

The device was set up in one room. Tin ducts carried the cool air to the next, Garfield's bedroom. While the device proved useful in cooling the air, it had the negative effect of generating additional humidity. The team overseeing the installation then set up another, larger box filled with ice on the outflow side, with the intention that "any excess of moisture would be absorbed by the ice in the large box," according to Simon Newcomb, a navy scientist who was part of the team, and the air further cooled in the process. Various combinations were also tested, including reversing the sequence of the boxes and opening and closing windows in the president's room according to what breeze was blowing.

The system went into use on July 12, 1881, and Professor Newcomb recorded that the air in the president's bedroom was "found to be cool, dry and ample in supply." *Scientific American* several weeks later, reporting on "The Presidential Cold Air Machine," said the device was capable of keeping the president's room at a steady 75°F. day and night with windows and doors open or at 60°F. with them closed, though this "gave the room an air of gloom." More important was a report subsequently written by navy engineers that went further in finding significance, hitting upon the essential qualities of what air conditioning would become in the twentieth century:

> *Our operations at the Executive Mansion have proved that it is possible to*
> *place dew-points, or relative humidity, of definite quantities of air, at any*
> *desired point, and there is no reason why this hygrometric condition may*
> *not be maintained with as much certainty as the amount and temperature*
> *of air supplied for proper ventilation and warming . . . and no reason why*
> *the atmosphere [in rooms of hospitals and public buildings] may not be*
> *made comfortable and healthful at all seasons and under all conditions of*
> *the outside air.*

Here, perhaps for the first time, was practical application of the principle of modern air conditioning. But its practicality was relative to the availability (and affordability) of ice in great quantities. A bill submitted by the Independent Ice Company of Washington reveals that it delivered 535,970 pounds of ice to the White House between July 10 and September 7, when Garfield was moved to his summer residence at Elberon, New Jersey, where he died September 19. That works out to nearly 9,000 pounds, or more than 4 tons, a day.

After Garfield's death, so far as is known, the system was dismantled and never used again. Its usefulness as a source of domestic comfort, as opposed to industrial use, was severely restricted by the fact that it needed so much ice to work effectively.

Twenty-eight years later, another entirely different ice-based cooling system was tried at the White House, this one for President William H. Taft. It was no longer a matter of improvising. Commercial air-cooling devices were purchased in the summer of 1909 from

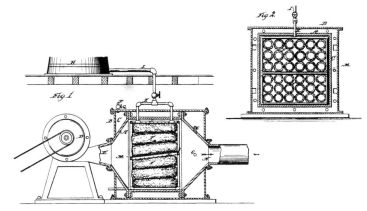

Forerunner of modern air conditioning: Jennings's Air-Cooling Apparatus of 1881, nucleus of the cooling system improvised for President James A. Garfield as he lay dying at the White House during the summer of 1881. Figure 1 shows the device itself with its wire cylinders wrapped in terry cloth. The blower is at the left; above it is the cistern supplying water that saturates the terry cloth through perforated pipe. Figure 2 is a transverse section showing the thirty-six terry-cloth covered cylinders. (U.S. Patent 246,013, August 23, 1881)

two separate firms and installed in the White House attic. These also depended on ice to achieve a cooling effect and used fans to force the chilled air through the ducts of the heating system. It was a much more ambitious plan than the cooling of one room—too ambitious. The system proved hopelessly inadequate and was apparently disassembled after a trial period. President Taft, only in his first year in office, seemed to have no alternative but to reconcile himself to Washington's humid and often sweltering summers for the rest of his term. But in May 1911, a smaller system was installed, serving only the president's office. This one worked—but it consumed very large amounts of ice each day. According to Taft's military aide, Archie Butt:

> We have just installed a marvelous system in the executive office for his [Taft's] comfort. We have an arrangement by which we pump cold air into his office. It is funny to go into his own room and see all the windows pulled down. . . . It seems to be too chilly for health, but the doctors say not. To go into the adjoining room is like going into a furnace. We use up 3,000 pounds of ice a day by the process, but if it makes life endurable for him I suppose the country has no cause for complaint.

Though the White House air coolers of 1909 apparently made use of chemical dehydrators of some sort to treat the air fanned through the heating ducts, ostensibly providing some degree of dehumidification, they were clearly no more effective than the system as a whole. Furthermore, ice as the basis of cooling technology was simply not feasible for widespread use (clearly so, when it took so much ice a day to cool one room). The key to modern air conditioning is mechanical cooling.

A mechanical cooling device was the eventual product of nineteenth-century experimentation, notably John Gorrie's ice machine. But comfort in warm weather is not a matter of coping with the heat alone; one also has to endure the humidity. In low humidity, body heat evaporates fairly readily. The higher the humidity, the less so. Hence at a given temperature, one may feel reasonably comfortable or absolutely uncomfortable, depending on the humidity. With the development of modern refrigeration, it was possible to generate cold air mechanically, but only when humidity was also controlled was it possible to have air *conditioning*, the standard by which comfort in the warm season is now measured.

The effective means of combining cooling and dehumidifying (as well as cleaning the air of dust particles and, where necessary, humidifying in winter to correct for dryness) was the contribution of Willis H. Carrier, namesake of the Carrier Corporation. His first installation in 1902 was at a lithography company in Brooklyn, New York. The firm printed in color, a process that required exact alignment of the paper through successive impressions of different color inks. Heat and humidity were the enemy, causing the paper to swell in size. Full-color printing was a new technology and, as happens so often, another unrelated technology was developed just in time to make it practical. The system designed by Carrier kept the printing plant at 55 percent relative humidity year-round and a temperature of 70°F. in winter and 80°F. in summer.

From there it was a matter of creating similar systems for business and industry, theaters and restaurants, museums and department stores, but commercial air conditioning did not begin to take hold until the 1920s. And then, once a small enough compressor unit was developed and safe refrigerants were available, air conditioning was possible for the home. The first household room unit was announced in 1928, during which year, another house — the U.S. House of Representatives — was being fitted out with air conditioning by Carrier, as was the Senate. The new systems went into use during the summer of 1929. The following year an air-conditioning system of the type usually supplied for small theaters was installed at the White House.

By 1930, units for home use had been, or were about to be, announced by Carrier, Frigidaire, General Electric, and Kelvinator. A typical unit, the Frigidaire of 1930, could cool a reasonably large room, but its usefulness was affected by outside temperature and humidity: it was only expected to cool the room to about ten degrees below the outside temperature and to reduce the humidity by 10 percent. It required a water connection, cost considerably more than a refrigerator, and used two to four times as much current as the latter.

Cooperative research between Carrier Engineering Corporation and York Heating and Ventilating produced the atmospheric cabinet, a popular early room air conditioner for both home and office that nevertheless still required a refrigeration unit outside the room. It went on the market early in 1932. Later that year Carrier brought out its first self-contained room unit, but sales of both these and the atmospheric cabinet languished as the Depression deepened. Central air was available by 1937 but was even more costly.

It was only after World War II that home air conditioning became common, along with another postwar sensation. "Air Conditioning: Booming Like Television" was how *Newsweek* headlined an article in July 1950. It was about how the nation's total electric power usage jumped 3 percent in just two weeks in June as homeowners all over the country turned on their new air conditioners. The number of room units in use had doubled in the last two years. A small unit was now reasonably affordable at $300, with three years to pay. So-called portable units became available during the 1950s, meaning not so much that one actually moved the air conditioner from room to room (though you could) as that one could install it oneself, cutting the overall cost.

Technological advance and mass production have continually made air conditioning more affordable. By the late 1990s roughly three of every four American homes had air conditioning in at least one room, and nearly half of American households had central air.*

ABOVE: *One of the early home air conditioners on the market was this Room Weathermaker introduced by Carrier in 1932.* (Courtesy of the Carrier Corporation)

RIGHT: *The postwar boom in home air conditioning brought with it the more compact window unit. This Carrier unit dates to 1954.* (Courtesy of the Carrier Corporation)

---

*While the benefits of air conditioning are generally too obvious to need elaboration, it may be worth taking note of a not-so-obvious virtue. A 1964 survey for Carrier Corporation revealed that people like to sleep covered. Twice as many feel more comfortable sleeping under blankets (meaning with the air conditioning on in summer) as without. Said one respondent: "I don't know why, but even on hot nights I have to have a sheet or something over me. Maybe it's for psychological reasons of security." (From Opinion Research, "Central Air," 25.)

Evaporator
Coil

Blower

Condenser
Coil

Compressor

How central air conditioning works: 1. An indoor thermostat automatically switches on the condensing unit of the central air conditioner, pumping high-pressure liquid refrigerant into the house through a closed loop of copper tubing. 2. At the evaporator coil inside the air-supply duct of the furnace, the refrigerant enters an expansion valve to be depressurized and chilled to about 40°F. The refrigerant flows inside the evaporator coil's tubing while the furnace blower forces indoor air up and around the coil. The refrigerant boils as it absorbs heat from the indoor air, turning from a liquid to a hot vapor. Ducts carry the cool, dry air throughout the house. 3. The vaporized refrigerant flows to the outdoor condensing unit and enters the compressor, where the gas is forced into increasingly smaller chambers, compressing it to a hot (about 120°F.) high-pressure vapor. 4. The compressor pumps the refrigerant over to the condenser coil. Here the refrigerant uses the coil's metal fins to release some of its captured heat to the air circulating in the condensing unit. The refrigerant condenses to a liquid again. A fan quietly blows the hot air out of the top of the unit. The refrigerant makes the loop back to the house, and the cycle continues until the desired temperature is reached. Then the thermostat automatically shuts off the condensing unit and blower motor. On a smaller scale, a window air conditioner works the same way. So too, essentially, does a refrigerator.

(Illustration by Barry Ross. Courtesy of the Carrier Corporation)

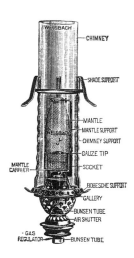

CHIMNEY

SHADE SUPPORT

MANTLE
MANTLE SUPPORT
CHIMNEY SUPPORT
GAUZE TIP

MANTLE
CARRIER

SOCKET

BOBESCHE SUPPORT
GALLERY
BUNSEN TUBE
AIR SHUTTER
GAS
REGULATOR
BUNSEN TUBE

LIGHTING

A BURNING QUESTION

Force of habit dictates our saying that a lightbulb "burns." Before the age of electricity, only combustion — in a candle, an oil lamp, or an early gas burner — produced light. The habit persists, and light continues to be identified with burning, even though modern lighting no longer involves combustion.

The commonest electric lightbulbs are incandescent (from the Latin *incandescere*, to glow). The bulb's essential feature is a filament that glows rather than burns inside its protective enclosure. Hence, whereas the candle literally burns up as it produces light, the electric lightbulb is not noticeably changed at all. Hundreds of hours after first being lit, it still looks the same. Minutes after being lit, the candle begins to disappear.

Paradoxically, the candle may also be said to be incandescent. It is not just the flame that provides illumination but also the glowing of particles of carbon from wick and wax, combusted to white-hot by the heat of the flame. But what is commonly recognized as incandescence is what made lighting modern, and that may be said to date from roughly the 1880s and the incandescent electric lightbulb.

Coincidentally there appeared the Welsbach gas mantle — also incandescent as we will see — which so revolutionized gaslight that its preeminence was taken for granted in 1895: "The Welsbach invention has so cheapened [the cost of] gas-light that it may be said it has no competitor but the heavenly bodies." Others expressed the same opinion. *Popular Science* that same year declared that "Notwithstanding the rapid development of electric lighting, the use of gas in dwelling houses, offices, and stores is undoubtedly so convenient and comparatively safe that for many years to come it will constitute the chief means of artificial illumination."

This great promise was offered by a new kind of gaslight developed by chemist and engineer Carl Auer von Welsbach of Vienna. Light from gas was originally produced by a flame issuing from a simple aperture in a pipe. The Welsbach invention, patented in 1885, was a mantle, or sheath, of fabric over and around the aperture; impregnated with metallic rare-earth elements, the mantle itself did not burn. Rather, it glowed brightly, or incandesced, from the heat of the gas flame. The idea of a mantle was not new, but the use of rare-earth compounds made it practical. Glowing at white heat, the Welsbach mantle gave off not merely more light but a steadier and more pleasing light as well.

Gaslight for a time remained preeminent. But it was Edison and not Welsbach who would light the new century, who would make a convert of even so enthralled a beholder of gaslight as Harry J. Thorne, the wonder-struck lad, encountered earlier, who was in his uncle's store when the gaslight first went on ("We beheld the glory of

the new wonder"). Born in the age of candlelight, he lived through one wonder to behold another, thus to write in the early twentieth century: "With some friends I found myself in front of one of the great theaters of the city the other night. Before we entered, I stood wonder struck at the brilliant spectacle. Night was

OPPOSITE PAGE: *The Welsbach gas mantle: incandescence applied to gas lighting. It is not the burning of the gas but rather its heat that produces light. The mantle is made of fabric impregnated with rare earths. The burning gas heats the mantle to white-hot, causing it to glow and produce a light that is steadier and more pleasing than the light produced directly by a gas flame.* (**Edward Byrn,** *Progress of Invention*)

ABOVE: *Probably the prototype of the electric incandescent lamp was this primitive device first described in Philosophical Magazine in 1845 by William Robert Grove, then professor of physics at the London Institution. It consisted of a coil of platinum wire (center top) inside an inverted glass set in a container of distilled water. The coil was hooked up to a voltaic battery by two copper wires and produced, Grove said, "a steady light."* (**Edward Byrn,** *Progress of Invention*)

changed to day, everywhere the glorious electric display delighted me. . . . what a marvel it all was!" Electricity, the ultimate in thumb-and-finger convenience, had emerged.

Experimentation with electric light began at the same time David Melville was lighting his house with gas. In England in 1807 Sir Humphry Davy created light with electricity using a device powered by a battery of two thousand pairs of plates. It sent a 4-inch electric arc between two sticks of charcoal.

The first practical use of arc lighting, once developed, was for lighthouses on the coast of England, beginning in 1858. Arc light could produce a brilliant beam that pierced the blackness, and in coming years was also found useful in lighting streets, railroad stations, freight depots, and factories. The Cleveland *Herald* in 1878 reported on a demonstration of a system, estimated to be equivalent to eight hundred gas burners, installed at the Union Steel Screw Company: "The effect was most brilliant. The rooms were flooded with a pure white light like the light of the sun, and it streamed out at all the windows, illuminating houses and streets for a long distance in every direction."

Such brilliance was fine for factories, railroad stations, streetlights, and lighthouses, but not for people's living rooms. Practical electric lighting for the household was an objective that occupied no few inventive minds and produced no few solutions—but nothing for the time being matched the simplicity and practicality of gaslight. For the opposite of simplicity there was this innovation, as described in 1877:

> *Messrs. Voison and Drouier, of Paris, have just patented a new scheme for obtaining light from an electric current. The apparatus consists of a single cell inclosed in a light mahogany case, in the top of which is a small central hole, through which projects a brass rod or "plunger," having a spiral spring and communicating with the zinc plate of the battery within the case. The battery is brought into play by pressing down the plunger so as to cause the immersion of the zinc plate.*

Thomas Edison's brilliance of mind would bring simplicity and practicality to electric lighting. In December 1879 a newspaper reported that

> *a short, thick-set man, with grimy hands led the way through his workshop, and willingly explained the distinctive features of what he and many others look on as an apparatus which will soon cause gas-light to be a thing of the past. The lamp which Mr. Edison regards as a crowning triumph is a model of simplicity and economy. In the lamp the light is emitted by a horseshoe of carbonized paper about two and a half inches long and the width of a thread. The horseshoe is in a glass globe, from which the air has been as thoroughly exhausted as science is able to do. . . . Here the inventor gave a practical illustration of his invention. He was standing just under an ordinary gas chandelier in which two of his lamps were burning. He took one of the lamps out, and it appeared simply as a glass globe. He placed it back in the burner, and immediately a brilliant horse-shoe of golden light illuminated the globe. Mr. Edison then, by turning a screw in the lamp, brought the light down to a spark, turned it off completely, as gas can be turned off, and turned it on again to a brilliant incandescence by a twist of his fingers. He certainly demonstrated in his own laboratory at Menlo Park [that] the electric light is as obedient to his will as the gas light is to the general public.*

The theory of the incandescent bulb was sound, but the practicality was still widely questioned. Edison's reputation as an extraordinary inventor did not guarantee success. "There are problems involved," said one writer, "which are far greater than any embodied in any previous invention or improvement of Mr. Edison." In 1879 Edison had made a lamp using carbonized cotton thread; it was the first he considered successful. Then he found that ordinary bristol board provided a carbon filament with an even longer life, and it was this that he demonstrated for reporters in his laboratory. Later he used bamboo and, in the 1890s, viscous cellulose.

In any case, a key to the incandescent lightbulb (along with a filament of high enough resistance) was the creation of a vacuum within the glass housing so that the filament would glow instead of burn up. The air was evacuated through a nipple at the top of the bulb. (This was the reason for the familiar pointed top of the early bulb; since the 1920s the air has been evacuated at the bottom, through a nipple covered over by the socket, leaving a tipless top.) Subsequently, reliance on a vacuum was superseded by the use of inert gas (nitrogen, argon), which allowed the filament to glow at a somewhat higher temperature. Hence, largely through the work of Edison, incandescence was made practical for electric lighting. In the protective, oxygenless environment of its glass bulb, a filament could glow, if not forever, at least for a thousand hours and more.

The Night the Lights Went On

Edison's Pearl Street Station in New York City went into operation on September 4, 1882, supplying electric light to an area bounded by Pearl, Nassau, Spruce, and Wall Streets. As it happened this included what was then the New York Times Building. The anonymous *Times* reporter who covered the story—writing with the new light—thus recorded not only broad historic detail but also the personal thrill of actually making history:

Although gaslight continued to be used in homes well into the new century, the decision of the public over time was likewise unanimously in favor of electric light, and

Edison's electric lightbulb, as illustrated in 1900. Its elements were described this way: A is the exhausted globe; B, carbon filament; CC, wires sealed in glass; D, line of fusion of two parts of globe; EF, insulating material; G, screw threads; HI, metal socket; J, fixture arm; K, circuit-controlling key. Today's lightbulb is still essentially the same. (**Edward Byrn**, *Progress of Invention*)

the lightbulb has changed little since those early years. Except for the use of tungsten for the filament and frosting to diffuse its glow, the lightbulb has perhaps undergone less modernization than any other household convenience.

The most significant addition to household illumination is another form of lighting that, by curious happenstance, was conceived at the time when both incandescent electric light and the Welsbach gas mantle were coming into use. But this one took much longer to reach household use: From *Popular Science* in 1880:

> *Dr. Phipson has proposed a new method of solving the question of a cheap household light. He has succeeded, with a comparatively feeble electric current, in perceptibly increasing the phosphorescence of certain bodies which are made faintly light by the rays of the sun. He incloses in a Geissler tube, containing a gas in a more or less rarefied condition, a phosphorescent body, the sulphuret of barium, for instance. By causing a constant current of a certain intensity to pass through the tube, he obtains a uniform and an agreeable light, at an expense he estimates to be less than that of gaslight.*

Here, well before its time, was the forerunner of fluorescent lighting. Not until 1938 did it become available for the home, and it came into general use only after World War II. Fluorescent light's virtues were as easy to recognize then as today. One writer observed in 1940 that fluorescent lamps "rival daylight in illumination but give out little heat . . . [and] their efficiency is also much higher than that of comparable incandescent lamps." The modern fluorescent lamp produces three and a half times as much light per watt as an incandescent, but it is also more costly.

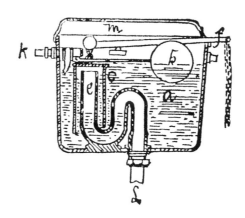

The Bathroom

Reflecting on Progress

Can you think of any room in the house which reflects the progress . . . of comfort and of convenience . . . more than the bathroom?

—House & Garden, September 1926

It was the bathroom that was changing fastest in the American home—or if not just changing, becoming in-house as opposed to outhouse.

How many homes had bathrooms in 1926? It is not possible to say. We may hazard a guess that perhaps no more than 15 percent of American homes had complete bathrooms in 1900. By 1940 the U.S. Census Bureau had begun to include such details of everyday life, and there is a firm figure—55 percent of American homes had at least one complete private bathroom that year. Keeping in mind that more than half of American homes in 1926 thus were not yet a part of this great change, it is nevertheless useful to see what was happening, for change there was, and it was significant.

The early bathrooms—those that included a water closet and a tub and sometimes a sink—were purely functional places that were probably occupied for no longer than necessary. Today's bathroom, on the other hand, serves a range of purposes. It is the scene of a wide assortment of daily routines that have nothing to do with bathing or elimination—brushing teeth, putting on makeup, shaving, cutting one's nails, inserting contact lenses, taking medication, cleaning and treating cuts and scrapes, weighing oneself, using a sunlamp, and even in some rare instances, where the bathroom is large enough and appropriately fitted out, exercising.

While the bathroom of the late 1920s was not quite so sophisticated, this description lets us see the change coming:

> Contrast our modern bathroom with its older prototype and note the difference. The old tin painted tub enclosed by stained pine boarding has gone, never to return. Its place is taken by a gleaming white vitreous china or porcelain one, built into a tiled floor. . . . The toilets of today are noiseless and well ventilated. Showers have solved the question of a morning bath in the minimum of time. No more is the bathroom itself a dingy closet with barely enough room for its fixtures and one small window. It is now given as much consideration in planning as any other room of the house. . . . It is now made into a pleasant and cheerful room. . . . Each bathroom has at least one large closet and a smaller medicine cabinet. Lights are placed so that the man may see his face distinctly in the mirror while shaving. Dressing tables have been introduced into the bathroom to hold the necessary toilet articles for the mistress of the house. The Spartan simplicity of the bathroom, until recently in vogue, is slowly dying out.
> (House & Garden, September 1926)

By the later 1920s the bathroom looked (and worked) as it does today. To see this more fully, let's look at its components: first at the water closet, which was becoming the "toilet" in the late 1920s—a sort of unofficial recognition of its coming of age by its being given a new name. And yet not all was new.

The use of water in conjunction with human elimination, as we have seen, goes back to the *latrinae* of ancient Rome and to even older primitive prototypes of water closets in Mohenjo Daro c. 2500 B.C. It was likewise to antiquity that sanitary engineers

OPPOSITE PAGE: *Winn's Syphon Tank, England, c. 1884. A cylinder (c) is raised by the lever (f) emptying water into and starting a siphon in the tubing (e), thus sending water into the bowl below through the outlet (l). Other parts shown are the tank (a), float (b), supply pipe (k), and cover (m). Here is the typical modern toilet tank in early but recognizable form.* (Brown, Water-Closets, 1884)

turned for one of the principal features separating the water closet of the 1860s from that of the twentieth century, the siphon.

The siphon is a natural pump. Archimedes and Hero of Alexandria were familiar with siphons, and the Greeks commonly used them in their water supply systems (the Romans to a lesser extent in conjunction with their massive aqueducts).

The useful qualities of the siphon were applicable to the bowl or tank of a water closet. To see how, let us take a closer look at what happens within a siphon. The siphon involves the use of a tube or pipe bent more or less into an inverted *U* with one leg shorter than the other. This shorter leg is inserted into a container from which liquid is to be drawn through the longer leg. The secret of the siphon is *net* atmospheric pressure (the difference between atmospheric pressure and the weight of the liquid). Atmospheric pressure alone is the same at both openings, but because the weight of the liquid in the shorter leg is less, the net pressure is greater. Hence the liquid in the first container is pushed up through that tube, over and across the inverted *U*, and down the other leg.

In the water closet the net reduction of pressure on the drain side helps atmospheric pressure push contents through. This fundamental change took the water closet from the nineteenth century—whether an archaic valve closet or the equally archaic pan closet—and made it the modern toilet. The flushing effect induced by the siphon is considerably greater than what happens when a valve is opened and the water merely flows down the drain by gravity.

Roughly speaking, the 1880s marked the beginning of the transition to the modern toilet—the Standard Sanitary Manufacturing Company, later American Standard, for example, produced its first water closet in 1885—and it was the application of the siphon that showed the greatest promise. Tanks based on the siphon principle were also being produced in England by the early 1880s. The Doulton Syphon Tank c. 1884 was described this way at the time:

> This tank is waste preventing, and its contents are emptied by means of a syphon. An annular syphon is surrounded by a cylinder, air tight on top and connected with the lever . . . [which] must be pulled down; this raises the cylinder and empties enough water into the syphon to start it into action. A two-gallon flush is obtained in this way without the necessity of holding the lever down for a moment. The supply is governed by the usual float-valve, and there is also an overflow in case the supply valve should leak.

Another form of siphon tank, Winn's (see diagram on page 220), looks remarkably similar to the modern-day tank, including its cover. Tank covers were common in England in the 1880s but not in America. Their purpose was to keep dust and impurities from settling in the water in the tank. By the very early 1900s tanks were beginning to be lowered from near the ceiling, where they had been since the days of Cumming and Bramah (before modern plumbing and water supply the height had enhanced water pressure). Now it was the "low down" water closet gaining popularity, and a covered tank was essential.

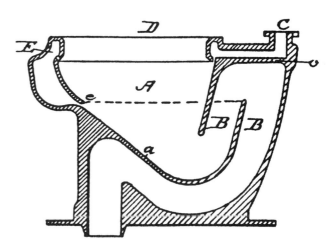

The siphon jet water closet, first U.S. patent, 1890. The bowl is a one-piece earthenware shell. C *is the intake from the tank. When flushed, some of the water is discharged through a "jet-forming orifice" (lowercase* c *at right), forcing out air in* B, *and producing a partial vacuum that starts the siphon action.* (U. S. Patent No. 441,268)

A bowl based on the principle of the siphon was patented in the United States in 1890. If we look at the illustration we can see that the bowl is a one-piece earthenware shell. The bowl of a pan closet or a Bramah was simply and literally that—a bowl, of chinaware or metal, with a hole in the bottom, the hole being sealed by a valve—a mechanical device. The 1890 siphon bowl, on the other hand, had no moving parts and hence was no longer mechanical. The siphon effect (rather than just gravity) caused the water and contents to empty while a trap that was part of the design sealed the opening to prevent sewer gas from backing up. This was also a far more sanitary device since it had no working parts to be fouled, as was notoriously the case with the pan closet. One of the earliest manufacturers, the Syphon Closet Company, explained in 1890 that the virtue of siphon design was "the exceedingly simple and natural working of its parts—its freedom from springs and unreliable valves; no openings likely to be choked, or become impure; absence of imperfect overflow devices and insecure traps that collect filth; and, in fact, the complete and perfect working of all its parts, in compliance with natural laws."

By 1910 all of the mechanical closets—the valve closet dating back to Cumming and Bramah, the pan closet so prevalent by the 1860s, and the plunger, a mid- to late-nineteenth-century version of the oldest form of all—were largely gone. Sanitary authority William Paul Gerhard in 1910 declared that, "At the present time pan-closets

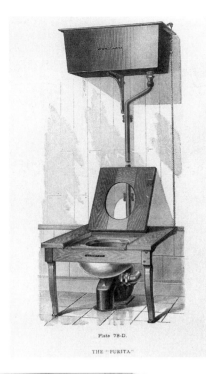

Plate 78-D.

THE "PURITA"

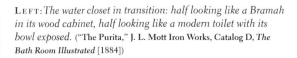

LEFT: *The water closet in transition: half looking like a Bramah in its wood cabinet, half looking like a modern toilet with its bowl exposed.* ("The Purita," J. L. Mott Iron Works, Catalog D, *The Bath Room Illustrated* [1884])

BELOW: *The essentially modern bathroom, 1933: Evergreen, Baltimore, Maryland. The low-tank toilet began to come into use shortly after the turn of the century.* (Photograph by the author. By permission of Evergreen/Johns Hopkins University)

are scarcely to be found, except in very old houses. In many cities and towns the plumbing regulations very properly prohibit their use altogether. Valve and plunger closets have likewise been discarded."

Combination of siphon action in both the tank and the bowl was considered essential. An authoritative account of the water closet in 1906 declared the siphon (more accurately the siphon jet) water closet "the best form of closet on the market. But it must be supplied from a flushing tank that is specially constructed to discharge the proper amount of water, preferably a siphon cistern."

Meanwhile, another element in the evolution of the modern toilet can be traced to the Bramah water closet: the flushing rim. The Bramah had a little flap inside the bowl (M in the illustration on page 86) that partially covered the inlet for water from the cistern. The purpose of this mouthpiece or fan (thoughtfully made removable in case it got clogged with sediment) was to make the water splash and thus wash out more of the bowl than would be the case with a simple stream—an innovative idea in 1778. In time the function of the fan came to be served by a device encircling the entire top of the bowl—the flushing rim. Furthermore, by this time, vitreous china was being used in all quality closets, and lead pipe, often prohibited by plumbing ordinances, was being restricted to

This typical modern toilet continues to use siphon jet action but needs only 1.6 gallons to flush as efficiently as older models did with 3.5 gallons. (Courtesy of the Kohler Co.)

soil and waste pipes, bends, and traps. Other metals—chiefly brass, copper, and iron—were coming into wider use for plumbing generally.

By 1915 the recognizably modern toilet—now with a low tank and siphon-powered—was a part of everyday life. According to plumbing authority R. M. Starbuck:

Modern water closets are superior to the old-style water closets of the pan, valve, and plunger styles in every respect. . . . Since the principle of siphonic action has been applied to the water closet . . . the siphon and siphon-jet fixtures have taken the precedence over all other forms, and it appears to be only a matter of time before they will supplant the less satisfactory forms entirely.

While there have been many refinements, and while some variations exist, the basic design of the average American toilet has changed little during the twentieth century. Most toilets now use siphon action, although some have a pressurized flush, which is usually noisier and more costly. There are also some with dual flushing mechanisms—one a mini-flush for liquid waste only. Some changes in the toilet have come as a response to a greater awareness of the need to conserve water. American toilets of the mid-twentieth century generally used 5 gallons per flush. This was subsequently reduced to 3.5, but federal law now mandates that all toilets manufactured after January 1, 1994, flush with a maximum of 1.6 gallons. This has been achieved with the use of either a pressurized tank or a standard flush toilet with a steeper bowl and a taller, slimmer tank to increase flow with less water.

Even in the simple little bathroom of the flat or the bungalow we have grown to expect much—soap recesses to hold the cake we once groped for or slipped on—fixtures made from such china as is used in dinner-plates—grab-rods by which we emerge from our tubbing with less danger of skidding—showers aloft, mirrors roundabout, and plate-glass shelves at hand; and also a fine, stout door with a lock on it.
— FAIRFAX DOWNEY, 1926

Other components of the modern bathroom have more prosaic stories than the water closet. The tub of 1926 was, for all practical purposes, the same tub one might find in the average home in the late twentieth century except that different materials—fiberglass in particular—are often used today.

The tub of 1926 still had the company of the old-fashioned tub that was its predecessor. Those tubs were still around. "It needs no old-timer," said Downey, "to recall the early type tin tub, with its broad wooden rim. Many of them are yet in use in old manses, and they are far from having attained the repose and dignity of museum pieces."

Although some such relics remained in use, however, the really old-fashioned tub had been on its way out for many years. Just before the turn of the century, plumbing manufacturer Jordan L. Mott recalled the bathtub that was "a wooden box lined with lead, a primitive and unsightly fixture. Following that came cast-iron bath-tubs, painted

An essentially modern bathtub—as opposed to a tin or copper shell inside a wooden cabinet—was available by 1878. Made of cast iron, it came in plain, galvanized, and enamel finish. Note the holes for faucets, which were now incorporated into the tub. It was available at either 54 or 60 inches in length. (J. L. Mott Iron Works, 1878 Illustrated Catalog)

The really up-to-date bathtub of the beginning of the twentieth century included a shower with a white rubber curtain (e) *and such accessories as a soap dish* (i), *a sponge rack* (j), *and a towel rack* (k). *The shower stall was also in use at this time but was only occasionally to be found.*
(**International Library of Technology,** vol. 71, 1906)

inside and out, and next a box lined with copper, which was the favorite bath for many years. A quarter of a century ago [c. 1870] was commenced here [New York] the manufacture of porcelain-lined bath-tubs, which for a long time were brought out exclusively by the company [J. L. Mott] of which I am the head."

The typical tub of 1926 was 5 feet long and made of cast iron coated with white porcelain enamel—inside and out if higher quality, coated inside and painted white outside if less expensive. Top-quality fixtures—sinks as well as tubs—were made of vitreous china. Cost also affected design. Less expensive tubs still had feet (often vague vestiges of the ball-and-claw feet that typify the 1890s and turn of the century) while higher-priced ones had a built-in look. While white was most common, colored fixtures were appearing in the bathroom as well as the kitchen. "Now we may have our bathrooms done in soft rose or warm brown tiles, with the frame of the tub tiled to match," noted Downey.

Showers were also in use, sometimes as separate stalls, sometimes incorporated into the tub. Downey's comment about "showers aloft" is probably a reference to the fact that in times past the "simple little bathroom" often had to make do with a flexible hose fixed to the bathtub faucet, the hose then being held over one's head in the tub. But a shower aloft meant a separate showerhead over the tub and a shower curtain suspended from a rod that encircled the tub. Or the tub might be built into an enclosure, so that the curtain need cover only the open side of the tub.

Also available was the shower stall, typically a steel enclosure with a duck curtain. For the really convenient shower there was the single-unit mixer faucet instead of separate hot and cold taps.

Although a bathroom of the late 1920s would look dated today, the average bathroom of modern America really represents no dramatic change. But such advances as single hot and cold water controls for convenience, the use of one-piece fiberglass tubs and showers for easier maintenance, and low-flow showerheads for water conservation attest to the continuing evolution of the American bathroom.

A really avant-garde shower at the turn of the twenty-first century simulates a return to nature. This 20-inch-wide cascade of water is said to drench the bather while soothing neck and upper back muscles. A custom installation, it is offered with a choice of wall coverings and shower doors. (Courtesy of the Kohler Co.)

APPLIANCES

"THEN THE MACHINE TAKES OVER"

For most American households in the early twentieth century, there were only hints of the revolution in comfort and convenience to come. Doing the laundry, for example, was usually the same drudgery it had been — something on the order of what was described (albeit with a little self-serving hyperbole) by the Acme Washing Machine Company in a 1905 brochure:

> There are today hundreds of thousands of women in this great land of ours, who spend every week four, five, and even more long, weary hours, standing over a hot, steaming wash-tub, rubbing away their health and strength on the old-fashioned wash-board. . . . And most of these hours are spent in rubbing, rubbing, rubbing — until their arms and shoulders ache, as if they had been pounded. And all the time they are inhaling the steam and odors arising from tub full after tub full of soiled garments, getting their own clothes wringing wet, which frequently means bad colds and rheumatism, when going out of doors to hang up the clothes. And when

PREVIOUS PAGE: *The first electric dryer, invented by J. Ross Moore in 1930, weighed 700 pounds. With its heating element underneath, it sometimes scorched the clothes. In later models Moore placed the element above and added a thermostat. The original design was purchased by Hamilton Manufacturing Company.* (Courtesy of Friday Associates International on behalf of General Electric Company)

ABOVE: *The mechanization of Monday. There was a time when laundry was traditionally done on Monday. With today's automatics, it can be done any or every day—or evening. Here is a chronology of the transition. 1. The Gravity Washer, c. 1900, still completely manual and little changed from the 1860s. 2. The Thor, made by the Hurley Machine Company, 1906. This first electric washer was chain-driven. 3. Maytag Model 90, 1927,was electrically powered, but it still required use of hand wringers. A one-cylinder gasoline motor was sold where electricity was not available. 4. The Jeep, 1947, made by Whirlpool and also marketed by Sears, Roebuck under the Kenmore brand name—one of the first automatics. It was top-loading and had three wash-rinse temperature settings. 5. Kenmore, 1971, designed for the permanent press era. The first washer with a permanent press cycle was marketed in 1965. 6. The Maytag Neptune, washer-dryer combination, 1998. This washer features a dispenser that automatically adds detergent, bleach, and softener at the right times.* (1. Whirlpool Corporation. 2. Friday Associates International on behalf of General Electric Company. 3. Maytag Company. 4. and 5. Whirlpool Corporation. 6. Maytag Company)

wash-day is over, then comes an hour or two of sewing on buttons, or
mending and repairing the damage done the clothes by the wash-board.

Although this gloomy narrative was meant to sell washing machines, it was probably a fair account of what laundry day was like for most American women. Writing in the *Ladies' Home Journal* in 1912, author Christine Frederick gave it as her opinion that, "Washing is done in most houses without washing machines and with only a common boiler [kitchen-range water heater]."

Even where there was a washing machine, it was probably still a simple device, commonly a tub with a hand-powered gyrator and wringer. Simple though it was, the fact that it used a gyrator to produce rotary motion as opposed to some mechanism simulating the action of the human arm, as had been the solution of many an inventor, made it ready for the new age.

In 1906 came the Thor, generally considered the first electric washer. It was chain-driven and was produced by the Hurley Machine Company. By about 1907 an electric washer was also being manufactured by the National Electric Supply Company. Operating on either AC or DC current, it had a one-tenth horsepower motor.

Meanwhile, rotary motion provided only half of the transition to the modern washer. Even though a crank, and later electric power, could effectively spin the clothes through sudsy water so as to produce a washing action, it was still necessary to use a wringer to extract the water before each new cycle, from soaking to final rinsing. Eliminating the need for a wringer may be regarded as the last significant step in the transition to the modern automatic washer. This came in 1926 with an Easy Company washer that used centrifugal force rather than a wringer to extract water.

Even so, it was not until after World War II that fully automatic washers became common. *McCall's* magazine in September 1945 announced the age of the automatic: "Only a few lucky women had such washers before the war. . . . [They] work without watching—after the clothes and soap have been put in, dials are set for time and temperature. Then the machine takes over: it washes and rinses thoroughly, removes much of the water, and shuts off."

Machines were slower to take over the other half of the laundry chore, drying. Even after the first electric washing machines were in use, the laundry was still being dried on a line in the backyard or on racks in the basement. The first electric dryer was devised in 1930 by J. Ross Moore, but it had two major shortcomings that kept it from being commercially viable: it weighed 700 pounds and had a tendency to scorch clothes. Because dryers remained little known until the end of World War II, they needed to be explained for the homemaker who was still using a clothesline: "While the second load of clothes is washing, the first load is transferred to the drier which tumbles them gently in heated air until dry." Homemakers caught on fast, and in the postwar years dryers became ever more popular. By the end of the century washers and dryers were commonly sold in pairs.

OTHER APPLIANCES

An early-twentieth-century survey on the use of labor-saving devices in the household offers some useful data on the evolution of appliances. The survey was included in a short book, *The Household Budget* (1917), by John B. Leeds and examined the use of labor-saving machinery among sixty families. The one machine used by all sixty was the sewing machine. Observed Leeds:

> *It would seem almost as strange to calculate the time saved by the use of a sewing machine as it would to credit the saving made by the use of a stove rather than an open fireplace for cooking, so accustomed have most of us become to the presence and use of this great labor-saving device. Possibly a generation hence our children will feel the same way regarding some of the implements with which we are just now commencing to experiment.*

How many of these sewing machines were electric, we do not know. Most were probably not. I. M. Singer and Company produced an electric sewing machine in 1889, but the treadle-operated model continued to predominate for many years. One writer in 1927 explained what an electric machine was like, suggesting that it was unfamiliar to most people:

A 1917 survey of sixty families found that the one appliance used by all sixty was the sewing machine. Some were electrics, but most sewing machines were still treadle-operated. Here, in Abilene, Kansas, Ida Eisenhower's treadle model. (Courtesy of the Dwight D. Eisenhower Library)

The electric sewing machine, as the name implies, is simply a sewing machine of whatever type is desired operated by a small electric motor rather than by foot power. . . . The function of the electrified sewing machine is to make anywhere from ten to fifty stitches grow where one grew before — in other words, an enormous acceleration of speed over that of the old foot-power machine. At the same time, fatigue on the part of the operator is largely eliminated.

Although the 100 percent saturation reported by Leeds could hardly hold true for the entire population, it is not an exaggeration to say that the sewing machine, whether foot-operated or electric, sooner or later found its way into nearly every home. In retrospect, however, a significant impact of the sewing machine was not its prevalence or even its own technology so much as its influence on the proliferation of other forms of household technology. It was the first widely advertised consumer product, and since the purchase price was high ($75 in the 1860s), I. M. Singer and Company offered installment buying. Hence to the sewing machine — ahead of its time, since installment buying did not become common until the 1920s — goes the distinction of pioneering the way in which countless Americans came to modernize their homes in the twentieth century.

The second most common appliance, in the new age of labor-saving devices, Leeds found to be the carpet sweeper, which was used by fifty-six of the sixty families in his survey. Roughly half also had vacuum cleaners. Both the carpet sweeper and the mechanical bellows vacuum we have seen.

The modern vacuum cleaner arrived with the age of electricity and steadily gained popularity. *McCall's* magazine in 1945 observed that "They have come to be a necessity in every home." And indeed, by the late twentieth century rare was the home without an electric vacuum cleaner. *McCall's* detailed twelve models, both uprights and tank-types, most with attachment tools. Except for minor styling changes and increased cleaning effectiveness, vacuum cleaners at the end of the twentieth century remained largely the same as those of fifty years ago.

The one major appliance that is common today but was used by absolutely no one interviewed for Leeds's survey is the dishwasher. "Expense" or "not needed" were the most common reasons his respondents cited. One participant actually replied that it was unnecessary because "dish washing [is] good training for girls"! In fact the dishwasher was still very rare in the household, although commercial models were not

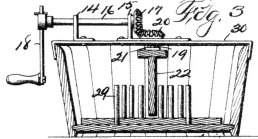

TOP: *A dish cleaner was first patented in 1863. It consisted basically of a tub with a crank and a slotted basket inside to hold the dishes. Still essentially the same was this Cyclone, with part of its dish receptacle apparently no longer intact. This device was patented in 1905, said its inventor, "to avoid the drudgery . . . incident to washing dishes." But since turning the crank fast enough to generate enough cleaning action, and from time to time reversing the cranking motion to clean the other side of the plates, was drudgery in its own right, this and similar devices seem to have attained little popularity. Like most real labor-saving household appliances, the dishwasher awaited the coming of the compact electric motor.* (Photograph by the author, courtesy of Museum Village, Monroe, New York)

LEFT: *Dish-washing machine. The Cyclone in a patent drawing.* (U.S. Patent 793,395, June 27, 1905)

BELOW LEFT: *The early vacuum cleaner. This Vacuette Model C, made by Scott & Fetzer, is based on a patent issued in 1917. Like many similar devices, its appearance, once manufactured, went beyond the essentials of its patent drawing.* (Photograph by the author, Museum Village, Monroe, New York)

BELOW RIGHT: *The Vacuette in a patent drawing.* (U.S. Patent 1,230,827, June 19, 1917)

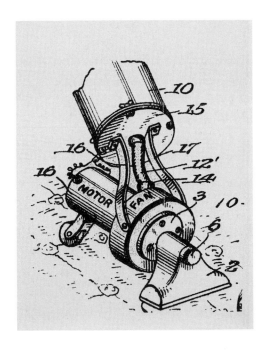

uncommon. The fact that Leeds asked about it is therefore interesting. Here was something on the horizon in 1917 — something that the housewife could look forward to.

The dishwasher in concept can be traced back to 1863 and the patenting of a "dish cleaner" that had the essential features of its modern counterpart. It consisted of a tub with a slotted wire basket inside. The dishes were to be placed in the slots, the tub filled with soap and hot water, and then the machine turned with a hand crank. Other similar devices were later produced; but until the coming of the compact electric motor, the degree of labor saving was negligible because of the need to turn the crank and to fill and empty the tub by hand.

A hand-operated dishwasher produced in 1909 by the Walker Brothers in the rear of their hardware store in Syracuse, New York, eventually turned the tide. Two years later they equipped it with a gasoline engine. And in 1913 the Walkers introduced their first electric-power model. Over the coming years the Walkers made a number of improvements, and by 1924 there was a compact unit small enough to be built into the

LEFT: *The first successful electric dishwasher, the Walker, also started out hand-cranked. It was then powered by a gasoline engine before becoming an "electric sink" in 1924. This was an actual convenience now, with its electric power. It was also simpler to use by being built into the plumbing supply so there was no need to fill it with water and empty it by hand.* (Courtesy of Friday Associates International on behalf of General Electric Company)

RIGHT: *Built in to the point of being almost unnoticed is this state-of-the-art modern dishwasher.* (Courtesy of General Electric Company)

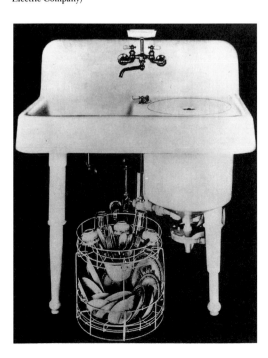

Over the years: a collection of KitchenAid mixers. (Courtesy of Whirlpool Corporation)

sink itself and filled through a circular lid in the drainboard. Further improvements in 1927 made the Walker lighter and more efficient. The propeller, valve, and overflow system incorporated into it remain essential features of the modern dishwasher. Walker Brothers was bought out by General Electric in 1930.

At roughly the time the electric dishwasher came into use there appeared another "appliance of the future" that in fact had a relatively brief future: the electric ironer. (A similar device, gas- or steam-heated, for table linens and sheets, had been offered by Montgomery Ward in 1895.) The ironer was a technological update of Benjamin Franklin's mangle, which so impressed George Washington because of the "facility with which it dispatched business." In its modern form, heated by gas or electricity, it used either a roller or a flat plate and was still most useful for flatwork like Franklin's tablecloths. The relatively brief popularity of the ironer declined as its usefulness was eclipsed by the automatic dryer and the use of permanent press fabrics, particularly since most ironers were console models that took up a significant amount of space.

The simple iron has enjoyed a more permanent career. Some early irons were hollow, so as to be filled with hot coals, glowing charcoal, or heated iron slugs; others, made of solid cast iron, were called sadirons. The first electric model was patented in 1882, although electrics did not come into wide use until after 1900. The first "steaming iron" appeared in 1926 and the first thermostatically controlled one in 1934. The spray-steam iron was an innovation of 1957, and Teflon coating was developed in 1965.

Of small appliances, particularly those that proliferated with the coming of electricity, there is a vast variety, more than can be described in detail here. It may therefore be useful simply to take note of what is known to have come into use and when.

- *1891: electric coffee or tea pot ($6.00), electric iron ($10.00), and electric pancake griddle, all from Carpenter Electric*
- *1893: electric fan, six blades, three speeds, Dakota model ($30.00), E. S. Greeley & Co.*
- *1901: electric chafing dish ($10.50 and up) and electric curling iron heater ($3.00) both from Western Electric*
- *1902: eight-inch electric frying kettle ($12.00) and electric waffle iron ($7.50) both from Electric Appliance Co., Chicago*
- *1909: electric corn popper ($5.75), five-inch electric frying pan ($6.50), and toaster ($4.50) all from General Electric*
- *1911: cigar lighter ($2.75) and heating pad ($6.40) from General Electric*
- *1915: lighted, battery-operated electric clock with double-bell alarm ($6.68) from Western Electric Company; portable hair dryer ($20.00) and vibrator ($15.00) both from Pacific States Electric; and a one-pint water heater, also for heating baby's milk ($6.00) from General Electric.*

THE KITCHEN

OUT OF THE BLUE

In today's kitchen is an appliance that had no precedent, no unwinding history of domestic evolution. Nothing quite like it ever existed until it came out of the blue. Literally. Out of the blue-turned-ashen skies of World War II, for that is when the principle behind the microwave oven emerged into practical application.

Radar first came into use during the Battle of Britain in 1940 and helped to end the Nazi rain of terror from the sky. Radar technology began in England, which shared it with the United States. The Raytheon Company, working in cooperation with the Radiation Laboratory of the Massachusetts Institute of Technology, was designated as the American firm to collaborate with England.

Radar (*radio detecting and ranging*) uses high-frequency radio waves generated by a magnetron tube. Even before the end of the war there was speculation about peacetime use of high-frequency radio waves in the kitchen. One writer in 1944 predicted that:

A post-war innovation of the frozen food processors will be the completely prepared dinner. The shopper will choose between menus offered

238

by competing companies. . . . Then, one minute before dinnertime, she will place the precooked frozen meal, in its sectioned, plastic container, into a special electronic oven. This oven will employ high-frequency radio waves which penetrate all foods equally, warming a whole chicken as fast as a portion of peas. In a few seconds a bell will ring and the whole dinner will pop up like a piece of toast — ready to serve and eat. Best of all, there will be no pots to scrape for the plastic container will be discarded after use.

This writer's incredibly accurate prediction was apparently extrapolated from a report of the development by the W. L. Maxson Company of New York of partly cooked frozen dinners for the armed forces. Immediately after the war, development of the "special electronic oven" began in earnest. Raytheon had turned out roughly half a million magnetrons during the war. With that kind of production capacity already intact, it made good business sense to find a peacetime application for the magnetron tube that made radar work.

The company wasted no time. The first microwave oven, called a Radarange, was unveiled and demonstrated for the press at the Waldorf-Astoria Hotel in New York on October 7, 1946. "News of Food: Stove Operating with Basic Radar Tube Will Cook Household Meals in Seconds," ran the headline in the *New York Times* the next day. The story explained how it worked:

OPPOSITE PAGE: *A typical component of the postwar kitchen: a 1948 Roper gas range with double oven.* (Courtesy of Whirlpool Corporation)

LEFT: *The Radarange, 1946. In size, it was the equivalent of five modern microwave ovens stacked one atop the other, and it was available only for commercial use. And even though it was not yet something for the countertop, it already had one hallmark of microwaves to come: "a screened oven door, so that foods may be watched as they cook."* (Courtesy of Raytheon Company)

When energy from the magnetron tube is beamed to food, the heat pene-
trates at once to the interior, and so cooking periods are cut amazingly . . .
as in all culinary processes up to now, heat has had to travel from the sur-
face to the center, and though the outside might be done relatively quickly,
the inside would not, and so preparation would be lengthened. But despite
the complicated electronic principle on which they are built, Radaranges
are easy and safe to use.

It might be somewhat simpler to say that microwaves cause molecules in the food to vibrate, and this vibration produces heat inside the food without heating the surrounding air. The result is much faster cooking.

Calling it the Radarange capitalized on a term then well known to the public and easy to accept, given the strange technology it brought into the kitchen. But once the device was in production, the generic term quickly became "electronic range" and then, by the early 1970s, was semiofficially changed to "electronic oven" by the American Home Economics Association. Eventually, in recognition of the technology that makes it work, "microwave oven" took hold, and that is how it is known today.

But terminology was moot in 1946. By any name, the microwave was at first impractical. The first Radaranges were intended exclusively for commercial use. Though in full production by 1947, they were used only in restaurants, on trains, and aboard ocean liners. A prototype for household use was demonstrated in 1949. At 5 feet high and 2 feet wide, it was still the size of a refrigerator. The magnetron alone cost some $500 to produce, so the oven was very expensive. Despite its size, there was already that feature so characteristic of later microwaves: a window in the oven door, allowing the user to watch the food as it cooks.

Befitting a place in the household, the device was introduced not in a hotel, like the commercial version, but in a test kitchen at Columbia University. And the promise of things to come made up for the lack of practicality. A reporter for the *New York Times* was impressed:

When the electronic ovens are available, housewives will be able to cook
oatmeal in fifteen seconds, half a chicken in two minutes and fresh corn
on the cob in forty-five seconds. . . . The range also does an excellent job of
warming over foods that have been cooked before. Miss Fairchild demon-

strated this for us with a dish of Spanish rice that had been baked the previous day. She reheated it in the oven for two minutes and it came out as good as new.

The oatmeal had to wait. Raytheon's household model never went into production. There was no microwave for the household kitchen until 1955, when Tappan bought the rights to Raytheon's patent and introduced the first domestic microwave oven, its Model RL–1. It was designed for in-the-wall installation but was adaptable also to placement on a countertop. Although not as compact as later ovens, with dimensions of 24 by 24 by 27 inches, it nevertheless no longer rivaled the refrigerator in size. The key to making it smaller was Tappan's development of an air cooling system to keep the magnetron from overheating. The Raytheon commercial model was water-cooled, requiring a connection to the plumbing. Tappan's oven was priced at $1,200. Only 54 units were sold the first year of production, but the figure was 1,552 the following year.

In 1967 Raytheon and Amana announced plans for production of a domestic oven, and other companies followed. By the early 1970s the price of a microwave oven was down to less than $500. It is estimated that between 100,000 and 125,000 ovens were sold in 1971. The price continued to come down with changing methods of producing ever cheaper magnetrons. The microwave also gained considerable popularity in Japan in the 1970s, further stimulating competition and driving down the price. By the end of the century, a microwave oven could be had for as little as $79. Today the microwave oven, long since a compact box stylishly suited to the average countertop, is everywhere.

OTHER STEPS TO THE FUTURE

One housekeeper . . . walked 105 needless miles each year . . . round and round in a poorly planned kitchen.

—*THE NEW YORK TIMES,* JULY 3, 1927

A striking thing about the kitchen of the 1920s was the emphasis on systematic planning. It went hand in hand with the development of the kitchen's components.

In an effort to find out how far the average housewife trekked from range to icebox to table to range and so on, a domestic science expert made a study that was reported in the *New York Times* in 1927. A housewife was watched as she set out to bake a cake.

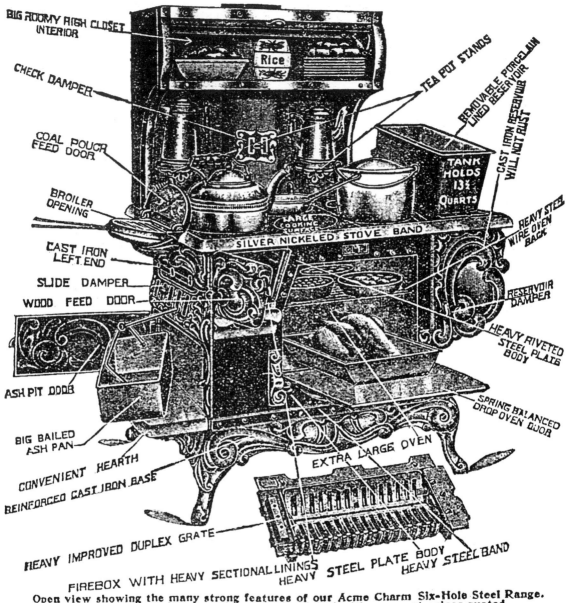

BIG ROOMY HIGH CLOSET INTERIOR

CHECK DAMPER

COAL POUCH FEED DOOR

BROILER OPENING

CAST IRON LEFT END

SLIDE DAMPER

WOOD FEED DOOR

ASH PIT DOOR

BIG BAILED ASH PAN

CONVENIENT HEARTH

REINFORCED CAST IRON BASE

HEAVY IMPROVED DUPLEX GRATE

Rice

TEA POT STANDS

REMOVABLE PORCELAIN LINED RESERVOIR

CAST IRON RESERVOIR WILL NOT RUST

TANK HOLDS 13½ QUARTS

HEAVY STEEL WIRE OVEN BACK

LARGE COOKING SURFACE

SILVER NICKELED STOVE BAND

RESERVOIR DAMPER

HEAVY RIVETED STEEL PLATE BODY

SPRING BALANCED DROP OVEN DOOR

EXTRA LARGE OVEN

FIREBOX WITH HEAVY SECTIONAL LININGS

HEAVY STEEL PLATE BODY

HEAVY STEEL BAND

Open view showing the many strong features of our Acme Charm Six-Hole Steel Range.
Cooking utensils illustrated are not furnished with range at prices quoted.

The turn-of-the-century range. Cooking appliances had been simpler in earlier times, and would become simpler again with the use of gas and electricity—and with the coming of other appliances. This is the coal- or wood-burning Acme Charm steel range. Its features included six burners, a porcelain-lined hot water reservoir, a warming closet, and a large oven with a thermometer on the door. (Sears, Roebuck and Co., catalog, 1908)

She mixed the ingredients, put the cake in the oven, baked it, took it out, and then cleaned up. Although her kitchen was only 15 feet square, she traveled 75½ feet preparing and baking the cake and another 32½ feet cleaning up. Extrapolated to a whole year's worth of cooking and baking that projected to 554,400 feet—or 105 miles—of walking back and forth.

"The old notion that a kitchen had to be a luxuriously large room of the house is passing," the *Times* reported. "A small, compact kitchen, where steps are routed and tools grouped, not only makes kitchen work less fatiguing but promotes health and happiness."

Efficiency was not a discovery of the late 1920s. In 1913, the year the Ford Motor Company began turning out Model T's on the first moving assembly line, author Christine Frederick, the wife of a corporate executive, wrote that the principles of industrial efficiency were just as important in the home as in the factory: "At first it did not occur to me that methods which were applicable to organized industries, like shoe factories and iron foundries, could be applied to my group of very unorganized industries—the home. Yet the more I studied it, the more possible it seemed . . . bringing the science of efficiency into the home." A half-century earlier, the Beecher sisters, Catharine Beecher and Harriet Beecher Stowe, were exploring new concepts of kitchen efficiency in their *American Woman's Home* (1869).

"It would be interesting to know how many thousands of unnecessary miles are traveled each year by American housewives because of poorly designed kitchens," the *Times* article of 1927 continued. The mammoth cast-iron or steel range of the period used up a lot of kitchen space, and its mass of metal generated heat, necessitating distance from the other components of the kitchen. The icebox was strategically placed away from the heat of the range and convenient for deliveries by the iceman. That meant that the icebox, with its butter and eggs, was probably some distance from the pantry with its mixing bowls and flour, and neither was likely to be immediately adjacent to the oven.

The keys to compactness were not simply a matter of design of the kitchen, however. It was the evolution of the components themselves that made compactness possible.

First, the range. Few elements of the house have made such rapid changes in appearance in so short a time as the range. In the late nineteenth and early twentieth centuries the range served assorted functions that had once been spread out on the open hearth. To this end, it had multiple burners, an oven, a warming chamber, a

LEFT: *Defying description is this prototype electric range, invented in 1904 by George A. Hughes. In the manner of a telephone switchboard of its day, it allowed for adjustment from low to medium to high by reinserting a plug in a three-stage electrical outlet. The Hughes Electric Heating Company eventually became a part of General Electric.* (Courtesy of Friday Associates International on behalf of General Electric Company)

RIGHT: *Curiously evocative of Hughes's range, with its little horizontal window, is this state-of-the-art GE electric wall oven. Any similarity ends with the window, however.* (Courtesy of General Electric Company)

teapot stand, a reservoir for storing hot water, a built-in thermostat (in later years), draft controls, and grates for burning either wood or coal, and so it was elaborate. Given the taste of the times, its design was elaborate as well. Hardly a square inch of surface escaped scrollwork or ornate floral patterns. Barely two decades later, however, modernity hit the kitchen, transforming the range into a thing of simplicity. In appearance, the 1920s range had barely a hint of its turn-of-the-century appearance. Stove black had given way to white and pastels, massiveness to compactness. Streamlined and efficient, it no longer dominated the kitchen as had the range of old but seemed content to accept a new role as merely one of the team.

This evolution reflects in large part the coming of the fuels of the twentieth century: gas and electricity. Gas was far more convenient for cooking than wood or coal — just turn a valve and light a match — and it was clean-burning. After 1915, when it was first offered by the American Stove Company, the oven regulator came into use, greatly enhancing the usefulness of the gas range. The regulator at first had settings numbered from 1 to 11. By the late 1920s the regulator wheel was being marked with the traditional degree settings — 300°F., 350°F., and so on.

Electricity for cooking was briefly experimented with late in the nineteenth century, and a conceptual electric kitchen with range, a boiler, kettles, and even a saucepan, all of them electrical, was exhibited at the World's Columbian Exposition in Chicago in 1893. A prototype of the first electric range leading to commercial production appeared in 1904, the creation of George A. Hughes. Something akin to a telephone switchboard, it used plug-in wires to adjust heat from high to medium to low. Hughes refined his concept and produced a more conventional-looking range by 1910; his Electric Heating Company later merged with Hotpoint (General Electric). GE meanwhile introduced an electric range of its own in 1913, the so-called Black Maria. A drawback to early electric heating devices was that their heating elements burned out quickly. Furthermore there was considerable use of electric current. Wider acceptance of the electric range was spurred by the development of an improved heating element, the Calrod, by Hotpoint in 1926. A range with an automatic timing control was introduced in 1930.

The modern electric range is the choice in six out of ten homes while gas, once the favorite, is used in the other four, the use of coal, wood, and kerosene being statistically negligible. Both gas and electric ovens have optional self-cleaning features. Some electric ranges have convection ovens that use a fan to blow hot air around and cook the food faster. Gas provides instant-on and instant-off heating and allows the cook to gauge the temperature visually by checking the height of the flame, but the electric stove heats more evenly.

The icebox remained the most common form of refrigeration well into the twentieth century; some iceboxes were still in use at midcentury. The use of mechanical refrigeration for the home was proposed, somewhat paradoxically, in *Ice Trade Journal* in 1887, and by 1895 there were several simple refrigerating machines on the market, though probably very few, if any, found their way into American households. More significant was a small domestic refrigerator that was developed in France and manufactured and marketed in the United States by the General Electric Company, beginning in 1911 and continuing until 1928. The invention of a French monk, Abbé Audiffren, it used sulfur dioxide as a refrigerant to cool salt brine circulating through the cooling system. By 1916 there were a number of other mechanical refrigerators on the market, but all were high in cost and unsatisfactory by later standards.

Three developments made the home refrigerator practical: automatic control, introduced by Kelvinator with its first model in February 1918, without which the compressor had to run continually or be manually controlled; a sealed unit, based on the Audiffren design and introduced by General Electric in 1925, to replace a separate motor- and belt-driven compressor (a noisy system prone to breakdown); and, in the early 1930s, the use of Freon-12 as a refrigerant to replace sulfur dioxide and methyl chloride, both of which are toxic. (Freon, too, would eventually be considered toxic to the atmosphere.)

Improvements notwithstanding, home refrigerators were rare in the early years. In 1923 only about 20,000 were in use in the United States. Iceboxes still outsold mechanicals. Not until 1930 was the balance reversed with the sale of 850,000 mechanical refrigerators that year. By 1944 mechanicals outnumbered iceboxes by more than two to one.

Appearance had been changing also. The early refrigerators looked like the iceboxes they were replacing; they even had the same dark wood exterior. But in the 1920s the refrigerator became more stylish along with the other components of the kitchen. It got a white enamel wrap to replace the old dark wood, and it acquired convenient features such as a freezer compartment to make ice cubes and store frozen food.* The postwar refrigerator had a freezer compartment "large enough to take a whole roast, chickens or chops, and several pounds of frozen fruits and vegetables," as Kelvinator claimed in 1945. More and more features appeared: a small compartment to keep butter spreadable, rustproof shelves, doors that opened from the right or the left, and utility bins for soda bottles and other assorted things.

It was also in the postwar years that the large home freezer began to sell in significant numbers. It had made its appearance in the late 1930s, but production was halted during World War II. When *McCall's* magazine in 1945 described all the glories of new household technology, it said of freezers, "You've heard about them, talked of them, longed for them — here they are." A 15-cubic-foot model offered by Carrier promised storage of from 500 to 600 pounds. It was an upright model that looked like a refrigerator. Most freezers, however, were the chest type. Some 200,000 were manu-

---

*Commercial frozen foods were first produced in 1929 in a Hillsboro, Oregon, plant that would later become a part of General Foods, and the first Birds Eye products appeared in 1930. Selections included peas, spinach, raspberries, loganberries, cherries, and various kinds of meat and fish. But frozen foods were sometimes more than twice as expensive as fresh produce. Frozen foods came into their own in the postwar years. The TV dinner arrived in the spring of 1954, an innovation of C. A. Swanson and Sons, of Omaha, Nebraska. The first was a meal of sliced turkey and gravy on corn bread with sweet potatoes and peas.

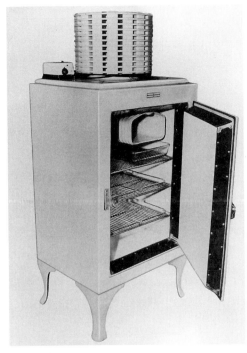

LEFT: *Perhaps the classic refrigerator was the General Electric Monitor Top, introduced in 1927. Its distinctive appearance owed to the coil on top, a location that appeared to offer greater efficiency. Its popular name derived from its resemblance to the warship* Monitor *of Civil War fame. Advertising at first promoted its efficiency and simplicity but later sought to generate snob appeal by capitalizing on its unusual looks.* (Friday Associates International on behalf of General Electric Company)

RIGHT: *Today's refrigerator: a built-in "side-by-side."* (Courtesy of General Electric Company)

factured in 1946, and by 1949 it is estimated that home freezers were in more than 1.2 million American homes.

By midcentury, with freezer compartments and a variety of foods to keep in them, the need for an old-fashioned pantry had virtually disappeared—though hardly the need for storage space, of which no kitchen has ever been known to have enough. By now the continuous counter with wall cabinets overhead offered a new degree of efficiency. Furthermore, the major components of the kitchen—the range, the refrigerator, and the sink, soon to be joined by the dishwasher and the microwave oven—were now being designed so as to be placed one next to the other. In 1945 major appliance manufacturers took this concept one step further by setting standard dimensions for cabinets, sinks, ranges, and refrigerators. For example, the height of the base cabinets was set at 36 inches, considered standard for a woman of average stature, and countertops were made 25¼ inches deep to accommodate an automatic dishwasher.

TOP LEFT: *The kitchen, c. 1927.* (Courtesy of Kohler Co.)

TOP RIGHT AND ABOVE: *The kitchen, c. 1940, two views.* (Courtesy of Kohler Co.)

The kitchen of today: recognizably traditional, yet a hint of things to come. (Courtesy of Whirlpool Corporation)

Recently such standardization has come into question because it is inconvenient for the handicapped and for people who are not of average size.

But the modern kitchen is more than the sum of its parts. It is perhaps the most dynamic part of the house. While the house as a whole is among the more traditional and conservative elements of society, the kitchen is quickest within the house to reflect new concepts of comfort and convenience. It is here one finds technology changing fastest. Yet the kitchen's traditional role as the hub of family life remains as durable as ever—whether that is evident in its being the locus of a household communications system or expressed in so simple a way as a note on the refrigerator door.

EPILOGUE

All we require is the greatest possible compactness, and convenience for the family expressed in the very comprehensive word comfort . . ."

The modern house would have delighted Benjamin Latrobe, with whose advice to a client in 1805 we began. The modern house captures his ideas of compactness and convenience. It expresses comfort more comprehensively than he ever imagined.

In the years since Latrobe, "convenience for the family," once only for the wealthy like the Walns and Markoes, has reached families throughout America. Technology and mass production, vastly altering expectations of comfort, have also made comfort technology attainable across the economic spectrum. Almost every home in our time contains an appliance or system that would have boggled the imagination in 1805 or 1860.

Of course, not all have perceived this progress as a flawless virtue. As the age of mass production took hold, George Canning Hill used a book called *Homespun* to take issue with the speed at which new technology was changing everyday life, complaining in 1867 that:

> *The Age we live in is an everlasting busybody. It invades every nook and corner, let it be ever so quiet and drowsy; like the tax-gatherer, it passes by no man's door.*

There were others, before and after Hill, who likewise saw modern convenience as unnecessary. Anne Longfellow Pierce, for example, whose family home was the Wadsworth-Longfellow House, in Portland, Maine. At the time of her death in 1902, it was the only residence in town with an outdoor privy. Wanting to preserve the house as it was in her childhood, Mrs. Pierce kept her privy by periodically applying to city officials for a special permit.

But for most Americans, technology has always been a welcome visitor at the door. The response has been to embrace, not bar, new forms of convenience. Yet there is a curious allure in looking back and seeing how seemingly simple were the origins of everyday comfort and convenience we take for granted:

- *a stone trough with a lead pipe and a stopcock (toilet);*
- *a brick chamber with a large stove inside it and some tin pipe sticking out the top (central heat);*
- *a barrel with a large handle (washing machine);*
- *a double-walled box interlined with powdered charcoal (refrigerator).*

Yet these innovations had an aura of complexity in their day; they were not always easy to understand, or trust, or make the most of. It was widely thought, for example, that ice, being expensive and hard to get, should be conserved by wrapping it in a blanket before placing it in the icebox. The ice did indeed last longer, but an icebox used that way didn't keep its contents very cold and was apt to be put down as another useless contraption.

New things could also be obstinate, finicky, and very unpredictable. Frances Breckenridge, talking about her new "Rotary" stove, described it's crank as having "the total depravity of inanimate things, [and] a trick of becoming useless." That was in the 1830s, but she could as easily have been complaining about the total depravity of an inanimate but cranky computer.

It is hoped, of course, that this account has been informative. It is also hoped it has provided new insight in seeing afresh new things in the light of old things.

Notes

Source notes are grouped under part numbers and then under subtitles. Full citations, other than periodicals, can be found in the bibliography. The following abbreviations are used:

CUR—archival and other material received directly from a curator or the curatorial staff.

HABS—Historic American Buildings Survey.

TECH—"The American Home and the Development of Domestic Technology," a survey conducted for this book and for the author's *Open House: A Guided Tour of the American Home* (New York: Henry Holt, 1999). The responses provided invaluable data on the technological evolution of more than three hundred historic American homes.

Introduction

Data for the 1990s generally is from U.S. Department of Commerce, *American Housing Survey 1995*, 5–6, "Selected Equipment and Plumbing, All Housing Units," 7, "Fuels, All Housing Units," Appendix A10–A12. For percentage purposes, a base of 106.4 million housing units is used. Other sources are *Eighty Years' Progress* (1869), 355 ("With the improved style of houses"); Martin, *Standard of Living*, 5–8 (economic impact of 1860s), 112 (New York, 1856), 127 (Baltimore, 1859); *Statistical Abstract of the United States*, 1935, 794, 1936, 814 (Real Property Inventory of 1934), 1969, 703 (plumbing, heating, cooking fuels, 1940 and 1960); U.S. Census of Housing, 1940, 8 (plumbing, 1940). Both the tables, "The American Household and the Evolution of Technology, 1856–1934," and "The American Household . . . 1940–1995" include data from the U.S. Census, 1940 and 1960.

PART 1. THE COMING OF MODERN: 1805
CUR, Gore Place; Latrobe, *Correspondence*, II, 36 ("All we require"); Smith, *Early Philadelphia*, 279 (laborer's wages)
PHILADELPHIA: 1805: Mease, *Picture of Philadelphia*, 25–26 (description generally), 311–14 (Peale's Museum); Scharf, *History of Philadelphia*, I, 486 (Ambrose & Co., gaslight, 1796); Sellers, *Mr. Peale's Museum*, 152–53 (use of State House). The "Athens of America" quote is attributed to Gilbert Stuart.
ARCHITECT OF CHANGE: Hamlin, *Latrobe*
BROADENING CONCEPTS: Cohen, *Drawings of Latrobe*, 184–85 (Waln House, "I should build for myself"); Goldstein, *Philadelphia and the China Trade*, 12, 53–54 (footnote on Waln); Hamlin, *Latrobe*, 197–99 (Waln's engagement, Waln House); Latrobe, *Correspondence*, III, 647 (Waln House in watercolor of 1847); Latrobe, *Journal*, 85–86 ("As far as I did observe"); *Times*, London, various dates 1790–1815 (real estate ads), July 5, 1790 ("genteel modern house").
COMFORT IN DESIGN and COMFORT IN TECHNOLOGY: Cohen, *Drawings of Latrobe*, 508–12, 521 (Markoe House); Hamlin, *Latrobe*, 341–42 (Markoe House); Ierley, *Open House*, 43–55, (Read House); Latrobe, *Correspondence*, II, 35–41 (Letter, March 26, 1805).
A HOUSE ELYSIAN: *Bibliothèque Britannique*, Sciences et Arts, XIX, 386, 391 (original version of quotations); Brown, *Benjamin Thompson*, 240–41 (Rumford's own kitchen); Ellis, *Memoir*, 425–29 (Pictet's description); Sparrow, *Knight*, 168–82 (Rumford's domestic technology generally), 193–94 (45 Brampton Row). The Thomson quotation, "Never been put to use," in the caption for "The Ultra-Modern Kitchen" is from *Annals of Philosophy*, London, April 1815, 243.
ANOTHER WORD FOR COMFORT: Brown, *Benjamin Thompson*, 278–79, 287 (windows at the auditorium of the institute); *European Magazine*, London, LV, 20–21 (epigraph); Sparrow, *Knight*, 168–82 passim, 177 (Board of Agriculture model kitchen, tradesman named Summers, number of roasters), 178–79 (lighting).
CONTRIVANCE AND CONVENIENCE: Adams, *Monticello*, passim, 99 (date of Margaret Bayard Smith's visit to Monticello, not included in her retrospection); McLaughlin, *Jefferson*, 210–11 (Hôtel de Langeac), 301–9 (Monticello generally), 301–2 (ice house), 309 (tea room stove, including quotation); New-York Historical Society, *Collections, 1878* (New York, 1879), 196–97 (Jefferson to Thomson, Paris, Nov. 11, 1784), 205 (Thomson to Jefferson, April 6, 1786, "not yet arrived"); Rice, *L'Hôtel de Langeac*, 8, 11, 13–14; Robins, *Story of the Lamp*, 112–13 (Argand); Rumford, *Collected Works*, IV, 34–35 (brilliancy of Argand lamp); Smith, *First Forty Years*, 386–87.

Power, Fuel, and Water Supply
MOVING TOWARD THE FUTURE: Baker, *Field Guide*, 3 (Flowerdew Plantation); Beedell, *Windmills*, 13 (earliest known English windmill), 19–44 passim; CUR, Old Economy Village, Ambridge, Pa. (Melish quote); HABS ("Old Windmill"); Park, *Wind Power*, Appendix 2.3 (wind power tables), 14 (Dutch windmills, improvements not copied in America); Rex Wailes, "Notes on Some Windmills in New England," *Old-Time New England*, Jan. 1931 (early windmills generally, output of Old Mill, 1661 gristmill, and 1673 fulling mill); Winthrop, *History*, I, 104.
THE COMING OF STEAM POWER: Ierley, *Place in History*, 26–31 (Hornblower, Schuyler engine), 38 (fire of 1768), 60–61, 64–65 (Roosevelt, Philadelphia waterworks).
ELECTRICITY: BARELY A HINT: Cohen, *Franklin*, 195, 200 (electricity for cooking).
FUEL: STILL MOSTLY WOOD: Ierley, *Open House*, 39 (Heyward House), U.S. Census Bureau, *Historical Statistics*, 1184 (coal imports, exports).
VERY USEFUL WORKS: Acrelius, *History*, 405–6 (Bethlehem waterworks); Bathe, *Evans*, 65 (specifications, Philadelphia waterworks), 66

(*Philadelphia Gazette* quote); Blake, *Public Health in Boston*, 151–59 (yellow fever in the colonies and early Republic), 156–57 (Boston Aqueduct); Brewster, *Rambles*, 211 ("Within a few feet"); CUR, Strawbery Banke, Portsmouth, N.H. (Portsmouth Aqueduct, Gilman); Caulkins, *New London*, 583–84 (yellow fever); Ierley, *Open House*, 85–89 (water supply generally); Latrobe, *Journal*, 94–95 ("But this very circumstance"), 95 ("the stratum in which the water runs"); Levering, *History*, 288–90 (Bethlehem); Mease, *Picture of Philadelphia*, 147–54, 152 (boring of pipe), 153 (700,000 gallons); Vadnais, Andrew, and Donald Woods, "The Water Power System at Hancock Shaker Village," *Old Mill News*, Society for the Preservation of Old Mills, Fall 1995, courtesy of Hancock Shaker Village ("A small stream of water comes down the mountains"); Watson, *Annals*, 706 ("There was little or no desire").

Heating

OVERCOMING "INCONVENIENCIES":
Elliott, *Technics*, 272 (Bouvier); Franklin, *Papers*, II, 424–25 ("Their inconveniencies"); *Histoire . . . Privée*, vol. 2, 496 ("*Pour le froit qui fait*"); Ierley, *Open House*, 161–72, passim.
A COPERNICAN THEORY OF THE HEARTH:
Gauger, *Fires Improv'd*, 10–15, including quote, "The common way of building"; *Dictionnaire de Biographie Française* (Paris, 1979) "Gauger" (brief biographical material).
THE Z FACTOR: De Bono, *Eureka*, 142 (Savot); Gauger, *Fires Improv'd*, 16–17; 23–26.
GAUGER "NEW-INVENTED": Ford, *Franklin*, 358–60 (stove of 1771); Franklin, *Autobiography*, 191–92; Franklin, *Papers*, II, 331 (1741 advertisement), 419–46 passim, 424–29 (various means of heating), 427 ("directly up the Chimney"), 428 ("Sieur Gauger"), 428–29 ("no Sight of the Fire"); Labaree, *Franklin Papers*, II, 419–46 (Pennsylvania Fireplace).
FROM STOVE TO FURNACE: Franklin, *Philosophical Papers*, 3 (definition of "rarified");

Gauger, *Fires Improv'd*, 25–26 ("Not only the air"); Ierley, *Open House*, "Keeping Warm" (orangeries, use of Franklin stove); Latrobe, *Correspondence*, II, 737 n, 801 n, 949 n. (brief biographical references to Pettibone); Pettibone, *Description*, passim; Pettibone, *Economy*, passim, 4 ("The principle, upon which"), 8–9 (Pettibone's dining room), 43–47 (biographical data). "American stove" is defined by James Sharp in *An Account of the Principles and Effects of the Pensilvanian Stove-Grates* (London: 1790) as one of those "which warm Rooms &c. by a continual Introduction and Exchange of dry fresh air," i.e., Franklin's, or one similar. Pettibone's hot-air furnace is described in Bishop, *American Manufactures*, II, 133, as appearing "to have been the earliest attempt in this country."
HOSPITAL-TESTED: Pettibone, *Description*, passim, 4 ("[My] improvements consist"), 10–11 (Pennsylvania Hospital); Pettibone, *Economy*, passim, 48 (Hewes and Rush endorsements); TECH, Wyck 1820; U.S. Patent Office, *List of Patents (1847)*, 146 (1808 Pettibone patent).

Lighting

A LIGHT, LATELY INVENTED: Elliott, *Technics and Architecture*, 234 (wicks soaked in boric acid, early lamps as shallow dishes); Luckiesh, *Artificial Light*, 54 (Argand lamp); New-York Historical Society, *Collections*, 1878 (New York: 1879), 196–97 (Jefferson to Thompson, Paris, Nov. 11, 1784); Thwing, *Flickering Flames*, 71–74 (Argand lamps).
INFLAMMABLE AIR: Bishop, *American Manufactures*, 67 (Ambrose & Co., exhibition of gaslight in 1796), 93 (background on Henfrey); Elliott, *Technics and Architecture*, 235–36 (Clayton quote); David P. Erlick, "The Peales and Gas Lights in Baltimore," *Maryland Historical Magazine*, spring 1985, passim, 9–10 (Henfrey, including *Federal Gazette* quote); *General Advertiser*, Philadelphia, July 29, 1796 ("Messrs. Ambrose, & Co. have the honor"); Peale, *Peale and His World*,

81 (Peale's Museum); Scharf, *History of Philadelphia*, I, 486 ("Ambrose & Co.," gaslight, 1796); Sellers, *Mr. Peale's Museum*, 200, 228–30, 237–38 (gaslighting of museum); Edith May Tilley, "David Melville and His Early Experiments with Gas in Newport," *Bulletin of the Newport Historical Society*, Jan. 1927, passim, 1 (Clayton), 4 ("inflammable air"), 15–16 (specifications of Melville's apparatus).

Stephens's *Philadelphia Directory*, 1796, lists an "Ambrose, Michael, fire work maker, 299 Arch St.," and *The Prospect of Philadelphia*, 1796, lists "Michael Ambrose, Fire-work maker" at 297 Arch Street, near Eighth.

Although 1806 is the year usually given — in the *Dictionary of American Biography*, for example — for Melville's historic use of gaslight, *American Gas-Light Journal*, Sept. 1, 1859, gives the "assurance of several prominent gentlemen there" as saying that Melville "lighted his own house in Newport . . . with gas in 1812"

Bathing

THE EVOLVING BATHROOM: Richard L. Bushman and Claudia L. Bushman, "The Early History of Cleanliness in America," *Journal of American History*, March 1988, passim, 1214 (Drinker quote, "not for 28 years"), 1226 (Nathaniel Waterman); CUR, Gore Place, George Read II House; Drinker, *Not So Long Ago*, 28–31; Richardson, *New Vitruvius*, "Donington Park."

The Water Closet

FROM CHUTES TO DITCHES: Brown, *Water Closets*, 14 (garderobe); James, *Ancient Inventions*, 442–46; Palmer, *Water Closet*, 13–21. THE METAMORPHOSIS OF THE JOHN: Aubrey, *Surrey*, II, 160 ("Here I saw a pretty Machine"); Brown, *Water Closets*, 16–20; Davies, *King in Toils*, 355 (George II); Fiennes, *Journeys*, 358 (Prince George); Harington, *Metamorphosis*, passim; Hellyer, *Lectures*, 189–94, 193 ("I found

two such water-closets"); Hibbert, *Virgin Queen*, 134 (Boorde quote); McNeil, *Bramah*, 24–25 (Prince George); Ogilby, *Africa*, 188 ("Round about the Mosques"); Palmer, *Water Closet*, 26–31 (Harington); Charles Scarlett Jr., "Governor Horatio Sharpe's Whitehall," *Maryland Historical Magazine*, Mar. 1951 (Whitehall generally), 21, 21 n. (Delft wall tile, marble floor tile); Waldman, *Elizabeth and Leicester*, 253–54 (Harington). A NEW GENERATION: Brown, *Water Closets*, 22–24; *Dictionary of National Biography*, "Aubrey," "Cumming"; Ierley, *Year That Tried Men's Souls*, 71–72 (Allen); Cumming, *Elements of Clock and Watch-work*, passim, copy at New York Public Library containing handwritten inscription with otherwise unpublished details about Cumming's life, notably his exhibits for and his receiving a pension from George III; McNeil, *Bramah*, 23–30 (6,000 water closets, spelling of Bramah). I am indebted to Orlando Ridout V, Maryland Historical Trust, for calling my attention to the little known water closet of c. 1765 at Whitehall. Whitehall was built by Governor Horatio Sharpe, who was subsequently called back to England. On his death he left Whitehall to his friend and secretary, John Ridout, who had cared for it after Sharpe's departure, and it was for many years the home of the Ridout family.

In and Around the Kitchen

SCIENCE MADE SAVORY: Primarily Rumford, "On the Construction of Kitchen Fire-places and Kitchen Utensils," *Collected Works*, III, 66 ("This unscientific and slovenly manner"); Rumford, "Of the Excellent Qualities of Coffee," *Collected Works*, V, 277 ("Nobody, I fancy, can be fonder"). CONCENTRATING THE HEAT: Brown, *Benjamin Thompson*, passim, 223 ("I was very desirous"); Brown, *Rumford, Physicist*, 74 ("cook the cook"), 75 (invented double boiler, etc.); CUR/TECH, Gardner-Pingree House, Gore Place, Homewood, Rundlet-May House; John Dornberg, "Count Rumford: the Most Successful

Yank Abroad, Ever," *Smithsonian*, Dec. 1994; Larsen, *American in Europe*, 18, 118 (Rumford as apprentice in Salem); Nylander, *Snug Fireside*, 217–18 (Rundlet); Rumford, "On the Construction of Kitchen Fire-places," *Collected Works*, III, 80 ("The loss of heat . . . noxious exhalations"), 88–89 (use of pasteboard and chalk), 88–90 (enclosed fireplace), 152–62 (roaster), 256 ("Bare inspection is sufficient"), 256–61 (family boiler), 282–85 (register stove).

THE BEGINNINGS OF REFRIGERATION: Anderson, *Refrigeration*, 7–8 (icehouses, 1780s–1790s); Ierley, *Open House*, 68–70; Moore, *Ice-Houses*, passim (details of "refrigerator"); TECH, Daniel Boone Homestead; Watson, *Annals of Philadelphia*, 202 (icehouses "have all come into use").

THE MISSING SINK: CUR, Silas Deane House, Ephrata Cloister, Hyde Hall; TECH, Menard Home. Particularly helpful was material on the Silas Deane House furnished by curator Donna K. Baron.

OTHER WORK FOR BARRELS AND BUCKETS: Chiefly the TECH survey. Also U.S. Patent Office, *Inventions and Designs*, 314–18 (washing machine patents, 1797–1847).

THE FUTURE: MORE RECOGNIZABLE 1830: CUR, Hyde Hall, Owens-Thomas House.

PART 2. BETWEEN THUMB AND FINGER: 1860

Chiefly Martin, *Standard of Living*, passim, 92 (stoves, 1830–1860), 93 (matches, 1860), 111 (Boston, 1860), 112 (New York, 1855–1856), 127 (Baltimore, 1859), 393 (wages in 1860). Also *Eighty Years' Progress*, 355 ("With the improved style of houses"); Goodrich, *Recollections*, 903, 905; Trollope, *North America*, 291 ("In Boston the houses").

ARCHITECTS, FATHER AND SON and THE VERY MODERN HOUSE, 1860: William Nathaniel Banks, "The Galliers, New Orleans Architects," *Antiques*, April 1997 (Tyrone Power

and related quotes; "I devoted every spare hour"); Gallier House, Guide Manual; Latrobe, *Impressions*, xxii–xxiii, 105 ("beyond Royal Street"); Martin, *Standard of Living*, 111–12 (water closets in New York and Boston); Rhonda Watts, "Gilt and Grace at Gallier House," *Tulanian*, Spring 1989.

Power, Fuel, and Water Supply

MAKING GIANT STRIDES: Goodrich, *Recollections*, 903, 905.

THE NEW POWER and A MOTOR THAT COULD TURN: Chiefly Byrn, *Progress*, 48–54 (early motors); Davenport, *Davenport*, 56–57 (visit to Crown Point and early experimentation); *Dictionary of American Biography* (Davenport; Henry); Giedion, *Mechanization*, 556–58 (early motors); U.S. Patent 132, Thomas Davenport, "Improvement in Propelling Machinery by Magnetism and Electro-Magnetism," Feb. 25, 1837 (specifications of Davenport motor).

THE AGE OF COAL and OTHER SLUMBERERS: Bishop, *American Manufactures*, II, 185 (early use of anthracite); Derby, *Anthracite*, 5 (effect of war of 1812), 46 ("Furnaces for burning wood," "No reason why illuminating gas"); Furnas, *Americans*, 304 ("whole town presents," "smoke of coals ascending"); Goodrich, *Recollections*, 904 ("Think of the labor performed"); U.S. Census Bureau, *Historical Statistics*, 1184 (coal in colonial period); U.S. Energy Information Administration (coal production statistics, 1800 and after); Watson, *Annals*, 707–9 (discovery of anthracite, early experience).

ILLUMINATING GAS: GOING PUBLIC: Chiefly David P. Erlick, "The Peales and Gas Lights in Baltimore," *Maryland Historical Magazine*, Spring 1985; Gerhard, *American Practice*, "Historical Notes on the Development and Progress of the Gas Industry."

THE AMERICAN WINDMILL: Baker, *Field Guide*, 3–7; Shepherd, *Development of the Windmill*, 31 (Eclipse windmill); Springfield *Union-News*, June 21, 1997, "Windmill Reclaims Place on Horizon" (Brimfield windmill, article furnished courtesy of Old Sturbridge Village); Torrey, *Wind-Catchers*, 92–94 (governor on Watt's engine); U.S. Patent No. 11,629, Aug. 29, 1854, Halladay Wind Wheel. The dating of the Brimfield windmill is based on material furnished by Saint Christopher's Church, Brimfield, Mass.

USEFUL WORKS CONTINUED: *American Almanac, 1850*, 187 (chronology of Philadelphia waterworks from 1801 through Fairmount), 193, 200–1 (Boston); American Society of Civil Engineers, *Proceedings*, Sept. 1927 vol. 53, "A Symposium: Historic Review of the Development of Sanitary Engineering in the United States during the Past One Hundred and Fifty Years," 1592 (Manhattan Company); *The Builder*, London, Aug. 19, 1865 ("The Croton aqueduct," "The hot-water supply is obtained"); CUR, Bryant Homestead, Hyde Hall; *Dictionary of American Biography* (Graff); Ierley, *Open House*, 87–89; Lyell, *Second Visit*, 180 ("A work more akin," "The rate of insurance"); Martin, *Standard*, 38–42 (public water supply generally, through 1860), 111 (Boston 1860), 112 (New York 1856); *National Aegis*, Worcester, Mass., April 17, 1822 (Ichabod Washburn); Nylander, *Snug Fireside* (Bryant Homestead, diary dates, amplified in correspondence with the author); Royall, *Sketches of History*, 210–11 ("I saw the old water-works"); Old Sturbridge Village, interpretation department, paper titled "Interpretation of a Gravity Water System Appropriate for Freeman Farm," by Robert Wilder, May 17, 1986 (gravity systems generally, including reference to *Barre Gazette*; OSV was also the source for the Worcester *National Aegis*); *Report of the Watering Committee*, 1801, 1816 (Philadelphia, numbers of customers); TECH (Frame House and salvaged pump, Park-McCullough House); Tomlinson, *Cyclopaedia*, I, 63–69 (chief source for Croton); U.S. Census Bureau, *Historical Statistics*, 1104 (federal budget 1842); Watson, *Annals*, 706 (costs and numbers of customers, Philadelphia waterworks).

Heating

KEEPING A WARM HOUSE: *The Builder*, Aug. 19, 1865, 582 (Chilson same as Boston furnace); Crawford County Historical Society, Meadville, Pa., bill of sale dated Aug. 14, 1857, from Cox, Richardson & Boynton to William Reynolds, Meadville, Pa., showing list price of $180 for two Boynton furnaces; CUR, Lindenwald, Kinderhook, N.Y. (Martin Van Buren Home, details of furnace), Wyck, Philadelphia (Haines, 1820 furnace); Downing, *Country Houses*, 475–77 (hot-air heat, Chilson furnace); *Journal of the Society of Architectural Historians*, Oct. 1962, 145 (Willard and Bulfinch); *Sheet Metal Worker*, "A Brief History of the Warm-Air Heating Industry," Jan. 1954, 58 (dates of Richardson & Boynton); TECH ("Like trying to heat a bird cage"); U.S. patent 4,133, Aug. 4, 1845 (Chilson furnace "humidifier"; but note that other furnaces of this period apparently had similar devices [Downing, *County Houses*, 475 n.]); Wheeler, *Homes for the People*, "General Warming Apparatus," 422–24 (Boynton furnace); Wheildon, *Willard*, 45–51, 47 (Willard quote, Safford), 48 (Bulfinch questions).

WARMING WITH PIPES: Arndt, *Economy*, 835–37 (specifications of heating pipe at Economy); Bathe, *Perkins*, 52 (Massachusetts Medical College, Shaw quote), 143 (Watt's attempt at steam heat, Guardian Fire Office); Robert Bruegmann, "Central Heating and Forced Ventilation: Origins and Effects on Architectural Design," *Journal of the Society of Architectural Historians*, Oct. 1978, 148 (Perkins's use of smaller pipe and high pressure); CUR, Old Economy Village, Ambridge, Pa. (Duke of Saxe-Weimar Eisenach quote); Depew, *One Hundred Years*, II, 362 (1845 installation still going strong in 1892), 363 ("For many years every steam-fitting firm"); Downing, *Country Houses*, 478–79 ("Heating by hot water"); Elliot, *Technics*, 279–81 (house of 1745, Bonnemain, Watt), 281 (British Museum, pipe "not thicker than your little finger"); Ferguson, "Central Heating," passim, 169–70 (Perkins's experimentation, drawbacks of high pressure), 170–71 (Gold's mattress radiator, Nason's pipe radiator), 171 (British Museum), 176–78 (Nason's installation at U.S. Capitol, Sumner quote, "there is no public edifice"); Holohan, *Lost Art*, 4–5 (Gold's mattress radiator); *National Cyclopaedia of American Biography*, Nason, Walworth; Plat, *Eden*, 50; Stifler, *Beginnings of a Century*, illus. following p. 64 (dating of Nason's pipe radiator); U.S. Patent Collection, No. 11,747, Oct. 3, 1854 (Gold's "Heating Apparatus").

STOVES: A PLACE IN HISTORY: *Appleton's Cyclopaedia of Applied Mechanics*, II, 813 (mica window for illumination); Depew, *One Hundred Years*, II, 358 (magazine concept first seen in 1770), 361 (stove production, 1830–1870); Elliott, *Technics*, 278 (Eliphalet Nott's stove); Mott, *Description and Design* ("the stove may be left for hours").

Lighting

TURNING UP THE LIGHT: Moss, *Lighting*, 77–78 (increase in price of whale oil), 80–81, 86 (comparison of costs of whale oil and burning fluid, reference to *Godey's Lady's Book*), 184 (solar lamp), 180 (astral lamp), 183–84 (sinumbra lamp); *Scientific American*, "From the Candle to Electricity," March 1928 (letter to the editor from Harry J. Thorne: "In our homes, each carried"), "The Horrors of Burning Fluid," Jan. 21, 1860 ("We long ago ordered this stuff out of our house").

A GOOD TIME FOR WHALES: *Living Age*, "A Good Time Coming for Whales," Sept. 29, 1860 (transformation of "quiet little farming community" of Titusville; quote, "As an illuminating oil it excels").

GASLIGHT: FROM CONCERN TO CONVENIENCE: Accum, *Practical Treatise*, 160–61 ("In fact, no danger can arise"); CUR, Merchant's House Museum, New York (reference to house and period gaslighting generally); David P. Erlick, "The Peales and Gas Lights in Baltimore," *Maryland Historical Magazine*, spring 1985 (street lighting in Baltimore in 1818, number of gas customers early 1830s); "Every House Occupant His Own Gas Manufacturer," catalog, n.d., in collections of National Museum of American History (as cited); Gerhard, *American Practice of Gas Piping*, 265–67 (New York, Manhattan, and Metropolitan Gas Companies); Martin, *Standard of Living*, 96–97 (number of gas companies by 1855, cities with gas at time of Civil War); Portable Oil Gas Company, advertisement, 1855, in collections of Henry Ford Museum and Greenfield Village Research Center (details of gas apparatus as described; text estimates use of 3 gallons at 15 cents per gallon for "a week's consumption to an ordinary family," or $23.40 a year; coal for heating the retort would be a nominal extra cost).

The Bathroom

A ROOM OF ITS OWN and AN INCREASING SENSE OF NECESSITY: Bayles, *House Drainage*, 85–89, 267 ("I know of nothing more disgusting"); Brown, *Water-Closets*, 61–62 ("Sanitary authorities agree"); CUR, Lindenwald, Kinderhook, N.Y.; Depew, *One Hundred Years*, "Plumbers and Steam Fitters' Supplies," 364–70 (half dozen plumbers in 1840s); Downing, *Architecture of Country Houses*, 326 ("Bathroom"); Hellyer, *Plumber*, 188–92 (pan closets), 188 ("It has always been a puzzle"), 189–90 ("The filth, splashed about"); John Jay Homestead, archives (No. 3 Third Avenue); Martin, *Standard of Living*, 111–12, 127 (numbers of water closets; actual figures given there, using various contemporary sources, are 10,384 water closets [1856] and population of 629,904 [1855] for New York; 9,864 water closets [1860] and population of 177,840 [1860] for Boston; 698 water closets [1859] for population of 212,418 [1860] for Baltimore; and 160 water closets [1859] for population of 62,367 [1860], Albany); J. L. Mott, Iron Works, Catalog "D," *The Bath Room Illustrated*, 1884; Vaux, *Villas*, 47 ("water-closet a necessity"); Waring, *Earth*

Closets, 21 ("complete suppression of odors"); Waring, *Sanitary Drainage*, 101 (Edinburgh 1872); Willich, *Encyclopedia*, V, 360 ("well calculated for travelling"). The patents of 1833 and 1835 are listed under "Household Furniture" in U.S. Patent Office, *Inventions and Designs*, 318; the 1847 patent is No. 4, 926, dated Jan. 13, 1847. BATHING ON THE INCREASE: Bushman (see below), 1225 (Philadelphia, number of tubs 1823, first plumbed tub 1826); Child, *Letters*, 168–69 ("We not only have the three large fountains"); CUR, Read House, New Castle, Del.; *Godey's Lady's Book*, May 1860; 464 Hamlin, *Latrobe*, 176 (Philadelphia 1815, number of tubs); Ierley, *Open House*, 98–99; Martin, *Standard of Living*, 111 (Boston 1860); J. L. Mott Iron Works, *1878 Illustrated Catalog*, 32 (specifications of cast-iron tub). Of particular help with this section was Richard L. Bushman and Claudia L. Bushman, "The Early History of Cleanliness in America," *Journal of American History*, March 1988.

Appliances

CATCHING UP WITH THE FUTURE: CUR, Webb-Deane-Stevens Museum, Wethersfield, Conn. (clock jack, Silas Deane House); *Oxford English Dictionary*, "mangle" (use by 1600, patent of 1774, general definition); U.S. Patent Collection, No. 81,539, Aug. 25, 1868 ("automatic fan"); Washington, *Diaries*, V, 183 ("Visited a Machine at Doctr. Franklins").
THE MECHANIZATION OF MONDAY: American Steam Washing Machine Manufacturing Co., *Description and Philosophy of James T. King's Patent Washing and Drying Apparatus*, New York, 1855, in the archives of the Smithsonian Institution, Warshaw Collection (King's washing apparatus); Bishop, *History of Manufactures*, II, 146 (early washing machines); Giedion, *Mechanization*, 560–67 (washing machines), Jacob A. Swisher, "The Evolution of Wash Day," *Iowa Journal of History and Politics*, Jan. 1940 (early history of wash day); U.S. Patent Office, *Inventions and Designs*, 131 (Bailey's steam jack), 314–18 (washing machine patents, 1797–1847).
OTHER PREVIEWS: Chiefly Giedion, *Mechanization*, 548–53 (dishwashers), 548, 582–86 (carpet cleaners).

The Kitchen

THE EVOLVING KITCHEN: CUR, George Read II House, New Castle, Del., Gardner-Pingree House, Salem, Mass.; Johnson, *Rural Economy*, 97–100; the illustration is plate VII, fig. 5. Virtually nothing is known of Stephen William Johnson. There is no record of any book by him other than *Rural Economy*, which is signed only "S. W. Johnson." Siegfried Giedion in *Mechanization Takes Command* suggests that Johnson was a friend of the inventor Oliver Evans, which is plausible; but Greville and Dorothy Bathe's definitive biography, *Oliver Evans*, makes no mention of Johnson.
SUCCESSORS TO THE DANCING FLAMES: This section leans heavily on Priscilla J. Brewer, "We Have Got a Very Good Cooking Stove: Advertising, Design, and Consumer Response to the Cookstove, 1815–1880," *Winterthur Portfolio*, Spring 1990, which was recommended to me, with good reason, by Frank G. White of Old Sturbridge Village. Also Brown, *Hundred Years*, 56–58 ("When we went to keeping house"); Giedion, *Mechanization*, 527–36; *Godey's Lady's Book*, Jan. 1866; Grow, *Kitchens* 10–16; Ann Howe, *The American Kitchen Directory and Housewife* (Cincinnati, 1868) ("meat is better roasted," as quoted in Brewer, 50); Janney, *John Jay Janney's Virginia*, 22 ("We had the first cooking stove ever seen"); William J. Keep, "Early American Cooking Stoves," *Old-Time New England*, Oct. 1931; U.S. Patent 25,532, Sept. 20, 1859 ("Electro-Heater").
THE NO LONGER MISSING SINK: Bacon, "Growth of Household Conveniences," 32 (c. 1865 sink); CUR, Hyde Hall, Cooperstown, N.Y.; Putnam, *Improved Plumbing*, 95 (need for thorough draining).

AN AMERICAN INSTITUTION: Anderson, *Refrigeration*, 8, 27, 36 (changes in diet), 13 (Wyeth ice cutter), 16 (ice cutting by 1850s), 22–23 (E. Leslie, *The House Book*, Philadelphia, 1840, wrapping blanket around ice, icebox in 1840s), 26–27 (ice consumption c. 1860); Ierley, *Open House*, 70–71 (Gorrie, Carré); *New England Farmer*, July 21, 1826 ("Refrigerators, manufactured"; courtesy of Old Sturbridge Village); *New-York Mirror*, July 14, 1838 ("It is but a few years"); Nichols, *Forty Years*, 162–63 ("In the long and almost perpetual summers"); Randolph, *Virginia House-Wife*, 1825 ed. (description of refrigerator).

THE FUTURE: MORE RECOGNIZABLE: 1900: CUR, TECH, Dwight D. Eisenhower Library, Abilene, Kan.; Eisenhower, *At Ease*, 32–33, 65–74 (boyhood home, early Abilene), 32 ("She rotated our duties"), 65 ("a glowing thoroughfare"), 72 ("house seemed a mansion"), 73–74 ("Some mornings were worse than others"); Miller, *Ike*, 67–71, 92–93, 92 ("Before that little potbellied stove," "There was always a scramble").

PART 3. THE PERFECTING OF COMFORT: THE 1920S TO THE PRESENT

Chiefly, *Literary Digest*, "An American House in Paris," Oct. 31, 1925 (including quotes ascribed to Albert Broisat). Also Faulkner, *American Economic History*, 534 (installment buying in 1920s); *House & Garden*, Jan. 1926, "The Rise of Comfort" (introductory quote); Sears, Roebuck and Co., catalogs for 1926 and 1927.

THE MODERN HOUSE OF THE 1920S: Substantially from Whitton, *The New Servant*, especially "Kitchen Assistants," 196–212, and "Other Useful Devices," 227–42; also, 116–20 (electric washing machines), 197–98 (description of "kitchen aid" and "anything but talk"), 214–17 (electric refrigerator), 227–32 (furnace blowers and stokers); "probably no machine in the entire galaxy," 204–5; "Indeed it is really unnecessary," 228–29; "the electric heating pad," 239–40; "the small electric hair dryer," 241. Also *Domestic Engineering Catalog Directory*, 1924, "Goetz Brass Co." (mixer faucet); Haines, Jones & Cadbury Company, Philadelphia, "Hajoca" plumbing catalog, 1913 (materials used for shower curtains, types of tubs and showers in use); *House Beautiful*, May 1927 (refrigerator ad, "colors to match the modern kitchen"); *House & Garden*, May 1927 (Walker Super-Sink ad); Elizabeth MacDonald, "Kitchen Equipment," *House Beautiful*, Feb. 1926 ("Ten years ago, when a building was started"); Sears, Roebuck and Co., catalog, 1927 (types of appliances and accessories in use).

TABLE — THE INCREASING ATTAINABILITY OF HOUSEHOLD TECHNOLOGY: Wages, 1805: chiefly Wright, *Industrial Evolution*, "Labor and Rates of Wages, 1790–1890," 215–18, corroborated by Blodget, *Economica*, 202 (rate for laborers, 1805); annual wages were computed using a fifty-two-week year. Costs, 1805: Construction records for Gore Place, Waltham, Mass., 1806 and 1807. All three items were almost certainly imported from England. The stove, not otherwise identified, was presumably for cooking. Wages, 1860: Chiefly Wright, corroborated by Martin, *Standard of Living in 1860*, "Family Income and Family Expenditures" and "An American Standard of Living," 393–427, using a fifty-two-week year. Costs, 1860: bill from Philbin & Quin, plumbers, to New York Central Railroad for "1 Pan Water Closet Complete," installed in office at 239 Broadway, New York City, on April 13, 1860 (Warshaw Collection, Smithsonian Institution). American Steam Washing Machine Manufacturing Co., New York, 1855 catalog (Warshaw Collection). The basic family washing machine ($50) was used here. A larger household model was also avauilable at $75. Wm. Reynolds, Meadville, Pa., bill dated Aug. 14, 1857, from Cox, Richardson & Boynton, New York, for Boynton Wood Furnace (Crawford County Historical Society). Wages, 1927: *Statistical Abstract of the United States*, 1935, "Average

Hours and Earnings in Manufacturing Industries," 310–11, and "Average Hourly Wage Rates Paid Common Labor," 314. The laborer was figured at 1927 national average of 42.6 cents per hour, using an eight-hour day; the machinist at 1927 average of 72.8 cents an hour using actual average of 47.7 hours per week; the auto worker at 1928 average of 75.6 cents an hour for actual average work week of 47 hours. Here a fifty-one-week year is used, allowing for a theoretical one-week vacation. Costs, 1927: Primarily 1927 Sears, Roebuck catalog, using either the model featured or the mid-priced model if there was a range of prices. The cost of 1805 water closet "as installed" includes $104.25 for purchase and/or installation of pipe shortly after purchase of water closet and presumably for that purpose; but no attempt was made to compute labor. The 1860 and 1927 water closets "as installed" were figured at 2.5 times cost of water closet based on the Philbin & Quin bill. The 1860 and 1927 furnaces "as installed" were computed at 3 times the cost of the furnace, based on actual figures in Federal Furnace League, *The Warm-Air Furnace*, pp. 94–95.

Power, Fuel, and Infrastructure

THE AGE OF TAMED LIGHTNING: Byrn, *The Progress of Invention*, 54; Davenport, *Davenport*, 56–58, 57 ("Like a flash of lightning"), 58; Kranzberg, *Technology*, I, Harold I. Sharlin, "Applications of Electricity," 563–78; *New York Times*, March 10, 1876 ("The great engine erected"), Feb. 3, 1882 (Philadelphia, Brush Electric), Sept. 5, 1882 ("Edison's central station"), May 13, 1893 (Electricity Building, "rival in brilliancy the sun itself"), June 2, 1893 (Tower of Light); *Scientific American*, Mar. 19, 1904 (Little Wonder Water Motor); Sears, Roebuck catalog, 1897, 898 (small electric motors).

A LOOK BACK AT THE FUTURE: A. E. Kennelly, "Electricity in the Household," *Scribner's Magazine*, Jan. 1890.

THE POWERING OF COMFORT: Elfun, *Walk in the Park*, 9 (GE appliances c. 1907); DuVall, *Domestic Technology*, 283 (wind farms); Judith Anne Gunther, "Power Houses: Who Needs a Roof? Cover Your House with Solar Cells Instead," *Popular Science*, May 1996 (photovoltaic cells incorporated into building materials), 78 (30 cents vs. 8 cents per kilowatt-hour); Halacy, *Earth, Water, Wind, and Sun*, "Power from the Wind," passim; Eric Herman, "Last Days of the World's Largest Windmill," *Mother Earth News*, June-July 1996 (Medicine Bow); Robert D. Kahn, "Harvesting the Wind," *Technology Review*, Nov.–Dec. 1984 (modern use of wind power in California); Kransberg, II, Bruce C. Netschert, "Developing the Energy Inheritance," 247–50 (electric power); Park, *Wind Power Book*, 16–17 (windchargers, pre-REA use); Righter, *Wind Energy*, 175–80 (Medicine Bow); Shepherd, *Development of the Windmill*, 33 (Brush windmill); *Statistical Abstract*, 1997, 596, quoting U.S. Energy Information Administration, *Annual Energy Review* (nuclear power statistics); U.S. Dept. of Commerce, *American Housing Survey 1995*, 7, "Fuels, All Housing Units" (solar energy statistics); *World Almanac*, 1929, 140–41 (production of electricity in 1927 and 1928, including comparison with 1912; "output equal to the rest of the world combined").

FUEL: CHANGING PREFERENCES: *House Beautiful*, "Oil Burners," Jan. 1926 ("Women have found no magic words"); *International Library of Technology*, LXXI (1906), 2–48, "Gas Making" (use of gas in early 1900s); Kranzberg, II, *supra*, 246–47 (natural gas); *Statistical Abstract of the United States*, 1996, 722, "Heating Equipment and Fuels for Occupied Units: 1950 to 1993" (household fuels); Whitton, *The New Servant*, 230–31 (30 tons of coal a year); *World Almanac*, 1929, 141 (natural and manufactured gas industries in 1927).

INFRASTRUCTURE: WATER AND SEWERAGE: American Society of Civil Engineers, *Proceedings*, Sept. 1927, 1585–1648, "A Symposium:

Historic Review of the Development of Sanitary Engineering in the United States during the Past One Hundred and Fifty Years," passim, 1578 (waterworks construction in the 1870s); *Datapedia*, 166, 170 (public water supply, 1990s); U.S. Census Bureau, *Historical Statistics*, 434 (public water supply 1900, mid-1920s).

Heating and Air Conditioning

FROM CENTRAL SUN TO CENTRAL HEAT: Carrier Corporation archives, 1959 ad for combination air conditioner and heat pump window unit, c. 1960 brochure, "How Carrier Heat Pump Weathermakers cool and heat with electricity ("think of it in terms of an ordinary household refrigerator"); *Consumer Reports*, Oct. 1993 "Heat Pumps"; Elliot, *Technics*, 294 (1880s hot-air furnaces, hot-water radiant heat); *House Beautiful*, "For Today's Houses: Heating and Air Conditioning," Summer 1940 (forced circulation hot-water heat in use); Charles L. Hubbard, "Heating and Ventilating," *Domestic Engineering*, April 15, 1901 ("In construction a furnace is a large stove"); Lescarboura, *Scientific American Home-Owners Handbook*, 375–86 (heating in the 1920s), 377 (original concept of hot-air heat as a stove within an enclosure is expressed thus: "The cold air, taken in through the cold-air duct, comes in contact with the hot stove, is heated, and then rises up through the risers to the various parts of the house"); Putnam, *Open Fire-Place* (jacketed furnace in 1882); Round Oak Co., 1942 catalog, Henry Ford Museum & Greenfield Village Research Center (1940s compact furnace); Dr. G. M. Sternberg, *Dr. G. M. Sternberg's Electro-Magnetic Regulator* (New York: n.d., early 1870s), copy in archives, History of Technology, National Museum of American History ("The regulative function of electricity," "In fact its possible and useful applications"); U.S. Dept. of Commerce, *American Housing Survey 1995*, 5, "Selected Equipment and Plumbing, All Housing Units" (percentages, types of heat in use); Whitton, *New*

Servant, 231 (1920s stokers); York International Corp., 1998 catalog, "Diamond 80" furnace (features of modern furnace).

INVENTIONS FOR COOLING: *Business Week*, "Home-made Weather Now Made at Home," Nov. 5, 1930 (early home air conditioners, esp. Frigidaire); Butt, *Taft and Roosevelt*, II, 659 (White House air-cooling apparatus, 1911, letter dated May 20, 1911); Cutler, *Life*, I, 269 (visit with Franklin); *Dictionary of American Biography*, "Carrier" (1902 Brooklyn printing plant); Elliot, *Technics*, 305–25 (air conditioning generally), 305 (1928 introduction of room air conditioner), 323 (Kahnweiler's chair); Ingels, *Carrier*, 84–85 (development of home air conditioner, early 1930s); *Literary Digest*, "The President's Weather," Sept. 13, 1930 (Taft, air conditioning of White House offices 1930); *Newsweek*, July 10, 1950 ("Booming like television"); *New York Times*, Sept. 16, 1882 (Independent Ice Co. bill); *Reader's Digest*, "Comfort for Millions," July 1950 (sales doubled in two years, $300 air conditioner, three years to pay); *Saturday Evening Post*, "He Manufactures Weather," May 25, 1929 (Carrier and air conditioning generally); *Scientific American*, "The Presidential Cold Air Machine," Aug. 6, 1881 ("75 degrees day and night," Garfield generally); Seale, *President's House*, 523–25 (Garfield), 524 (Newcomb, "cool, dry, ample"), 759 (Taft); Skolfield, *Electric Fans*, electric fans generally, 2 (Thebes 1700 B.C.), 9 (desk fan 1882); U.S. Navy Dept., *Reports of Officers*, 1882 (Garfield air cooling apparatus generally), 4 ("any excess of moisture would be absorbed," quoting Simon Newcomb), 10 ("Our operations at the Executive Mansion have proved"); U.S. Patents 12,106, Louis Stein, Dec. 19, 1854 ("Revolving Fan," "rotary motion imparted by electromagnets"), 246,013, Ralph S. Jennings, Aug. 23, 1881 (air-cooling apparatus), and 387,954, Ransom F. Humiston, Aug. 14, 1888 (maiden with urn, "During the summer season the weather often becomes").

Lighting

A BURNING QUESTION: Depew, *One Hundred Years*, 299 ("The Welsbach invention . . . no competitor but the heavenly bodies"); Heyn, *Century*, 65 (Davy and early arc light); New York *Sun*, quoted in *Popular Science Monthly*, Dec. 1878, 235 ("There are problems involved"); *New York Times*, Oct. 22, 1877 ("Messrs. Voison and Drouier"), April 22, 1878 ("The effect was most brilliant," quoting Cleveland *Herald)*, Dec. 28, 1879 ("a short, thick-set man"); *Popular Science Monthly*, 1895, quoted in Heyn, *Century*, 70 ("Notwithstanding the rapid development of electric lighting"); Harry J. Thorne, "From the Candle to Electricity," letter to the editor, *Scientific American*, March 1928, 274–76 ("With some friends I found myself").

THE NIGHT THE LIGHTS WENT ON: Heyn, *Century of Wonders*, 67 (*Popular Science* quote, "Dr. Phipson has proposed a new method"); *New York Times*, Sept. 5, 1882 ("It was about 5 o'clock yesterday afternoon"); Harold P. Strand, "Pointers on Installing the New Fluorescent Lamps," *Popular Science*, Jan. 1940, 136 ("They rival daylight in illumination").

The Bathroom

REFLECTING ON PROGRESS: Brown, *Water-Closets*, 144–49 (Doulton, Winn tanks), 148 ("This tank is waste preventing"); *Consumer Reports*, "Low Flow Toilets," Feb. 1995 ("dual flushers," pressurized flush, late twentieth century generally); *Consumers' Research*, Jan. 1994 (low-flow toilets); Gerhard, *Water Supply, Sewerage, and Plumbing*, 137 ("At the present time pan-closets are scarcely to be found"); *House & Garden*, Sept. 1926 "Development of the Bathroom" ("Can you think of any room" and "Contrast our modern bathroom"); *International Library of Technology*, LXXII (1906), 16 ("the best form of closet on the market"); Thomas McKeown, "Siphons," *Journal of the Association of Engineering Societies*, June 1900, 339 (Manchester), 340–41("the reason we have not had siphons"); Jordan L. Mott, "Plumbers' and Steam-Fitters' Supplies," in Depew, *One Hundred Years*, 364–70 (water closets and plumbing generally, c. 1895); Standard Sanitary Mfg. Co. catalog, July 1, 1937, "After Fifty Years," 89–91 (brief recap of water closet design, 1885–1930s); Starbuck, *Modern Plumbing*, 115 ("Modern water closets are superior to the old-style"), 118 (use of vitreous chinaware), 271 (increasing use of brass, copper, and iron instead of lead); Syphon Closet Co., *Syphon Supplement*, 1 ("the exceedingly simple and natural working of its parts").

EXPECTING MUCH: *Domestic Engineering Catalog*, 1924, 529 (mixer faucet), 547 (showers and accessories); Fairfax Downey, "Bathtubs, Early Americana," *Scribner's Magazine*, Oct. 1926, 440–43 ("It needs no old-timer to recall," "Even in the simple little bathroom," and "Now we may have our bathrooms done"); Jordan L. Mott, "Plumbers' and Steam-Fitters' Supplies," in Depew, *One Hundred Years*, 365 ("a wooden box lined with lead").

Appliances

"THEN THE MACHINE TAKES OVER": Acme Washing Machine Co., Columbus, Ohio, brochure, 1905, in Warshaw Collection, Smithsonian Institution ("There are today hundreds of thousands of women"); Elfun, *Walk Through the Park*, 21 (1906 Thor as first electric washer, 1926 Easy as first use of centrifugal force instead of wringer, 1930 dryer of J. Ross Moore); Christine Frederick, "The New Housekeeping," *Ladies' Home Journal*, Sept. 1912 ("washing is done in most houses"); Kane, *First Facts*, 650 (Smith, rotary motion washing machine, 1859); *McCall's*, "Automatic washers and dryers," Sept. 1945 ("Only a few lucky women," "All of these washers work without watching," and "While the second load of clothes is washing"); National Electric Supply Co. catalog, c. 1907, Smithsonian Institution, Electrical Collections.

OTHER APPLIANCES: DuVall, *Domestic Technology*, 201–2 (irons generally, Montgomery Ward 1895); Elfun, *Walk Through the Park*, 22–23 (Walker diswasher); Giedion, *Mechanization*, 548–49, 590–95 (carpet sweeper, vacuum cleaner); Leeds, *Household Budget*, 79–83 (survey of sixty families and "good training for girls"); Lifshey, *Housewares Story*, 238–39 (irons generally: 1882 patent, 1926 steam iron, 1934 thermostatic control, 1957 spray steam, and 1965 Teflon), 290–91 (carpet sweepers); *McCall's*, Sept. 1945 (ironers), Nov. 1945 (vacuum cleaners); Whitton, *The New Servant*, 234 ("the electric sewing machine . . . as the name implies"). The compilation of earliest known dates of various electrical appliances is based primarily on material in Electrical Collections, National Museum of American History, Smithsonian Institution. The reference to Leeds is from Cowan, *More Work for Mother*.

The Kitchen

OUT OF THE BLUE: *Appliance Service News*, Dec. 1991 (presentation to Smithsonian Institution of first Tappan microwave, with details of what it was like); S. S. Block, "New Foods to Tempt Your Palate," *Science Digest*, Oct. 1944 ("A post-war innovation of the frozen food processors"); Heyn, *Century of Wonders*, 288 (development of radar); *International Directory of Company Histories*, II, 85 (Raytheon, half-million magnetrons); *New York Times*, Oct. 8, 1946 ("Stove Operating with Basic Radar"), Mar. 14, 1949 ("Radarange among Future Home Marvels"); Raytheon Company, letter to the author Aug. 27, 1998 (chronology pertaining to Raytheon); Van Zante, *Microwave Oven*, xiii–xiv (microwaves in 1970s, over 100,000 in sales, high of $1,500, popularity in Japan).

OTHER STEPS TO THE FUTURE: Anderson, *Refrigeration*, 100 (mechanical refrigerator proposed 1887, several on market 1895), 101 (Audiffren), 194–99 (home refrigerators generally), 195 (first Kelvinator 1918), 196–97 (automatic control, sealed unit, Freon-12), 213 (number of refrigerators in 1921, 1930, 1944), 298–99 (home freezers generally, 1.2 million in 1949); *Consumer Reports*, March 1996, "Cooking with Gas" (gas ranges), Oct. 1996, "Choices for Cooks" (electric ranges); Du Vall, *Domestic Technology*, 116 (automatic timing control for electric range); Elfun, *Walk Through the Park*, 16 (Audiffren), 18–19 (George Hughes, GE 1913); Frederick, *New Housekeeping*, viii ("At first it did not occur to me"); Giedion, *Mechanization*, "Mechanical Refrigeration after 1800," 599–603, 602 (number of refrigerators in 1923, 1933, and 1941, start of production by Kelvinator and Frigidaire); Ierley, *Open House*, 72 (frozen food), 75 (early gas and electric cooking); *McCall's*, Sept. 1945, "Refrigerators," "Freezers" ("large enough to take a whole roast"), "Gas Ranges"; *National Cyclopaedia of American Biography*, XLII (George Hughes, 1904); *New York Times*, July 3, 1927, "Kitchen Planning in Modern Homes" ("The old notion that a kitchen," "It would be interesting to know how many thousands," "The old-time kitchen used to have"), July 13, 1945, "Makers Agree on Standard Sizes to Aid Kitchen Equipment Problem" (standardization of sizes); Sears, Roebuck and Co. archives, "Historical Review: Refrigerators and Freezers," 1995; Sears, Roebuck catalog, 1908, 638–39, "Acme Charm Steel Range" (features of the turn-of-century range); Strasser, *Never Done*, 36–42 (turn-of-the-century ranges, reference to study of range maintenance chores in 1899).

EPILOGUE: Breckenridge, *Recollections*, 185 ("The crank, too, with the total depravity"); Hill, *Homespun*, 18 ("The Age we live in"); TECH, Wadsworth-Longfellow House, Portland, Maine.

BIBLIOGRAPHY

Books

Accum, Fredrick. *A Practical Treatise on Gas-Light.* London, 1815.

Acrelius, Israel. *A History of New Sweden.* Philadelphia, 1876.

Adams, William Howard. *Jefferson's Monticello.* New York: Abbeville Press, 1983.

Anderson, Oscar Edward, Jr. *Refrigeration in America: A History of a New Technology and Its Impact.* Princeton, N.J.: Princeton University Press, 1953.

Appleton's Cyclopaedia of Applied Mechanics. New York, 1895.

Arndt, Karl J. *Economy on the Ohio.* Worcester, Mass.: Harmony Society Press, 1984.

Aubrey, John. *The Natural History and Antiquities of the County of Surrey.* London, 1718–1719.

Avery, Madalyn. *Household Physics.* New York: Macmillan, 1938.

Bathe, Greville, and Dorothy Bathe. *Jacob Perkins: His Inventions, His Times, and His Contemporaries.* Philadelphia: Historical Society of Pennsylvania, 1943.

——*Oliver Evans: A Chronicle of Early American Engineering.* Philadelphia: Historical Society of Pennsylvania, 1935. Reprint, New York: Arno Press, 1972.

Bayles, James C. *House Drainage and Water Service.* New York, 1880.

Beckmann, Johann. *A History of Inventions, Discoveries and Origins.* 4th ed. London, 1846.

Beecher, Catharine E., and Harriet Beecher Stowe. *The American Woman's Home.* New York, 1869.

Beedell, Suzanne. *Windmills.* New York: Scribner's, 1975.

Bent, Silas. *Slaves by the Billion: The Story of Mechanical Progress in the Home.* New York: Longmans, Green, 1938.

Bernan, Walter [Robert Meikleham]. *On the History and Art of Warming and Ventilating.* London, 1845.

Bertram, Anthony. *The House: A Summary of the Art and Science of Domestic Architecture.* London: Adam & Charles Black, 1945.

Bibliothèque Britannique. Geneva, 1802.

Bishop, J. Leander. *A History of American Manufactures from 1608 to 1860.* 3d ed. Philadelphia, 1868.

Blake, John B. *Public Health in the Town of Boston, 1630–1822.* Cambridge, Mass.: Harvard University Press, 1959.

Blodget, Samuel. *Economica: A Statistical Manual for the United States of America.* Washington, D.C., 1806.

Breckenridge, Frances A. *Recollections of a New England Town.* Meriden, Conn., 1899.

Brewster, Charles W. *Rambles about Portsmouth.* Portsmouth, N.H., 1869.

Bridenbaugh, Carl. *Cities in the Wilderness.* 1938. Reprint, New York: Capricorn Books, 1955.

Brown, Glenn. *History of the United States Capitol.* Washington, D.C.: U.S. Government Printing Office, 1900.

——*Water Closets: A Historical, Mechanical and Sanitary Treatise.* New York, 1884.

Brown, Harriet Connor. *Grandmother Brown's Hundred Years, 1827–1927.* Boston: Little Brown, 1929.

Brown, Richard D. *Modernization: The Transformation of American Life, 1600–1865.* New York: Hill & Wang, 1976.

Brown, Sanborn C. *Benjamin Thompson, Count Rumford.* Cambridge, Mass.: MIT Press, 1979.

——*Count Rumford, Physicist Extraordinary.* London: Heinemann, 1964.

Butt, Archibald. *Taft and Roosevelt: The Intimate Letters of Archie Butt.* Garden City, N.Y.: Doubleday Doran, 1930.

Byington, Margaret F. *Homestead: The Households of a Mill Town.* 1910. Reprint, Pittsburgh: University Center for International Studies, 1974.

Byrn, Edward W. *The Progress of Invention in the Nineteenth Century.* New York, 1900.

Cardwell, Donald. *Norton History of Technology.* New York: Norton, 1995.

Caulkins, Frances Manwaring. *History of New London.* New London, Conn., 1895.

Child, [Lydia] Maria. *Letters from New York.* New York, 1845.

Clark, Clifford E., Jr. *The American Family Home.* Chapel Hill, N.C.: University of North Carolina Press, 1986.

Cleaveland, Henry W., William Backus, and Samuel Backus. *Village and Farm Cottages.* New York, 1856.

Cohen, I. Bernard. *Benjamin Franklin's Science.* Cambridge, Mass.: Harvard University Press, 1990.

Cohen, Jeffrey A., and Charles E. Brownell. *The Architectural Drawings of Benjamin Henry Latrobe.* New Haven, Conn.: Yale University Press, 1994.

Colden, Cadwallader. "Observations on the Fever Which Prevailed in the City of New-York in 1741 and 2." *American Medical and Philosophical Register*, vol. 1 (1814).

Cooke, Lawrence S., ed. *Lighting in America: From Colonial Rushlights to Victorian Chandeliers.* Pittstown, N.J.: Main Street Press, 1984.

Cooper, Thomas. *Some Information Concerning Gas Lights.* Philadelphia, 1816.

Cowan, Ruth Schwartz. *More Work for Mother: The Ironies of Household Technology from the Open Hearth to the Microwave.* New York: Basic Books, 1983.

Cumming, Alexander. *The Elements of Clock and Watch-work Adapted to Practice.* London, 1766.

Cutler, Manasseh. *Life, Journals and Correspondence of the Rev. Manasseh Cutler.* Cincinnati, 1888.

Davenport, Walter Rice. *Thomas Davenport.* Montpelier: Vermont Historical Society, 1929.

Davies, J. D. Griffith. *A King in Toils.* London: Lindsay Drummond, 1938.

De Bono, Edward, ed. *Eureka! An Illustrated History of Inventions.* New York: Holt, Rinehart, 1974.

Depew, Chauncey M., ed. *One Hundred Years of American Commerce.* New York, 1895.

Derby, George. *Anthracite and Health.* Boston, 1868.

Derry, T. K., and Trevor I. Williams. *A Short History of Technology from the Earliest Times to A.D. 1900.* London: Oxford University Press [1970].

Downing, Andrew Jackson. *The Architecture of Country Houses.* New York, 1850.

DuVall, Nell. *Domestic Technology: A Chronology of Developments.* Boston: G. K. Hall, 1988.

Eastman, R. O., Inc. *Zanesville and 36 other American Communities: A Study of Markets and of the Telephone as a Market Index.* New York: Literary Digest, 1927.

Eighty Years' Progress of the United States ("By Eminent Literary Men"). Hartford, Conn., 1869.

Eisenhower, Dwight D. *At Ease: Stories I Tell to Friends.* Garden City, N.Y.: Doubleday, 1967.

Elfun Historical Society. Franklin Friday, author and editor. *A Walk Through the Park: The History of GE Appliances and Appliance Park.* Louisville, Ky.: Elfun Historical Society, 1987.

Elliott, Cecil D. *Technics and Architecture: The Development of Materials and Systems for Buildings.* Cambridge, Mass.: MIT Press, 1992.

Ellis, George E. *Memoir of Sir Benjamin Thompson, Count Rumford.* Boston, 1871.

Evans, Oliver. *The Young Mill-Wright & Miller's Guide.* London, 1795.

Faulkner, Harold Underwood. *American Economic History.* 8th ed. New York: Harper & Row, 1960.

Federal Furnace League. *The Warm-Air Furnace.* [Albany, N.Y.], 1909.

Ferguson, Eugene S. *Bibliography of the History of Technology.* Cambridge, Mass.: MIT Press, 1968.

———"An Historial Sketch of Central Heating: 1800–1860," in Charles E. Peterson, ed., *Building Early America.* Radnor, Pa.: Chilton, 1976.

Fiennes, Celia. *The Journeys of Celia Fiennes.* Edited by Christopher Morris. London: Cresset Press, 1949.

Ford, Paul Leicester. *The Many-Sided Franklin.* New York, 1899.

Franklin, Benjamin. *An Account Of the New Invented Pennsylvanian Fire-Places.* Philadelphia, 1744.

———*The Autobiography of Benjamin Franklin.* Edited by Leonard W. Labaree et al. New Haven, Conn.: Yale University Press, 1964.

———*The Papers of Benjamin Franklin.* Edited by Leonard W. Labaree. New Haven, Conn.: Yale University Press, 1960.

———*Philosophical and Miscellaneous Papers.* London, 1787.

Frederick, Christine. *The New Housekeeping: Efficiency Studies in Home Management.* New York: Doubleday, 1913.

Furnas, J. C. *The Americans: A Social History of the United States, 1587–1914.* New York: Putnam, 1969.

———*How America Lives.* New York: Henry Holt, [1941].

Gallier, James. *American Builders' Price-Book and Estimator.* New York, 1833.

Garrett, Elisabeth Donaghy. *At Home: The American Family, 1750–1870.* New York: Harry N. Abrams, 1990.

Gauger, Nicolas. *Fires Improv'd.* Trans. J. T. Desaguliers. London, 1715.

——*La mécanique du feu*. Paris, 1714.

Gerhard, William Paul. *The American Practice of Gas Piping and Gas Lighting in Buildings*. New York: McGraw, 1908.

——*Hints on the Drainage and Sewerage of Dwellings*. New York, 1884.

——*The Water Supply, Sewerage and Plumbing of Modern City Buildings*. New York: Wiley, 1910.

Giedion, Siegfried. *Mechanization Takes Command*. New York: Oxford University Press, 1948.

Girouard, Mark. *Life in the English Country House*. New Haven, Conn.: Yale University Press, 1978.

Gold, Stephen J. *Gold's Patent Low Pressure Self-Regulating Steam Heating Apparatus*. New York, 1868.

Goldstein, Jonathan. *Philadelphia and the China Trade, 1682–1846*. University Park: University of Pennsylvania Press, 1978.

Goodrich, S. G. *Recollections of a Lifetime*. New York, 1856.

Gowans, Alan. *Images of American Living*. New York: Harper & Row, 1976.

Grier, Katherine C. *Culture and Comfort: People, Parlors, and Upholstery, 1850–1930*. Rochester, N.Y.: Strong Museum, 1988.

Grow, Lawrence. *The Old House Book of Kitchens and Dining Rooms*. New York: Warner Books, 1981.

Halacy, D. S., Jr. *Earth, Water, Wind, and Sun*. New York: Harper & Row, 1977.

Hamlin, Talbot. *Benjamin Henry Latrobe*. New York: Oxford University Press, 1955.

Harington, John. *Sir John Harington's New Discourse of a Stale Subject, Called the Metamorphosis of Ajax*. Edited by Elizabeth Story Donno. London: Routledge & Kegan Paul, 1962.

Harrison, S. A. *Hints on Warming and Ventilating Public and Private Buildings*. Philadelphia, [1850s?].

Hellyer, S. Stevens. *Lectures on the Science and Art of Sanitary Plumbing*. London, 1882.

——*The Plumber and Sanitary Houses*, 4th ed. London, 1887.

Heyn, Ernest V. *A Century of Wonders: 100 Years of Popular Science*. Garden City, N.Y.: Doubleday, 1972.

Hibbert, Christopher. *The Virgin Queen: Elizabeth I, Genius of the Golden Age*. Reading, Mass.: Addison-Wesley, 1991.

Hill, George Canning [Thomas Lackland]. *Homespun*. New York, 1867.

Histoire de la vie privée. Edited Philippe Aries and Georges Duby. Paris: Seuil, 1985–1987.

Hodges, Henry. *Technology in the Ancient World*. New York: Knopf, 1970.

Holohan, Dan. *The Lost Art of Steam Heating*. Bethpage, N.Y.: Dan Holohan Associates, 1992.

Howell, John W., and Henry Schroeder. *The History of the Incandescent Lamp*. Schenectady, N.Y.: Maqua Company, 1927.

Ierley, Merritt. *Open House: A Guided Tour of the American Home, 1637–Present*. New York: Henry Holt, 1999.

——*A Place in History: North Arlington, New Jersey: A Centennial Chronicle of the Birthplace of Steam Power in America*. North Arlington, N.J.: North Arlington Public Library, 1994.

Ingels, Margaret. *Willis Haviland Carrier, Father of Air Conditioning*. Garden City, N.Y.: Country Life Press, 1952.

International Directory of Company Histories. Chicago, St. James Press, 1988. Place of publication varies with successive volumes.

International Library of Technology. [Scranton, Pa., 1903 —]

James, Peter, and Nick Thorpe. *Ancient Inventions*. New York: Ballantine Books, 1994.

Janney, John Jay. *John Jay Janney's Virginia: An American Farm Lad's Life in the Early 19th Century*. McLean, Va.: EPM

Publications, c. 1978.

Jennings, Jan, and Herbert Gottfried. *American Vernacular Interior Architecture, 1870–1940.* New York: Van Nostrand Reinhold, 1988.

Johnson, S. W. *Rural Economy.* New York, 1806.

Johnson, Thomas H. *The Oxford Companion to American History.* New York: Oxford University Press, 1966.

Kranzberg, Melvin, and Carroll W. Pursell Jr. *Technology in Western Civilization.* New York: Oxford University Press, 1967.

Kurian, George Thomas. *Datapedia.* Lanham, Md.: Bernan Press, 1994.

LaFollette, Marcel C., and Jeffrey K. Stine, eds., *Technology and Choice: Readings from Technology and Culture.* Chicago: University of Chicago Press, 1991.

Larkin, Jack. *The Reshaping of Everyday Life, 1790–1840.* New York: HarperCollins, 1988.

Larsen, Egon. *An American in Europe: The Life of Benjamin Thompson, Count Rumford.* London: Rider, 1953.

Latrobe, Benjamin Henry. *The Correspondence and Miscellaneous Papers of Benjamin Henry Latrobe.* Edited by John C. Van Horne and Lee W. Formwalt. New Haven, Conn.: Yale University Press, 1984.

——*Impressions Respecting New Orleans.* Samuel Wilson Jr., ed. New York: Columbia University Press, 1951.

——*Journal of Latrobe.* [New York, 1905].

Leeds, John B. *The Household Budget: With a Special Inquiry into the Amount and Value of Household Work.* Philadelphia: Privately printed Ph.D. diss., Columbia University, 1917.

Lescarboura, Austin C. *Scientific American Home-Owners Handbook.* New York: Scientific American, 1924.

Levering, Joseph Mortimer. *A History of Bethlehem, Pennsylvania 1741–1892.* Bethlehem, 1903.

Lifshey, Earl. *The Housewares Story: A History of the American Housewares Industry.* Chicago: National Housewares Manufacturers Association, 1973.

Longmate, Norman. *King Cholera: The Biography of a Disease.* London: Hamish Hamilton, 1966.

Luckiesh, Matthew. *Artificial Light: Its Influence upon Civilization.* New York: Century, 1920.

Lupton, Ellen, and J. Abbott Miller. *The Bathroom, the Kitchen, and the Aesthetics of Waste: A Process of Elimination.* Cambridge, Mass.: MIT List Visual Arts Center; New York: Princeton Architectural Press, c. 1992.

Lyell, Charles. *A Second Visit to the United States.* New York, 1849.

Lynd, Robert S., and Helen Merrell Lynd. *Middletown: A Study in Contemporary American Culture.* New York: Harcourt, Brace, 1929.

Martin, Edgar W. *The Standard of Living in 1860.* Chicago: University of Chicago, 1942.

McGaw, Judith A., ed. *Early American Technology: Making and Doing Things from the Colonial Era to 1850.* Chapel Hill: University of North Carolina Press, 1994.

McLaughlin, Jack. *Jefferson and Monticello: The Biography of a Builder.* New York: Henry Holt, 1988.

McNeil, Ian. *Joseph Bramah: A Century of Invention, 1749–1851.* Newton Abbot, England: David & Charles, 1968.

——ed. *An Encyclopedia of the History of Technology.* London: Routledge, 1990.

Mease, James. *The Picture of Philadelphia.* Philadelphia, 1811.

Meikleham, Robert. *On the History and Art of Warming and Ventilating Rooms and Buildings.* London, 1845.

Metcalf, Leonard, and Harrison P. Eddy. *Sewerage and Sewage Disposal.* New York: McGraw-Hill, 1930.

Miller, Merle. *Ike the Soldier: As They Knew Him.* New York: Putnam, 1987.

Moore, Thomas. *An Essay on the Most Eligible Construction of Ice-Houses. Also, a Description of the Newly Invented Machine Called the Refrigerator.* Baltimore, 1803.

Morton, Thomas G. *The History of Pennsylvania Hospital.* Philadelphia, 1897.

Moss, Roger W. *Lighting for Historic Buildings.* Washington, D.C.: Preservation Press, 1988.

Mott, J. L., Co. *Description and Design of Mott's Patented Articles.* New York, 1841.

Nichols, Thomas Low. *Forty Years of American Life.* 1864. Reprint, New York: Stackpole, 1937.

Nylander, Jane C. *Our Own Snug Fireside: Images of the New England Home, 1760–1860.* New York: Knopf, 1993.

Ogilby, John. *Africa.* London, 1670.

Orton, Vrest. *The Forgotten Art of Building a Good Fireplace: The Story of Count Rumford and His Fireplace.* 2d ed. Camden, Me.: Yankee Books, 1974.

Packard, Francis R. *Some Account of the Pennsylvania Hospital.* 1938. Rev. Philadelphia: Pennsylvania Hospital, 1957.

Park, Jack. *The Wind Power Book.* Palo Alto, Calif.: Cheshire Books, 1981.

Peale, Charles Willson. *Charles Willson Peale and His World.* Edited by Edgar P. Richardson, Brooke Hindle, and Lillian B. Miller. New York: Harry Abrams, 1983.

Peirce, Josephine H. *Fire on the Hearth.* Springfield, Mass.: Pond-Eckberg Co., 1951.

Peterson, Charles E., ed. *Building Early America.* Radnor, Pa.: Chilton, 1976.

Petroski, Henry. *Invention by Design: How Engineers Get from Thought to Thing.* Cambridge, Mass.: Harvard University Press, 1996.

Pettibone, Daniel. *Description of the Improvements of the Rarifying Air-Stove.* Philadelphia, 1810.

———*Pettibone's Economy of Fuel.* Philadelphia, 1812.

Philadelphia in 1824. Philadelphia, 1824.

Philadelphia's First Water Works. Philadelphia: Benjamin F. Emery, 1925.

Plante, Ellen M. *The American Kitchen, 1700 to the Present.* New York: Facts on File, 1995.

Plat, Hugh. *The Garden of Eden.* London, 1653.

Pursell, Carroll W., Jr., ed. *Technology in America: A History of Individuals and Ideas.* Cambridge, Mass.: MIT Press, 1981.

Putnam, J. Pickering. *Improved Plumbing Appliances.* New York, 1887.

———*The Open Fire Place.* Boston, 1881.

———*Plumbing and Household Sanitation.* Garden City, N.Y.: Doubleday Page, 1911.

Randolph, Mary. *The Virginia House-Wife.* 2d ed. Washington, D.C., 1825.

Report of the Watering Committee. Philadelphia, 1801 — . (Title varies. The edition of 1801 is titled *Report of the Committee for the Introduction of Wholesome Water*).

Rice, Howard C. *L'Hôtel de Langeac.* Charlottesville, Va: Thomas Jefferson Memorial Foundation, 1947.

Richardson, George. *The New Vitruvius Britannicus.* London, 1802–1808.

Righter, Robert W. *Wind Energy in America: A History.* Norman: University of Oklahoma Press, 1996.

Robins, F. W. *The Story of the Lamp.* London: Oxford University Press, 1939.

Roth, Rodris. "Recording a Room: The Kitchen." In *Historic America.* Washington, D.C.: Library of Congress, 1983.

Royall, Anne. *Sketches of History, Life, and Manners in the United States.* New Haven, Conn., 1826.

Rumford, Benjamin Thompson, Count. *Collected Works of Count Rumford.* Cambridge, Mass.: Belknap Press, 1968–1970.

———*The Complete Works of Count Rumford.* Boston, 1870–1875.

Russell, Loris S. *Handy Things to Have Around the House.* New York: McGraw-Hill, 1979.

Scharf, J. Thomas, and Thompson Westcott. *History of Philadelphia.* Philadelphia, 1884.

Schivelbusch, Wolfgang. *Disenchanted Night: The Industrialization of Light in the Nineteenth Century.* Translated by Angela Davies. Berkeley: University of California Press, 1988.

Seale, William. *The President's House: A History.* Washington, D.C.: National Geographic Society and White House Historical Association, c. 1986.

Sellers, Charles Coleman. *Mr. Peale's Museum.* New York: Norton, 1980.

Seymour, John. *The Forgotten Household Tasks.* New York: Knopf, 1987.

Shammas, Carole. *The Pre-Industrial Consumer in England and America.* New York: Oxford University Press, 1990.

Sharp, James. *An Account of the Principles and Effects of the Pensilvanian Stove-Grates.* London, [1790].

Shepherd, Dennis G. *Historical Development of the Windmill.* Washington, D.C.: National Aeronautics and Space Administration, 1990.

Sherman, Steve. *Heating with Coal.* Harrisburg, Pa.: Stackpole Books, 1980.

Skolfield, W. K. *A Century of Electric Fans.* Bridgeport, Conn.: General Electric, 1957.

Smith, Billy G., ed. *Life in Early Philadelphia: Documents from the Revolutionary and Early National Periods.* University Park: Pennsylvania State University Press, 1995.

Smith, Margaret Bayard. *The First Forty Years of Washington Society.* New York: Scribner's, 1906.

Sparke, Penny. *Electrical Appliances.* London: Unwin Hyman, 1987.

Sparrow, W. J. *Knight of the White Eagle: A Biography of Sir Benjamin Thompson, Count Rumford.* London: Hutchinson, 1964.

Starbuck, R. M. *Modern Plumbing Illustrated.* New York: Norman W. Henley, 1915.

Stifler, Susan Reed. *The Beginnings of a Century of Steam and Water Heating.* Westfield, Mass.: H. B. Smith, 1960.

Stowe, Harriet Beecher, and Catharine E. Beecher. *The American Woman's Home.* New York, 1869.

Strasser, Susan. *Never Done: A History of American Housework.* New York: Pantheon, 1982.

Syphon Closet Co. *Syphon Supplement.* [Trenton, N.J.], 1890.

Thuro, Catherine M. V. *Oil Lamps: The Kerosene Era in North America.* Greensboro, N.C.: Wallace-Homestead, 1976.

Thwing, Leroy. *Flickering Flames: A History of Domestic Lighting through the Ages.* Rutland, Vt.: Charles Tuttle, 1958.

Time-Life editors. *How Things Work in Your Home.* New York: Time-Life Books, 1975. Reprint, New York: Henry Holt [1994].

Tobey, Ronald C. *Technology as Freedom: The New Deal and Electrical Modernization of the American Home.* Berkeley: University of Califoria Press, 1996.

Tomlinson, Charles, ed. *Cyclopaedia of Useful Arts and Manufactures.* London and New York, 1854.

Tredgold, Thomas. *The Principles of Warming and Heating.* 3d ed. London, 1836.

Trollope, Anthony. *North America.* London, 1862.

U.S. Census Bureau. *A Century of Population Growth: From the First Census of the United States to the Twelfth, 1790–1900.* Washington, 1909.

——*Historical Statistics of the United States, Colonial Times to 1970.* Washington, D.C., 1975.

U.S. Commerce Department and Department of Housing and Urban Development. *American Housing Survey for the United States in 1995.* Washington, D.C.: U.S. Government Printing Office, 1997.

U.S. Navy Department. *Reports of Officers of the Navy on Ventilating and Cooling the Executive Mansion during the Illness of President Garfield.* Washington, 1882.

U.S. Patent Office. *List of Patents for Inventions and Designs Issued by the United States from 1790 to 1847.* Washington, 1847.

Usher, Abbott Payson. *A History of Mechanical Inventions.* New York: McGraw-Hill, 1929.

Van Zante, Helen J. *The Microwave Oven.* Boston: Houghton Mifflin, 1973.

Vaux, Calvert. *Villas and Cottages.* New York, 1857.

Waldman, Milton. *Elizabeth and Leicester.* London: Collins, 1944.

Walford, Edward. *Old and New London.* London, [1877].

Waring, George E., Jr. *Earth-Closets and Earth Sewage.* New York, 1870.

——*Earth-Closets: How to Make Them and How to Use Them.* New York, 1868.

——*The Sanitary Drainage of Houses and Towns.* New York, 1876.

Washington, George. *The Diaries of George Washington.* Edited by Donald Jackson and Dorothy Twohig. Charlottesville: University Press of Virginia, 1979.

Watson, John F. *Annals of Philadelphia.* Philadelphia, 1830.

Wheeler, Gervase. *Homes for the People.* New York, 1858.

Wheildon, William W., *Memoir of Solomon Willard.* [Boston], 1865.

Whitehead, Russell F. *Good Houses.* Saint Paul, Minn.: Weyerhaeuser Forest Products, 1922.

Whitton, Mary Ormsbee. *The New Servant: Electricity in the Home.* Garden City, N.Y.: Doubleday Page, 1927.

Williams, William H., *America's First Hospital.* Wayne, Pa.: Haverford House, 1976.

Willich, A. F. M. *The Domestic Encyclopedia; or A Dictionary of Facts and Useful Knowledge.* Philadelphia, 1804.

Wilson, Mitchell. *American Science and Invention.* New York: Simon & Schuster, 1954.

Winkler, Gail Caskey. *The Well-Appointed Bath.* Washington, D.C.: Preservation Press, 1989.

Winthrop, John. *The History of New England from 1630 to 1649.* Boston, 1853.

Wright, Carroll D. *The Industrial Evolution of the United States.* New York, 1895.

Wright, Lawrence. *Home Fires Burning: The History of Domestic Heating and Cooking.* London: Routledge & Kegan Paul, 1964.

Unpublished Works

"The Account Book of Lucius R. Dodge, 1889–1946." Baker Library, Harvard University Graduate School of Business Administration, Boston, Mass.

Anderson, Cheryl P. "Foodways at Hancock Shaker Village: An Interpretive Manual." Pittsfield, Mass., Hancock Shaker Village, 1993.

Bacon, Elizabeth Mickle. "The Growth of Household Conveniences in the United States from 1865 to 1900." Ph.D. diss., Radcliffe College, 1942. Harvard University Archives.

Basye, Katherine. "Evolution of Electrical Outlets in Domestic Applications," in "Research in Building Technology," a series of papers for the Maryland Historical Trust. George Washington University, 1996.

Opinion Research Corporation. "Central Air Conditioning: Its Effect on Living Patterns and Attitudes. A Depth Interview Study for Carrier Corporation." Princeton, N.J., 1964.

Miscellaneous

A Symposium: Historic Review of the Development of Sanitary Engineering in the United States during the Past One Hundred and Fifty Years. American Society of Civil Engineers, *Proceedings*, Sept. 1927 (vol. 53, pp. 1585–1648).

ACKNOWLEDGMENTS

"Victory has a hundred fathers."* In a somewhat different context, the same may be said of a book as comprehensive as this one. Hereby acknowledged are the hundred fathers and mothers whose contributions, large and small, make this work all the richer, more rounded, and more complete.

I am deeply appreciative, in particular, of those who read and evaluated all or major portions of the manuscript: At the National Museum of American History, Smithsonian Institution, Washington, D.C.: Dr. Bernard S. Finn, curator, Electrical Collections; Anne M. Serio, assistant curator, Division of Social History; and William E. Worthington Jr., assistant curator, Division of the History of Technology. Also: John L. McKnight, professor of physics, College of William and Mary, Williamsburg, Virginia, and Elizabeth B. Leckie, curator, Historic House Trust of New York City. My thanks

also to Eric Johnson, manager of editorial services, Carrier Corporation, for reading the section on air conditioning and for arranging for the cutaway drawing of central air conditioning that appears herein; John McTear, vice president for projects and technical resources, General Public Utilities International, for reading the sections relating to power and fuel; William Sigafoos, vice president, export and product development, plumbing products, American Standard Companies, Inc., the section on modern plumbing; and Elliot Sivowitch, museum specialist, Electrical Collections, National Museum of American History, Smithsonian Institution, for his assistance. And to Mimi Sherman, curator of the Merchant's House Museum, New York City, my great appreciation for reading the page proofs from the perspective of her own considerable knowledge of household technology.

My sincere thanks to Doron Weber, program director, Alfred P. Sloan Foundation, not only for the reality of a grant for this project but for the remark-

---

*"Victory has a hundred fathers, but defeat is an orphan." Count Galeazzo Ciano, 1942. Oxford Dictionary of Quotations, 4th ed.

able streamlining of the grant application procedure (mechanization of bureaucracy, in a sense).

In the course of researching and writing this book as well as its predecessor, *Open House*, I developed a close working relationship with the Historic House Trust of New York City, which I warmly acknowledge. My thanks in particular to Scott P. Heyl, executive director; Nancy Zeigler, development director; and Liz Leckie, curator.

I am especially appreciative of the wonderful original artwork of Dolores Malecki-Spivack that appears in this book. In addition to being an accomplished illustrator she is a registered architect, thus providing a uniquely informed perspective to the illustrations that appear here.

My sincere thanks to the following corporations, all major contributors to the evolution of domestic technology in their own right, for furnishing illustrations and background material: American Standard Companies, Inc., Piscataway, N.J., Lisa Glover, communications manager; Carrier Corporation, Syracuse, N.Y.; General Electric Company, Louisville, Ky., Chip Keeling; and Frank Friday, Friday Associates International, Louisville, Ky. on behalf of General Electric; Kohler Company, Kohler, Wisc., Jill M. Cavil, public relations manager, and Christopher J. Thiede, communications specialist; Maytag Corporation, Newton, Iowa, Ron Krajnovich, manager of employee communications; Raytheon Company, Lexington, Mass., Toni Simonetti, director of media relations, and Michelle A. Ross, media relations specialist; Sears, Roebuck and Company, Vicki Cwiok, public affairs department; Whirlpool Corporation, Benton Harbor, Mich., Cinda Noffke, administrative assistant for global communications; York International Corporation, York, Pa., Eunice Luckenbaugh, supervisor, corporate marketing services, and David Rieker, communications program manager. Photographs and other materials sent by these various corporations, over and above what were used in this book, have been given to the Smithsonian Institution.

My particular thanks to the following curators who helped in many ways with material relating to their historic houses: Dennis H. J. Medina, museum curator, Dwight D. Eisenhower Library, and Kathleen A. Struss, audiovisual archivist, Eisenhower Home, Abilene, Kans.; Jan C. Bradford, chief curator, Hermann-Grima/Gallier Houses, and Mary Strickland, former curator, Gallier House, New Orleans, La.; Karin J. Lodinsky, executive vice president, and Douglas R. Kent, former executive vice president and curator, Hyde Hall, Cooperstown, N.Y.; Olivia E. Alison, curator, Owens-Thomas House, Savannah, Ga.

And my thanks to the following for their contributions: Steve Somers, curator, Ephrata Cloister, Ephrata, Pa.; Lawrence J. Yerdon, director, Hancock Shaker Village, Pittsfield, Mass.; John Page, director, and Diane Barsa, assistant director, the Hermitage, Ho-Ho-Kus, N.J.; Lili R. Ott, director of historic houses, and Catherine Rogers Arthur, curator, Homewood, Johns Hopkins University, Baltimore, Md.; Jennifer Ambrose, assistant curator of prints and photographs, Erika Piola, curatorial assistant, and Jennifer Sanchez, former coordinator for rights and reproductions, Library Company of Philadelphia; Orlando Ridout V, chief, office of research, survey, and registration, Maryland Historical Trust, Crownsville; Anthony Knipp, president of the board of trustees, and Donald O. Mavros, executive director, Museum Village, Monroe, New York; Emogene A. Bevitt, program specialist, National Park Service, Washington, D.C.; Raymond V. Shepherd, director, Old Economy Village, Ambridge, Pa.; Jack Larkin, director of research, collections and library, Frank G. White, curator of mechanical arts, and J. Edward Hood, research historian, architecture and material life, Old Sturbridge Village, Sturbridge, Mass.; Barbara Katus, manager, rights and reproductions, Pennsylvania Academy of the Fine Arts, Philadelphia; Carol Wojtowicz Smith, archivist, Philadelphia Contributionship; Mark J. Sammons, director of research, Strawbery Banke Museum,

Portsmouth, N.H.; Donna K. Baron, curator, Webb-Deane-Stevens Museum, Wethersfield, Conn.; E. Richard McKinstry, librarian, Joseph Downs Collection of Manuscripts and Printed Ephemera and Winterthur archivist, Winterthur Museum, Winterthur, Del.

An invaluable research tool for this book and for my earlier book, *Open House* (New York: Henry Holt, 1999) was a survey titled "The American Home and the Development of Domestic Technology" that was sent by the respective publishers to historic site administrators around the country. This book makes use of replies for both books. The following people are acknowledged and thanked specifically for their response to the survey for this book:

Arrow Rock State Historic Site, Arrow Rock, Mo., Michael Dickey, site administrator; Athenaeum Rectory, Columbia, Tenn., Carolyn Hunter and Alice Algood; Audubon House and Tropical Gardens, Key West, Fla., Teresa Ashley, administrator; Clara Barton National Historic Site, Glen Echo, Md., National Park Service; Beauvoir, Biloxi, Miss., Michael S. Wright, collection manager; Bement-Billings Farmstead, Newark Valley, N.Y., Harriet Miller, executive director, Newark Valley Historical Society; Blount Mansion, Knoxville, Tenn., Brooke Hamby, director of education; Daniel Boone Homestead, Birdsboro, Pa., James A. Lewars, administrator; Boscobel, Garrison, N.Y., Sarah Allaback, archivist-registrar; Botto House National Landmark, Haledon, N.J., Dr. Angelica M. Santomauro, executive director; Buhl House, Zelienople, Pa., Joyce M. Bessor, director, Zelienople Historical Society; Burrows House, Newport, Ore., Steve Wyatt, curator; Byers-Evers House, Denver, Colo., Kevin Gramer, administrator; Campbell House Museum, Saint Louis, Mo., Jeff Huntington, executive director; Buffalo Bill Cody's Home, North Platte, Nebr., Tom Morrison, superintendent; Crawford House, Newburgh, N.Y., Allynne Lange, Russell Lange, Anne Coone, and Tom Porfidio; Deshler-Morris House,

Philadelphia, Pa., Karie Diethorn, chief, Museum Branch, Independence National Historical Park; Jean Baptiste Faribault House, Mendota, Minn., Lisa A. Krahn, site manager; Farmington, Louisville, Ky., Deborah Spearing, executive director, and Kelly A. Hanna, associate director; William Farnsworth Homestead, Rockland, Maine, Janice Kasper, historic site coordinator, Farnsworth Art Museum; Fort Robinson Museum, Crawford, Nebr., Thomas R. Buecker, curator; Fosterfields, Morristown, N.J., Mary Chatfield, collections care manager; Garland Homestead, West Salem, Wis., Errol R. Kindschy, president, West Salem Historical Society; Gibson House, Boston, Mass., Edward W. Gordon, executive director; Gore Place, Waltham, Mass., Susan Robertson, director, Susanne Olson, curator, and Lana Lewis, assistant curator; Graeme Park, Horsham, Pa., Brenda Reigle, eastern regional curator, Pennsylvania Historical and Museum Commission; Haas-Lilienthal House, San Francisco, Calif., Anastasia Fink, director of education and curator; President Warren G. Harding Home, Marion, Ohio, Phillip Payne, site manager; Harpers Ferry National Historical Park, Harpers Ferry, W.Va., Judith Mueller, curator; Ezekiel Harris House, Augusta, Ga., Cherie Blizzard Prickett, preservation assistant; Hatton-Eielson Museum, Hatton, N.Dak., Eileen O. Mork, curator; Heurich House, Washington, D.C., Barbara Franco, executive director, Historical Society of Washington; Thomas Hill House, Bangor, Maine, Dr. Deborah Thompson, architectural historian, on behalf of the Bangor Historical Society; Historic New Harmony, Ind., Julienne Rutherford, historic preservation coordinator; Herbert Hoover Birthplace Cottage, West Branch, Iowa, Bill Wilcox, historian; Hope Lodge, Fort Washington, Pa., Brenda Reigle, eastern regional curator, Pennsylvania Historical and Museum Commission; Ivy Green, Tuscumbia, Ala., Sue Pilkilton, director; Kearney Mansion, Fresno, Calif., Suzanne B. Smith, collections and operations manager; Thomas P. Kennard House, Lincoln, Nebr., John R. Lindahl, site supervisor; Martin Luther King Jr. National Historic Site, Atlanta, Ga., Dean Rowley, historian; Lincoln Log Cabin State Historic Site, Lerna, Ill., Susan Nordmeyer, lead interpreter; Lloyd House, Alexandria, Va., Joyce A. McMullin, manager; Lockwood-Mathews Mansion, Norwalk, Conn., Zachary N. Studenroth, executive director, and Kathleen Maher, curator; Mabry-Hazen House, Knoxville, Tenn., Barry K. Davis, administrator; McConnell Mansion, Moscow, Idaho, Joann Jones, curator; Magnolia Manor, Cairo, Ill., Timothy W. Slapinski, curator; Mission Houses Museum, Honolulu, Hawaii, Sarah Fishman, curatorial assistant; Moody Mansion, Galveston, Tex., Margaret Doran, curator; Senator George Norris State Historic Site, McCook, Nebr., Linda Hein, tourism facilities operator, Nebraska State Historical Society; Oakleigh Historic Complex, Mobile, Ala., Opal W. Matthews, manager; O Henry House, San Antonio, Tex., Bill West, curator; Pardee Home Museum, Oakland, Calif., David Nicolai, director; Park-McCullough House, North Bennington, Vt., Ann M. Pistocco, guest curator; Passavant House, Zelienople, Pa., Joyce M. Bessor, director, Zelienople Historical Society; Petersburg Museums, Petersburg, Va., Roswitha Rash, curator of collections; Frank Phillips Home, Bartlesville, Okla., Susan J. Lacey, curator; The Pillars, Bolivar, Tenn., Evalyn M. Harris, recording secretary, Hardeman County Chapter, Association for the Preservation of Tennessee Antiquities; Plum Grove Historic Home, Iowa City, Leigh Ann Jero, curator; James K. Polk Ancestral Home, Columbia, Tenn., John Holtzapple, director; Narcissa Prentiss House, Prattsburgh, N.Y., Rena Davis, president, Prattsburgh Community Historical Society; Rancho Los Cerritos, Long Beach, Calif., Steve Iverson, historical curator; Ramsey House Plantation, Knoxville, Tenn., Helma Sickles, director; Sagamore Hill National Historic Site, Oyster Bay, N.Y., Amy Verone, curator; Saint Christopher's Church, Brimfield, Mass, site of the Brimfield windmill, Valerie Bernier, administrative assistant; Salisbury Mansion, Worcester, Mass., Holly V. Izard, research curator; Thomas Sappington House, Crestwood, Mo., Jane Lewis, president; Andrew Finley Scott House, Richmond, Ind., Michele L. Bottorff, director, Wayne County Historical Museum; Henry H. Sibley House, Mendota, Minn., Lisa A. Krahn, site manager; Skolfield-Whittier House, Brunswick, Maine, Amy L. Poland, curator; William Tanner House, Aurora, Ill., Roger Behrens, curator; Todd House, Philadelphia, Ann Marie Dubé, associate curator, Independence National Historical Park; Robert Toombs House, Washington, Ga., Marcia Campbell, interpretive specialist; Wadsworth Longfellow House, Portland, Maine, Joyce Butler, curator of museum collections, Maine Historical Society; Bishop White House, Philadelphia, Karie Diethorn, chief, museum branch, Independence National Historical Park; Williams Residence, New Orleans, Ann Elise Tenold, registrar; Woodrow Wilson Birthplace, Staunton, Va., Patricia A. Hobbs, curator of collections; John Wornall House Museum, Kansas City, Mo., Betsy Johnson, director; Wren's Nest House Museum, Atlanta, Ga., Carole Mumford, executive director and curator.

Discussion of water supply in this book took note of the fact that New York City's Croton Aqueduct of 1842 used a receiving reservoir at Fifth Avenue and Forty-second Street. Once no longer needed for water supply, the site was rebuilt as a reservoir of knowledge—the New York Public Library. It was the most used resource library for this book, and I wish to thank the many helpful staff members who, in their own way, were essential to this project.

Finally I extend sincere thanks to my editors at Clarkson Potter, Roy Finamore, special projects editor, and Chris Smith, editorial assistant, and my agent, Faith Hamlin, and her associate, Nancy Stender, of Sanford J. Greenburger Associates.

INDEX

Page numbers in italics indicate illustrations.